Inside
Plea Bargaining

THE LANGUAGE OF NEGOTIATION

Inside
Plea Bargaining

THE LANGUAGE OF NEGOTIATION

Douglas W. Maynard

University of Wisconsin
Madison, Wisconsin

Plenum Press • New York and London

Library of Congress Cataloging in Publication Data

Maynard, Douglas W., date–
  Inside plea bargaining.

  Bibliography: p.
  Includes index.
  1. Plea bargaining—United States. I. Title.
KF9654.M38   1984   345.73'072   84-9809
ISBN 0-306-41577-1   347.30572

© 1984 Plenum Press, New York
A Division of Plenum Publishing Corporation
233 Spring Street, New York, N.Y. 10013

Printed in the United States of America

To JOAN

Preface

Negotiation is a ubiquitous part of social life. Some even say that social order itself is a negotiated phenomenon. Yet the study of negotiation as an actual discourse activity, occurring between people who have substantial interests and tasks in the real social world, is in its infancy. This is the more surprising because plea bargaining, as a specific form of negotiation, has recently been the center of an enormous amount of research attention. Much of the concern has been directed to basic questions of justice, such as how fair the process is, whether it is unduly coercive, and whether it accurately separates the guilty from the innocent.

A study such as mine does not try to answer these sorts of questions. I believe that we are not in a position to answer them until we approach plea bargaining on its own complex terms. Previous studies that have attempted to provide a general picture of the process as a way to assess its degree of justness have neglected the specific skills by which practitioners bargain and negotiate, the particular procedures through which various surface features such as character assessment are accomplished, and concrete ways in which justice is administered and, simultaneously, caseloads are managed.

My investigation into the skills, procedures, and routines involved in plea bargaining is aided by the use of tape-recorded negotiations that I collected in a court in "Garden City," California. I owe a large debt to the judges, district attorneys, public defenders, private attorneys, clerks, bailiffs, and other personnel in the court system there. They facilitated this study in many ways, graciously allowing my presence in delicate situations, answering a great number of questions, and offering other services. Of particular help were the Chief Public Defender of Garden County, and two judges in the municipal court. My deep gratitude goes to all of these persons, whom I cannot name for reasons of anonymity.

I received important financial support during the course of my research. The study was initiated, and early versions of Chapters 2, 6, and 7 were written, as part of my dissertation research while I held a Regents' Fellowship at the University of California. Chapters 3, 4, 5, and 8 are based on work that I did after joining the University of Wisconsin faculty; some of that work was done under the auspices of a grant from the Graduate School.

Three persons at the University of California—Donald R. Cressey, Thomas P. Wilson, and Don H. Zimmerman—provided inspiration, direction, and ideas as I gathered and analyzed data and wrote my dissertation. Their interest and enthusiasm continued even after I finished the dissertation and moved away. I owe a very large debt to Cressey, who was not only instrumental in helping me obtain access to the Garden City court (see Chapter 1) but who also made extensive editorial comments on a draft of this manuscript, so that much of what is readable is due to his efforts. Furthermore, his own work on plea bargaining and thoroughgoing sociological approach to the topic set the stage for much of what I have done. I owe no less of a debt to Wilson and Zimmerman, whose teaching and research stimulated my interest in the study of face-to-face interaction, ethnomethodology, and conversational analysis. They also introduced me to the work of Harold Garfinkel, Erving Goffman, and Harvey Sacks, all of whom I cite repeatedly in this study, although a citation count probably would not measure the extent of their influence. Not least important, Wilson and Zimmerman provided encouragement in many nonintellectual ways.

A number of other people have provided detailed criticisms on drafts of one or more of the chapters. At the University of Wisconsin, Howard Erlanger, Warren Hagstrom, Jack Ladinsky, Gerald Marwell, and Aage Sorensen, none of whom is very familiar with the style of work I do, nonetheless exposed core problems in some of my early analyses and made percipient suggestions for improvement. From a variety of other places, Charles Goodwin, Gail Jefferson, Dave Luckenbill, Anita Pomerantz, and Emanuel Schegloff took time to write comments that have been nothing short of invaluable to the development of particular chapters. Lynn Mather, as an outside reviewer, provided beneficial remarks on all chapters.

For typing the many drafts that I tend to write, I thank Chris Peters, Toni Polglase, and especially Virginia Rogers. John Demetrion did an admirable job of locating miniscule spelling and referencing errors.

The friendship and regard of four special people made some of the rough spots involved in the experience of writing the manuscript just smooth enough to get across. Dave Luckenbill was an endless source of good advice on the practicalities of crafting a book. (He also let me "borrow" what has been an indispensable resource—a copy of Deering's California Penal Code—for the last five years.) Rich Hilbert's brand of impracticality probably gives him one of the best listening ears I have ever come across. I poured out many a trouble to him and he set me right by somehow hearing what I was trying to say. Maureen Hallinan was an enthusiastic and needed local source of support. And Joan Maynard was simply an inseparable part of the sustained effort required to do all of the tasks involved in, and surrounding, the writing of this book.

Parts of this manuscript, in different forms, have appeared in *Human Studies, Law and Society Review, Semiotica, Social Problems,* and *The Sociological Quarterly.*

Contents

CHAPTER 1

The Language of Negotiation

Plea bargaining, the major means by which cases are funneled through the criminal justice process, is not a new practice. There is evidence of its presence in the United States before the Civil War, and it became a predominant means of administering justice shortly thereafter. What is new is the amount of attention it has received recently. Plea bargaining was only sporadically discussed in the early decades of this century, though in the 1920s various states surveyed their criminal courts and discovered just how dominant plea bargaining had become. It was not until the 1960s, however, that plea bargaining emerged as a national issue, and numerous professions and disciplines, including law, political science, and sociology, began to focus on the practice. In the 1970s, there was a virtual explosion of published material, as over two-thirds of the extant books, articles, and studies concerning plea bargaining were written during the decade.[1] Despite all this attention, and although we have learned much by the use of surveys, interviews, and firsthand observations, the picture we have of courtroom negotiation is largely an outside view.

This book takes a look inside plea bargaining in two major senses. First, the practice usually escapes scrutiny because it is carried on by professionals in their offices, in hallways, over the telephone, or, as in the jurisdiction studied here, in open courtroom conferences that are ritually protected from intrusion. Even when ethnographers gain access to these secluded talks, they necessarily have to make hurried notes as

[1]This figure was obtained by a count of articles in an extensive bibliography of plea bargaining compiled by Matheny (1979). The percentage also tallies with one cited by Miller, McDonald, and Cramer (1978: iii), although the two-thirds figure pertains to publications appearing in the decade prior to their study (1968–1978).

1

they overhear or are allowed to watch what are sometimes rapid-fire conversations. Otherwise, researchers must rely on the participants' retrospective interpretations of what they do, or on their comments regarding hypothetical cases. This report, however, investigates the tape-recorded negotiations of defense attorneys, district attorneys, and judges as they discuss actual cases in a municipal-court setting.

Second, plea bargaining is often depicted as a *response* to such outside factors as overcrowding in the courts or abstract laws and harsh penalties established by state legislatures. This volume views plea bargaining not as a *re*action, but as participants' *en*action of taken-for-granted discourse and negotiational skills, which exhibit neglected aspects of social organization. Thus, the other sense of plea bargaining as an inside activity refers to its being derived from practitioners' own cultural knowledge and praxis rather than from outside social pressures. The chapters dealing with specific bargaining practices make this point clear.

More generally, this book investigates the structure of negotiation as a generic phenomenon that occurs in the daily interaction among prosecutors, defense attorneys, and judges in a local United States jurisdiction. And it examines discretion as it is actually exercised in the criminal justice process.

Most previous studies of negotiation have been carried out almost exclusively in experimental settings, to the neglect of everyday interaction in such particular settings as courthouses. Where researchers have examined negotiation in natural settings—whether it be industry (e.g., Gouldner, 1954), national politics (e.g., Riker, 1962), international relations (e.g., Ikle, 1964), and so forth—their reports tend to take a narrative form, analyzing only one or two cases, and either omitting the structural context within which negotiation occurs or focusing on that context while neglecting the microscopic analysis of the negotiations themselves (Strauss, 1978: 97–101).

Thus, there is a need to explore negotiation directly, which is done here by close scrutiny and analysis of tape-recorded and transcribed talk concerning 52 misdemeanor criminal cases processed over a five-month period in a California municipal court. While the emphasis is on the microanalysis of plea bargaining discourse, attention is also given to wider contexts within which it occurs, including the court, the criminal justice process, and the society that relies on discretionary activities of courtroom professionals for administering justice.

Discretion in the criminal justice process has been of great social scientific concern for at least the last 15 years. Difficult choices are made at every major point in this process—detection, apprehension, and conviction. These decisions, which implement the criminal law but also reflect a multitude of factors not covered by the law, determine who will get further processed, and how this will be done. The network of decisions has been likened to a sieve. At each stage, various acts and actors are screened out of the process through the discretionary practices of key decisionmakers. Accordingly, only a small percentage of crimes committed are reported, and only one-third to one-half of all arrests are filed in court. Depending on the court, from 10 to 50 percent of these cases are dismissed as a matter of judgment. Of those defendants not dismissed, 90 percent plead guilty to charges agreed upon—and sentences arranged—in informal discussions between attorneys.[2] Thus, only 10 percent of the cases coming before the court are handled by means of trial, where strict rules of evidence, lawyer and judicial decorum, procedure, and so on, adhere; and the percentage of cases resulting in trial is even smaller when related to reported or filed offenses. As Rosett and Cressey (1976: 45) have remarked, "Informal discretionary choices, rather than formal courtroom choices, determine the outcome of all but a small portion of criminal cases."

This fact heightens the importance of this study from another standpoint. Recently, a number of researchers have examined *trial* discourse, giving attention to forms of questioning (Churchill, 1978; Danet and Kermish, 1978; Phillips, 1982), terminological manipulations (Danet, 1980a; Loftus and Palmer, 1974; Loftus and Zanni, 1975), language styles (Conley and O'Barr, 1977; Conley, O'Barr, and Lind, 1978), silences (O'Barr and Atkins, 1978), interruptions (Lind and O'Barr, 1979), storytelling (Bennett, 1978, 1979) and accusatory sequences (Atkinson and Drew, 1979) in the courtroom.[3] Important as these studies are to the understanding of trials, they touch only the tip of the iceberg as far as com-

---

[2]The figures cited in this paragraph vary from study to study (e.g., Feeley, 1979b; Mather, 1974; Neubauer, 1974; Rosett and Cressey, 1976), and depend upon jurisdictional reporting practices and whether felonies only, felonies and misdemeanors, or misdemeanors only are included in the count.

[3]Many of these studies (and related ones) are reviewed, and their findings summarized, in Danet (1980b: 519–541). Maynard (1983) reviews and critiques three books on trial discourse that concern speech styles (O'Barr, 1982), storytelling (Bennett and Feldman, 1981), and accusation sequences (Atkinson and Drew, 1979).

prehending the bulk of the linguistic processes through which decisions are made in the court. Since most decisions are made informally rather than formally, the inspection of the discourse of plea bargaining permits us to turn away from the linguistic practices involved in a comparatively rare and ceremonial event and to focus on the speech forms by which justice is administered as a routine, everyday matter for the bulk of cases coming before the court.

THE APPROACH

This is a study of recorded discourse, and it offers a unique understanding of plea bargaining not provided by any of the now-substantial number of excellent ethnographies of courtroom negotiations. In doing ethnography, researchers attempt to draw pictures of what some phenomenon looks like to an insider for an audience that wants to know about it. Researchers investigating plea bargaining have hung around courtroom halls, corridors, backrooms, and chambers, watching and interviewing until they feel that they have an adequate idea of what is going on. They then write about this conception and describe such prominent features of plea negotiations as charge bargaining, sentence bargaining, character assessment, discussion of facts, compromise, reaching a decision, and so forth. From their reports, we do have a rich sense of the plea-bargaining enterprise. The trouble is that ethnographers rely on unnoticed abilities to record and recognize such features, just as participants rely on uninvestigated abilities in producing them. How bargaining, character assessment, and other activities are organized in practical and methodic ways remains to be fully explored. Plea bargaining as an orderly phenomenon needs to be appreciated not only for its more prominent features (i.e., charge and sentence bargaining, discussion of character and facts, etc.), but also for those deep-level discourse procedures wielded to accomplish its various surface characteristics. The question is: How are these features or surface characteristics put together, assembled, and thus made recognizable?

Such deep-level assembly procedures are the "seen but unnoticed methods" (Garfinkel, 1967), the routine practices, that make negotiation and its related properties a skilled accomplishment of participants. That they are "seen" is evidenced by the fact that observers and practitioners recognize and produce standard plea bargaining behavior. But the involved patterns and practices are taken for granted as common sense or trivial and thus remain "unnoticed." For this reason, they are rarely the subject of genuine social scientific inquiry. The presumption here, contrariwise, is that a social organization worthy of intense scrutiny is deeply rooted in members' ongoing production of those interactional products that get labeled as *plea bargaining, character assessment, deciding facts,* and so forth.

Treating courthouse talk as a production or as an organized achievement sets off this study from other plea bargaining research. It distinguishes it also from experimental social psychology and most studies of trial discourse. By and large, social psychologists have studied the influence of conditions such as attitudinal commitment, prior experience, group and individual differences, and the like on *outcomes* of negotiation. Similarly, research on trial talk regularly investigates the *effects* of various factors on jury perceptions and decisions. Here, the focus is on the social process itself, rather than on its product.

Two recent books on trial discourse exemplify the contrasting approaches. *Linguistic Evidence* (O'Barr, 1982) illustrates the drawbacks of the product- or outcome-oriented research. *Order in Court* (Atkinson and Drew, 1979) exhibits what I consider to be advantages of process-oriented research.

Linguistic Evidence reports how variations in four patterns of talk— (1) powerlessness, (2) narrativeness, (3) hypercorrection, and (4) simultaneous speech—affect the perceptions that mock jurors have of witnesses and lawyers. One set of subjects (mock jurors) heard tapes of actual misdemeanor, felony, and capital trials. Another set of subjects heard tapes of actors presenting the same substantive information while varying the speech styles in which it was presented.

First, O'Barr employed Lakoff's (1975) descriptions of women's speech to measure the "power" of a speech style. Women are said to use more hedges—polite forms of discourse, question forms, adverbial qualifiers, indirect statements, and similar conversational devices—that indicate their subordinate social status. Such devices, however, seem to be tied more to socioeconomic status in general than simply to gender. That is, O'Barr found that males with low socioeconomic status exhibited a high percentage of women's language features, and high-status females displayed a low percentage. Defining speech as powerful or powerless depending on the presence of hedges, qualifiers, and so on, O'Barr played for his subjects tapes of courtroom testimony representing these two styles. They rated both male and female witnesses who utilized a powerful speech style as more convincing—truthful, competent, intelligent, and trustworthy—than those who employed a powerless style.

The second type of speech that O'Barr explored was that of narrative testimony, in which a witness provided extended answers to an attorney's questions. The contrast condition involved a witness producing shortened responses, or speaking in "fragmented" style. The hypothesis was that witnesses who spoke narratively would be evaluated more positively than witnesses who talked in fragments. Indeed, when reactions to fragmented and narrative styles differed significantly it was in the direction of favoring witnesses who spoke narratively.[4]

A third phenomenon that O'Barr investigated was hypercorrection, which refers to the overuse of precise enunciation, sophisticated vocabulary, correct grammar, and other speech refinements. Mock jurors were presented with a condition in which hypercorrection was prevalent and one in which ordinary formal speech was used. Subjects evaluated the witness who employed the ordinary style as significantly more convincing, competent, qualified, and intelligent than the one who produced hypercorrect speech.

Finally, O'Barr examined how the occurrence of simultaneous speech between witnesses and lawyers would affect perceptions of their interaction. Whenever there was overlapping speech, which implies a violation of the rule that only one party at a time should speak, the witness was regarded as having greater control of the situation. This did not imply a negative opinion of the lawyer; to the contrary, if the lawyer overpowered the witness by continuing to speak after overlap first occurred, he was viewed with more disfavor than when the witness was allowed to continue.

These findings are provocative, and O'Barr suggests in his con-

---

[4]The results of the experiments on "narrative" and "fragmented" style testimony were not uniform and are thus difficult to interpret. For example, subjects rated males who spoke in a narrative style more highly than males who did not, but there were no significant differences in response to females who spoke narratively and females who talked in a fragmented style. Subjects evaluated males' fragmented style negatively, O'Barr argues, because they figured that it reflected lawyer control over, and disapproval of, the witness' testimony. On the other hand, if women provided fragmented answers to lawyers' questions, subjects would expect this to be a female trait and would not view it negatively. This assumption seems reasonable except that it is inconsistent with the results of the previous experiment in which the use of "powerless" speech even by females negatively affected respondents' ratings.

cluding chapter that coaching lawyers and witnesses on speech styles may improve their credibility before juries. However, we have to consider the following problems with this kind of research.

One problem concerns the distinction between statistical significance, which can indicate that a relationship between variables exists, and substantive significance, which refers to the *amount* of influence that is exerted by an independent variable on a dependent variable. Although the findings in *Linguistic Evidence* demonstrate possible relationships between various speech styles and subjects' evaluations of lawyers and witnesses, we do not know the extent to which these evaluations are based on such styles. And there may be other factors, including age, education, sex, class, race, and perceived moral character, that by themselves, with each other, or in combination with speech style, explain more of a juror's response to a witness than does speech style considered separately.[5] A further trouble is that the experiments examine only the relation between speech styles and the *perceptions* that the subjects have of lawyer and witness. Even if there were a substantial impact of styles on perceptions, the question remains whether such perceptions, in turn, influence the *decisions* that jurors might make. Clearly, a multivariate research design is called for, but that requires a sophisticated theory of trial discourse and a research design that can handle the complexity of courtroom interaction. Neither of these exists (Dane and Wrightsman, 1982), which highlights the importance of studying the discourse process as an entity in its own right, rather than regarding it as a vehicle for transmitting the effects of this or that variable.

Another shortcoming of this research derives from the use of doctored data for the experiments. Such data are necessary in order to probe the effects of contrasting speech styles, because there must be experimental and control conditions. The doctored tapes, however, distort actual speech by overemphasizing the way in which elements of style may be tied to a single speaker and ignoring how such styles may be elicited, suppressed, or coaccomplished by one's interactional partner. Consider the example of powerless, "women's speech." In cross-sex conversations, Zimmerman and West (1975) and West (1979) have shown

[5]Dane and Wrightsman (1982) review a number of studies showing that such characteristics do influence jurors' reactions. The problem, as Miller and Burgoon (1982) observe, is that "a hesitant, nonfluent witness of acknowledged impeccable character is likely to be perceived as nervous or uncertain, but a witness of shady reputation who manifests the same behaviors probably will be viewed as an unconvincing liar."

that males interrupt females much more than the reverse. A possible explanation for this is that women *invite* such interruptions because of their own speech habits, such as talking more than men, and not asserting themselves when they are interrupted to reclaim rights to produce a full turn of talk. However, if anything, males talk more than females during cross-sex conversations (West and Zimmerman, 1983) and women respond to interruptions in the same way as males, thus not permitting interruptions any more than men do (West, 1979). The disproportionate amount of male interruptions is not a response to characteristics of women's speech *per se*, but it reflects a system in which differential rights to talk are distributed by way of interaction. The lesson is that any speech style is not necessarily a stimulus condition that prompts a given type of reaction. Powerless speech and other styles of talk can be investigated as outcomes of socially organized practices.

A third and related problem concerns the use of a coding format to make analytical decisions about what is occurring in the talk. Even though the investigator might use prior theory and research to establish well-informed coding categories, when these categories are imposed on given utterances they eliminate a crucial element of the context of those utterances. That element is the *sequential environment* wherein utterances occur, which can be an important resource for deciding how to characterize a given piece of talk.[6] The following example of actual testimony contains what O'Barr considers to be "fragmented" speech on the part of the witness.

1. Q: Now, calling your attention to the twenty-first day of November,
2.   a Saturday, what were your working hours that day?
3. A: Well, I was working from 7 to 3
4. Q: Was that 7 A.M.?
5. A: Yes
6. Q: And what time that day did you arrive at the store?
7. A: 6:30
8. Q: 6:30. And did uh, you open the store at 7 o'clock
9. A: Yes, it has to be opened by then. (O'Barr, 1982:76–77)

---

[6]It is not that O'Barr is unaware of this problem. In Chapter 6 of *Linguistic Evidence* (1982) he discusses the crucial role that context plays in determining how some conversational feature is constituted. Components of style do not exist in isolation from their interactive environments, including "various attempts to control or mitigate or even magnify their significance" (O'Barr, 1982: 110). However, the overriding concern with the effects of style on audience perception necessitates a certain inattention to contextual matters.

O'Barr suggests that it was "necessary for the lawyer to pose additional questions" to elicit information lacking in the witness's first answer (line 3). However, the "lack of information" in that answer is not an inherent quality of it. It is only by observing the question–answer sequences that follow it that counsel's need for further facts becomes manifest. Moreover, each answer (lines 3, 5, 7, and 9) is closely fitted, and entirely responsive, to the question that precedes it. That is, each question is formed so as to expect a yes/no type of answer, which the witness provides.[7] If the witness had answered in the following hypothetical manner, O'Barr argues that she would have been speaking in a "narrative" style:

Q: Now, calling your attention to the twenty-first day of November,
    a Saturday, what were your working hours that day?
A: Well, I was working from, uh, 7 A.M. to 3 P.M. I arrived at the store
    at 6:30 and opened the store at 7.

As a response to the key part of counsel's question about working hours, however, the answer is insuccinct, provides nonessential information, and could appear strange in actual courtroom discourse. Thus, a sequential analysis of both examples reveals quite different characterizations of the answers than does a procedure that simply codes responses as "fragmented" or "narrative" without attention to the preceding and following utterances. That is, an analysis of the original answers in context and without predetermined categories would suggest that their form was elicited by the style of preceding questions. It would be a dubious procedure to count the answers as instances of a fragmented style of talk.

In contrast to O'Barr's study, Atkinson and Drew's *Order in Court* (1979) is not concerned with the effects that the characteristics of trial discourse have on the perceptions of judge or jury. Instead, it is concerned with how the discourse is organized by the participants as an ongoing part of their interaction. Features of courtroom testimony are not intrinsic to isolated turns of talk; they are achieved collaboratively by counsel and witness. Finally, the authors do not rely on a coding

---

[7]Technically, the question–answer sequences in the example are "adjacency pairs" (Schegloff and Sacks, 1974: 239). A feature of such units is that the first pair-part selects the form in which a second pair-part is properly delivered, a feature to which the witness is clearly alive.

scheme to examine the data. Rather, they analyze pieces of talk in relation to, and as defined by, their sequential environments.

Of particular interest in *Order in Court* is how lawyers engage in
accusing and blaming witnesses and how the latter respond with justifications and excuses. Accusations, Atkinson and Drew found, are built
through series of question-and-answer sequences designed to elicit
agreement from the witness concerning the "facts" of a case. Such facts,
however, are not objective characterizations of an event. Rather, they
are chosen to project an interpretation in which a defendant's activities
are found blameworthy. Even though the defendant, during examination, can foresee the accusatory direction of a series of questions, it is
difficult to resist collaborating with an attorney's line because the elicited
information does have the appearance of being "merely" descriptive.

Once counsel produces an accusation, witnesses handle it by using
a *rebuttal* plus an *account*. In the English Tribunal of Inquiry that Atkinson
and Drew studied, the prosecution issue was a failure by police to take
sufficient action during a Protestant–Catholic conflagration in Northern
Ireland.

COUNSEL: In any event, when you mounted that second baton charge, you took no steps
to prevent the Protestant people following you
WITNESS: I was not in a position to take any steps [rebuttal]. If I had taken any steps to
prevent them I would have left more than half my party and the other three
or four of us would have had no effect on chasing them . . . [account]. (Atkinson and Drew, 1979: 162)

The rebuttal contradicts the factual premise of the noticing of failure to
take action (i.e., that the witness *could* have done so); the account provides a *reason* for the lack of action.

Identifying practices for accusing, denying, and other courtroom
actions necessitates close attention to transcripts of the tribunal hearing.[8]
It bears repeating that Atkinson and Drew, unlike O'Barr, do not offer
propositions about the *effectiveness* of different blaming or defending
strategies on the perceptions of those who attend to the discourse for
the purpose of making a judgment. The concern is with describing and
demonstrating in the transcripts how each of these strategies is orga-

---

[8]Only one part of one hearing was investigated in the Atkinson and Drew book. This is
in part necessitated by the extraordinary attention to detail, but use of other, similar data
would have strengthened the analysis.

nized across turns of talk and in relation to the other. Thus, Atkinson and Drew demonstrate how patterning in legal discourse need not be thought of as a mere reflection of inherent tendencies (speech styles) of participants. Patterns of talk are continuously and contingently constructed as participants act and react in real time. Furthermore, the microanalysis of Atkinson and Drew is extraordinarily powerful in its description of an apparatus for engaging in accusing and denying that is general enough to apply to nontrial situations. Thus, we learn about the structure of social action *per se,* and not just a special, institutionalized aspect of it.

In focusing on the process of plea bargaining discourse, this study is more like the research of Atkinson and Drew and less similar to that of O'Barr, other courtroom studies, and social psychological perspectives which are outcome oriented. There is frequent attention to transcripts of plea-bargaining conversation, which enables the study of how negotiation is organized in and through the participants' concrete speaking practices. Thus, the starting point for analysis is not a theory or coding format, but rather the discourse itself. In addition to internal characteristics or utterances, sequential and other contexts within which utterances appear are primary analytic resources for describing structures of the bargaining discourse.

We will see that studying discourse processes in this way is important in at least three interrelated ways. First, it is possible to increase our understanding of spoken language, direct interaction, and their social structure. There is throughout an emphasis on transsituational patterns of talk and conduct. Bargaining and negotiation, after all, are not confined to the back rooms and corridors of courthouses. Since they are ubiquitous activities that occur in many arenas of social life, a formal analysis in one arena should aid a comprehension of how they occur in many other circumstances. This proposition concurs with the thrust of much of the conversational analysis literature, including the work of Atkinson and Drew. Rather than exploring aspects of discourse indigenous to a particular situation, analysis has focused on structures of talk, such as the turn-taking system, that transcend diverse settings (Sacks, Schegloff, and Jefferson, 1974). Subsequent chapters on bargaining sequences and person descriptions, for example, fit this tradition.

Still, it is impossible to ignore that plea bargaining occurs in a particular institutional environment. Relatively unexplored in conversational analysis is how such an environment provides instrumental tasks to which members must attend by way of their talk and action. More specifically, the setting of plea bargaining is more than an incidental part of the discourse. It is a feature of the criminal-justice process and the court that *results*—in the form of decisions about criminal defendants and their cases—must always be produced. This feature has consequences for the patterns of talk that emerge in plea bargaining. Put differently, organized aspects of the discourse are often occupied with meeting the participants' institutional mandate to process cases. A second aim of this research, as exemplified in chapters on sentencing and on the system of negotiation, is to explore forms of talk as decision-producing routines.

Finally, the approach here makes it possible to relate concrete social structure to general criminal-justice concerns, such as whether and how bias exists in sentencing and why so many cases result in guilty pleas rather than trials. A perennial complaint about research that has explored these problems is that it has focused on the *mechanics* of the criminal-justice process—its inputs and outputs—and has paid little attention to its *dynamics* (Neubauer, 1974: 197). As Sarat (1979: 59) has observed, major paradigms used to view the court fail to capture its complexities and difficulties. Needed are

> new paradigms for describing and evaluating criminal courts, paradigms which are close to what those courts in fact do and which would be recognizable to those who are involved in processing criminals as well as those who study such behavior.

Although the effort here is to meet this mandate, it is not because of a first-order interest in how well the courts are performing, whether plea bargaining is "fair," or whether justice is being done. Such concerns require first adopting some standard with which to compare the court and its operation, and result in what ethnomethodologists call a "contrastive analytic" approach. This is the strategy of taking a point of view, a definition, or a theory regarding some phenomenon, comparing it to the everyday world of social activities, and reporting as findings the fit between the point of view, definition, or theory, and the world.[9]

An obvious example of a contrastive analysis of the criminal-justice process is Blumberg's (1967) study of "Metropolitan Court." Starting

---

[9]For further general discussion of the issue, see Garfinkel (1967: 277) and Coulter (1979: Chapter 1). With respect to the courts, in particular, see Atkinson and Drew (1979) and Dunstan (1980).

with the idea of a fully adversary system that presumes innocence, he roundly criticizes plea bargaining because it is not adversarial and it relies on a presumption of guilt (Blumberg, 1967: 6). In recent years, as investigators have employed differing conceptions of justice, plea bargaining has been less an object of condemnation. For example, Utz (1978) argues that the proper role of the courts is to administer substantive justice—where individuals and circumstances take precedence over procedural norms. To the extent that the social and political climate of the court allows plea bargaining to render this sort of justice, it is to be admired. Indeed, after finding that Alameda County in California permits the administration of substantive justice, Utz (1978: Part 3) comments favorably on that county's criminal-justice process. Thus, her answer to the question of whether justice is being done in plea bargaining is much different from Blumberg's, but the contrastive analytic procedure is the same.

The presumption here is that an appreciation of what courts in fact do necessitates the suspension of *a priori* notions of justice, theories of court operation, and so on. Such suspension enables one to view orderly aspects of interaction in the criminal-justice process as resulting from socially organized practices that reflect the participants' orientations, standards, and theories, as these are embedded in actual episodes of interaction. This strategy directs immediate attention to the phenomena of talk and behavior. Subjects' concerns are exhibited in the organization of their discourse and may or may not coincide with those matters of abstract interest to social scientists. Once the orientations of the participants are understood, and the orderliness of plea bargaining discourse is appreciated as an achievement directed to handling their practical problems, we can more fully address some of those issues that preoccupy professionals who study the courts.

COLLECTION OF DATA AND THE SETTING

This study emerged from my interest in using a natural setting to obtain tape-recorded talk for the purpose of conversational analysis. At the University of California, I one day conferred with Donald R. Cressey, who had coauthored a book on plea bargaining (Rosett and Cressey, 1976). Citing his own interest in negotiation processes within the court system, he suggested that I record plea-bargaining conversations. We agreed that an ethnomethodological and conversational analysis perspective would help to make sense of them and would contribute to a fuller understanding of bargaining and negotiation as generic processes.

The problem, of course, would be to gain access and permission to make such recordings. Professor Cressey knew the Chief Public Defender in "Garden City," the fictional name of a medium-sized community of approximately 147,000 people (including suburbs) which is the county seat of "Garden County," California. He called the public defender and set up an appointment to talk over my proposed research.

A week later we were sitting in the public defender's office presenting our interests. I carried a letter stating my concerns and intentions. In the letter, and in talking to the public defender, I noted that my main interest was in conversational patterns of agreement, disagreement, and negotiation. I remarked that these processes had been examined in conversations in nonlegal settings but that, because they most likely are particularly salient in lawyers' conversations, it would be desirable to obtain recordings of conversations between defense attorneys and prosecutors. I assured the public defender that the privacy and anonymity of all participants would be protected.

Happily enough, the public defender was vaguely familiar with conversational analysis, having recently observed a distinguished sociologist as an expert witness on language. The public defender agreed to help in whatever way he could. His immediate suggestion was that I study misdemeanor plea bargaining because it took place in a scheduled manner twice a week during pretrial and settlement conferences in the municipal court. Such regularly scheduled sessions would facilitate observation and, eventually, tape recording of negotiations. Attempting to observe and record felony plea bargains, he said, would be much more difficult because they were not on any court agenda. I responded that the municipal court sessions would probably suit my purposes.

The Garden City municipal court is one part of the court system in Garden County, which is divided into a north district and a south district. The north area is served by two trial departments of the superior court and two departments of a municipal court in a city of 60,000 (including suburbs). In Garden City, the south area is served by a superior court with five departments and a municipal court with four departments. In addition, there are single municipal departments in two small communities in outlying areas of the county.

Strictly speaking, it is difficult to know the extent to which the municipal court in Garden City is representative of other lower courts.

Nearly 30 years ago, Kalodner (1956: 321) discussed wide variation in the structure of America's lower courts. Then, ten years ago, Long (1974: 183) suggested that misdemeanor courts were becoming more homogeneous and similar to felony courts. However, more recent studies document a great amount of diversity in lower courts, especially between urban and rural jurisdictions (Alfini and Doan, 1977) but also among states (Alfini, 1981; Ryan, 1981) and even within states (Alfini, 1981). Variation occurs, for example, along the following dimensions: number of full-time judges; types of cases handled; range and severity of sanctions; and case-processing practices, including the incidence of plea negotiation, the availability of defense counsel, and the presence of state prosecutors (Alfini, 1981: 11–14). The Garden City Municipal Court was structured in this way: it had three fulltime judges handling civil, traffic, and ordinance violations in addition to criminal cases; it had indeterminate sentences (with responsibility for all criminal cases that involved penalties of up to a year and/or $1000 fines); there was a high rate of plea bargaining (see Chapter 8); it employed public defenders for indigent defendants; and it utilized district attorneys (as opposed to police officers) for prosecution.

Concerning the provision of public defenders, the use of district attorneys, and the negotiation of charges and sentences in the bulk of cases, the Garden City court is similar to the majority of lower courts in large- and medium-sized (but not small) American cities, according to a survey of judges conducted by the American Judicature Society and the Institute for Court Management (Alfini, 1981: Appendix B). Qualitatively speaking, the court appeared to process its large caseloads in a seemingly chaotic manner, similar to that described in various ethnographic studies (see Chapter 2). In a number of ways, then, we might characterize the municipal court in Garden City as an average urban court.

The afternoon that we talked to the public defender was one of the days set aside for pretrial and settlement conferences, so the public defender took us over to the court and introduced us to the judge who was administering the conference that day. The public defender explained my interest to the judge and the several lawyers present in his chambers, and immediately we were able to sit in on some negotiations. We left after an hour, but during the next week I returned and talked to other public defenders, district attorneys, and judges to explain my research interest more fully. I furnished identical copies of the letter I had given to the chief public defender and a paper I had written on topic change in conversation. Some were initially hesitant, but after two weeks I was able to begin tape-recording conversations at the conferences. I also began three months of observing municipal court operations, interviewing public defenders, district attorneys, probation officers, and judges, and collecting data from court records. Most of the information reported in later chapters was collected during this period, although I continued regular observations (but not tape recordings) of pretrial conferences for another two months.

Field notes from observations, interviews, and court records are the primary source of data for Chapter 2, which describes the courtroom social structure. I also obtained court transcripts of various defendants entering their pleas and of judges issuing sentences at pretrial conferences, and these are also used in Chapter 2.

The tape recordings of plea negotiations comprise the data for Chapters 3, 4, 5, 6, 7, and 8. Nearly 10 hours of recordings on 52 cases were done in 3 locales within the court: (1) The pretrial conferences were conducted in open court, where tape-recording was not allowed. On two occasions I arranged for the public defenders and district attorneys to discuss their cases in an unused jury room where I was able to record. These were two-party conversations, involving a single district attorney and a single public defender, although there were periodic interruptions. Taped discussions of 24 cases were obtained here, and amounted to 3 hours of talk. (2) Another set of recordings was made in the judges' chambers where the district attorneys and public defenders would retreat when they needed help in resolving particular cases. These were essentially three-party conversations among the judge, public defender, and one district attorney, although other public defenders, district attorneys, probation officers, or bailiffs would sometimes enter the conversation. Approximately 6 hours of negotiations, involving 30 cases, were taped here. (3) Sometimes, if plea negotiations were unsuccessful at the pretrial stage and a case were scheduled for trial, the judge, defense lawyer, and district attorney would make one last attempt at settlement by discussing the case immediately before trial. One hour of taped conversations regarding 4 cases was obtained in judges' chambers on the day that trials were scheduled to begin.[10]

The 52 cases I collected included 15 involving theft, 11 drunk driv-

---

[10]The cases from (1), (2), and (3) add up to 58 (instead of the total of 52 mentioned earlier) because six cases were discussed in two locales.

ing, 8 battery, 3 drinking in public, 3 exhibition of speed, 2 fighting in public, and 2 loitering offenses. There was one case each of hit-and-run driving, reckless driving, resisting public officers, assault with a deadly weapon, removing vehicle parts, carrying a switchblade, vandalism, and burglary. (In cases where there was more than one charge, I tallied the initial charge on the docket sheet for this enumeration.)

METHODS

Chapter 2 is an observation study of the courtroom where defendants assembled, lawyers conducted their negotiations, and judges heard pleas. Chapters 3–8 describe and analyze plea-bargaining conversations. Thus, two preliminary comments seem necessary—one regarding ethnography, the other concerning conversational analysis. Some remarks about observer influence and the generality of this study are also appropriate.

Participant Observation

That plea bargaining in misdemeanor cases in Garden City took place in a public courtroom facilitated an observational study of how negotiations were conducted even while a variety of other official and unofficial activities occurred. In the courtroom, I was free to sit in different areas, watch, and take notes on the behavior of the courtroom officials, the defendants, and members of the public.

A distinction is often made between the known and unknown observer in field research (Lofland, 1971: 93–99). I rather straddled the fence with respect to this dichotomy, whose extremes are probably nonexistent in actual research (Roth, 1962). On the one hand, I had been introduced to the judges and most of the lawyers; they knew who I was and that I was doing research. On the other hand, some of the district attorneys and defense lawyers appearing in court had not been introduced to me. And, of course, the vast number of defendants and members of the public who were present did not know of my research. I believe that most of them considered me to be another lawyer. The fact that I was taking notes was plausible given this typification and setting.

The progress of the observation study was somewhat similar to that described by Glaser and Strauss (1965: 289). First, I took notes on a wide variety of happenings and rather confusedly tried to document everything that occurred. Gradually, however, I became interested in the way in which everyone present seemed to be engaged in the careful work of producing what Goffman (1963: 10) called a "public order"—a system of face-to-face interaction that regulates what people do with and to each other. This interest led to a more focused approach in my observations and note taking and to the eventual development of provisional hypotheses. Such hypotheses are used to help further sensitize an observer to particular behaviors in the setting being studied (Bogdan and Taylor, 1975: 80) and to guide the search for supporting data and negative cases (Becker, 1958; Cressey, 1953). This is not to say that the final analysis is contemporaneous with the collection of data. Rather, some analytic work occurs even while the researcher is in the setting, and this helps in the collection of the data (Spradley, 1980).

Conversational Analysis

An important concern of conversational analysis, long ago noted by Sacks (1963), is that language ought not to be part of an analytic apparatus until it has been described. Sociologists and other researchers, instead of investigating language as a phenomenon in its own right, have often treated it as a taken-for-granted resource in analyzing, describing, and explaining social realities. But, according to Sacks, language ought to be treated as a *feature* of social settings and not as a *means* for addressing other sociological questions.

Conversational analysis is in a tradition consistent with Wittgenstein (1958), Searle (1969), and Austin (1965) that distinguishes language as an *activity*, a mode of doing things, and not just a vehicle of "communication" (cf. Labov, 1972a: 298). In and through naturally occurring talk, a variety of features of ordinary social settings are accomplished. These features include roles, norms, types of relationships, types of settings, properties of those settings, and so on, which largely are discussed as social "facts" rather than social activities.

How does one then analyze the discourse activities in a setting? Briefly, the procedure is to identify patterns exhibited in talk that are nontrivial because participants produce and are "oriented to" them. This means that conversationalists themselves describe and analyze what they are doing in their talk, and notice and attempt to repair breaches of conversational order. Observers, therefore, must be concerned with

members' meanings, categories, and ways of exhibiting—to themselves
and others—what is happening in the interaction at any given moment
(cf. Sacks et al., 1974: 228). In other words, orderliness occurs in discourse because it is produced, recognized, and used by participants as
an ongoing basis for inference and action (cf. Schegloff and Sacks, 1974:
234). The problem of whether some observed phenomenon is an instance
of an answer, or an argument, or a denial, or any other item cannot be
resolved by reference to a body of theory or a list of necessary features.
It must be resolved by examining how the phenomenon is treated by
the participants within the conversation.

An illustration will make the point clearer. One obvious feature of
conversation is that only one person may properly speak at a time. When
more than one person is talking, one will drop out and may ritually offer
an "excuse me," which allows the other to proceed (Sacks et al., 1974:
723–4). When no one talks, other devices are used to repair or restore
the one-person-talking feature, such as making a query about who was
spoken to ("Who me?"), invoking a topic change (Maynard, 1980), and
so forth. Thus, keeping one and only one person speaking at a time is
a problem for participants, as exhibited in their speaking practices. Using
the criteria that participants have for determining the salient features of
interactional episodes lends to an analysis that is not an *interpretation* of
their conduct. Rather, analysis is based on, and made valid by, the
participants' own orientations, characterizations, and exhibited
understandings.

Also involved in the analysis of discourse is what Mehan (1979:
20–21) calls "comprehensive data analysis." This involves developing a
set of propositions that makes sense of patterns exhibited by all cases
in a corpus of data. One begins with a small group of cases, generates
a provisional analytic scheme, compares another set of cases to the
scheme, and modifies the scheme as necessary until the corpus is ex-
hausted. Negative or discrepant cases are neither ignored nor accommodated by a search for additional variables to explain them. Instead,
the researcher attempts to find deeper levels of organization in the data
that encompass every case.

Thus, in studying a corpus of nearly 500 telephone calls, Schegloff
(1968) formulated a rule that "answerer speaks first." This rule worked
in all calls except one, in which the caller spoke first. Rather than ignoring
this instance, minimizing its importance, or explaining it away in an *ad
hoc* fashion, Schegloff pursued an analysis of summons–answer se-

quences. If the ring of a telephone call is the first part of such a sequence, and an answer to the ring is the second part, then the rule that answerer speaks first reflects the obligation to respond appropriately when summoned. An inappropriate response occurs when a called person picks up a receiver and says nothing. The caller might know that a recipient is present at the called number, but would not know if the person is available for further interaction. The caller may then reissue the summons by saying hello or otherwise speaking first. Therefore, the answerer speaks first rule was not broken in Schegloff's deviant case. A second summons was produced because a complete answer to the first one had not been provided, and the rule clearly operated within the structure of summons–answer sequencing.

Examining the negative case forced Schegloff to modify his provisional framework and describe deeper and more general interactional structures. The consequence of analyzing data comprehensively is a model that completely describes the patterning of a given phenomenon. Such comprehensiveness and completeness are sought in this study with respect to a variety of phenomena, including the use of "person-descriptions," "bargaining sequences," and other units of negotiational discourse. Generalizations are derived from an examination of every instance of these units and from particular attention to cases that do not fit preliminary analyses.

Analyzing discourse may involve the use of audio and videotapes and transcriptions of these tapes. Because I did not make videotapes of the plea bargaining sessions, some organizational features of the data are not accessible. For example, by examining gaze behavior in videotaped casual conversations, Goodwin (1981) has shown how otherwise disorderly appearing hesitations, pauses, and restarts are involved in achieving mutual orientation between co-participants. Similarly, Frankel (1983) has shown how gaze, touch, and talk are finely coordinated aspects of a single interactional system operative in doctor–patient encounters. Ideally, students of microinteraction in the court would collect data by videotape, but that strategy is obviously more disruptive of day-to-day routines than the use of audiotape. My assumption is that any phenomena lost because I made no video record of the plea-bargaining conversations, though relevant to other issues in the organization of talk, are not critically germane to the analyses and generalizations offered in the following chapters. That assumption can be put to the test by future research.

My tape recordings were transcribed according to the system devised by Gail Jefferson (see Appendix 1). Those conventions are designed to preserve and reproduce much detail from the actual conversations. One reason is that the kinds of phenomena that reveal important patterns in conversation are often found in what are sometimes regarded as minor features of talk, such as errors, false starts, hesitations, appositional particles, pauses and their durations, overlapping speech, and so forth (Terasaki, 1976: Appendix II). A second reason for maintaining close attention to detail is to promote the kind of rigor that makes for reliable results, which could be replicated in repeated observations and by others examining the data. A third reason for using technical transcription is to obtain a record that does not depend upon what the researcher thinks is interesting or important before analyzing the data. The transcript is an attempt to reproduce the actual interactive process as faithfully as possible and to include as many of its elements as can be practically rendered in written form.

I have not, however, presented plea bargaining excerpts in the full detail in which they were originally transcribed. Neither have I completely "normalized" the talk appearing in excerpts. Instead, I have simplified the segments in the text to make for easier reading. The visibility of silences, overlapping talk, hesitations, and other conversational features is preserved only when they are necessary to make a particular descriptive or analytic point (cf. Goodwin, 1981: 47). And, following Labov and Fanshel (1977: 40–41), there is no well-developed phonetic system used in the transcripts, but excerpts do contain some well-recognized dialect pronunciations, such as *ya* for *you*, *wanta* for *want to*, *arright* for *all right*, and so on.

Observer Influence: Generality of the Study

I was present at all recording sessions, to monitor the tape recorder and also to take notes on the interaction. This raises obvious problems as to whether my presence influenced the conversations in any direction. Labov (1972b: 209) has addressed the "observer's paradox" involved:

> The aim of linguistic research in the community must be to find out how people talk when they are not being systematically observed; yet we can only obtain these data by systematic observation.

Two factors work to minimize observer influence. One is that "the natural interaction of peers can overshadow the effects of observation and help us approach the goal of capturing the vernacular of everyday life in which the minimum amount of attention is paid to speech" (Labov, 1972a: 256). Indeed, it seemed that once the lawyers whom I was observing asked their questions about my recording equipment, and began talking about their cases, their conversation took on a character that could not have been very much removed from their unobserved talk. There is a reason for this, as Labov (1972a: 256) notes: the "vernacular is the property of the group" and its "consistency and well-formed, systematic character is the result of a vast number of interactions." Thus, to suddenly produce a nonstandard form of conversation, if not difficult for the participants, would be noticeable to them and out of keeping with the constraints developed through the production and maintenance of the courtroom subculture.[11]

Another factor minimizing observer influence is that participants have a practical interest in what they are doing and are unlikely to let an outsider interfere with the normal performance of their jobs. Gumperz (1972: 15–16) has argued that speakers utilize knowledge of their audience and its members' possible social identities to determine what constraints might be operating on their own choice of interactional strategies. Determining what effect I might have had, then, would necessitate finding out the extent to which I was perceived as a relevant audience by the lawyers and whether—if I was considered as an audience—my social identity would affect their choice of negotiation strategies. The assurances that I made about the research being primarily concerned with language were meant to imply that I represented an audience of no concern to the participants. And that the anonymity of everyone concerned would be preserved further implied that the discussants did not need to be concerned about who might eventually see what was said. My impression was that, after initial questions regarding the recording equipment, the involved parties mostly disattended both it and myself, since I was careful not to talk or laugh or otherwise make myself interactionally available.

In all, two judges, six public defenders, three private attorneys, and six district attorneys were recorded. I obtained recordings from these different attorneys, and at varied locales and times, in order to correct for any factors that might be unique to any one time, place, or set of participants within the court.

That plea bargaining was studied within only one misdemeanor

---

[11]The courtroom subculture is discussed in later chapters. See especially Chapter 6.

court may limit the general implications of the findings, but three points should be considered. First, misdemeanor criminal justice has been understudied, a situation stemming from a tradition of legal and social scientific scholarship that has considered misdemeanor courts to be trivial even while advocating radical reform (Alfini, 1981: 1–11; Klonoski and Mendelsohn, 1970: xiii–xiv; Long, 1974: 173; Mileski, 1971: 477; Brickey and Miller, 1975: 688).[12] The consequence is that it would be difficult to do comparative research in a number of courts even if one wanted, because of the lack of a developed frame of reference or theory on which to base the research.[13] One student of lower criminal courts has observed:

> I am not convinced that current knowledge of criminal court processes is well developed, and unless or until there is a substantial body of carefully drawn descriptive and inductive research on which typologies can be drawn and until classifications are made, the benefits of an analysis of a single setting may be as great as, if not greater than, those of comparative studies. (Feeley, 1979c: xvii)

Because of the previously mentioned heterogeneity among America's lower courts, the need for case studies is particularly acute. The intensive analysis of one court, in one city, can lead toward the development of a "grounded theory" (Glaser and Strauss, 1967) that then can guide later comparative analysis.

A second question is whether misdemeanor (lower court) plea bargaining is comparable to felony (higher court) plea bargaining. Myers (1982) demonstrates differences in misdemeanor and felony decision-making processes, but they are complex and do not explain a large proportion of variance in case outcomes. The tendency among observers of the court is to emphasize how misdemeanor plea bargaining resembles felony plea bargaining and how lower courts have emerged as similar

---

[12]One researcher has noted:

> This state of affairs is ironical because statistically misdemeanor courts are the most frequent type of criminal courts and because many people assess the justness of the entire court system by their encounters with its "lowest" division. Preoccupied with the grandeur of the Supreme Court and the notoriety of felony courts, researchers forget the insight of the President's Commission on Law Enforcement and Administration of Justice [1967] that "most of the cases in the criminal courts consist of what are essentially violations of moral norms or instances of annoying behavior, rather than of serious crimes," and that "almost half of all arrests are on charges of drunkenness, disorderly conduct, vagrancy, gambling, and minor sex violations." (Long, 1974: 173)

[13]This problem in the theoretical literature regarding the courts is examined more thoroughly in Chapter 2.

to higher courts. While comparing district courts with the state superior courts in Massachusetts, Buckle and Buckle (1977: 63) were "unable to detect any systematic differences between the [plea bargaining] processes of the two systems, which would tend to alter our findings." In his study of Connecticut courts, Heumann (1977: 34–46) argues that though plea bargaining in the superior courts is carried on in a more decorous atmosphere than in circuit courts, negotiations are substantially similar in the two systems. In an Illinois city, Neubauer (1974: 216) found that felony cases often involve greater preparation and discussion by attorneys and that felony cases were treated with less flexibility than misdemeanors. Otherwise, however, such considerations as the seriousness of an offense, the suspect's past record, the strength of the prosecutor's case, and the particulars of a defendant's biography were characteristic of both felony and misdemeanor plea bargainings (Neubauer, 1974: 217–219). Finally, Feeley (1979c: 7) attributes the similarity between courts to the "constitutional revolution" that gave misdemeants as well as felons the right to counsel, and which has led to greater formalization of the lower courts.

Third, patterns of talk and interaction are presumed to reflect a common system of speaking and acting skills (Zimmerman, 1978), whether acquired by virtue of participation in the general society or in particular (e.g., professional) subgroups. Following a procedure in conversational analysis, it is possible to "extract" from the plea bargaining data those orderly phenomena that are independent of the particular court situation, particular kinds of cases, and particular individuals involved (Sacks et al., 1974: 699).[14] The structures or practices (orderly phenomena) identified by this means are also context-sensitive and thus reflect and accomplish particular aspects of given settings. In short, the *duality* of interaction is captured in this research. Because structures or practices are the very means by which the particulars of a situation, case, or individual are attended to, the details of actual negotiations are not lost. By examining formal practices, however, it is possible to transcend mere description and obtain an analysis of general cultural and subcultural skills used in the constitution of the objective-appearing features of plea bargaining.

---

[14]The independence of bargaining practices from their context is given critical attention in Chapter 3.

PLAN OF THE BOOK

The observed plea bargaining conversations took place at pretrial and settlement conferences in a public courtroom. Chapter 2 first shows that a variety of other official and unofficial activities took place concurrently and then explores the social organizational means by which the business of the court is made to occur. It examines, among other things, why defendants, who are evidently the most alienated by courtroom routines, contribute to its ongoing stability. This latter discussion provides an introduction to plea bargaining practices, including character assessment and the negotiation of case outcomes, which are more closely examined in subsequent chapters.

The *context* of plea bargaining discourse is given further attention in Chapter 3. Drawing on Goffman, the chapter discusses how attorneys *frame* the positions that they take in plea bargaining. Their framing practices display the importance of the relationships that attorneys have with other persons, such as defendants and witnesses; with their own offices and professions; with other agencies, such as the police; and with the court and its activities, such as trial. These relationships need to be understood as part of the context to which organized bargaining sequences (discussed in following chapters) are sensitive. Chapter 3 also critiques the view of plea bargaining as a process of "information exchange," and argues that a dramaturgical perspective is needed to understand the way in which "facts" are presented and positions are taken.

Usually, plea bargaining is defined as a process in which charge and/or sentencing concessions are traded for a defendant's guilty plea, but it is well known that a much wider array of transactions takes place in actual negotiations. Chapter 4 shows that behind the diversity of transactions is the "bargaining sequence," wherein one party presents a position and the other responds to it. Elaboration of the bargaining sequence yields various characteristic features of plea bargaining, such as "exchange," "compromise," "disagreement," and so on. Procedures for leading into, and exiting from, the sequence relate it to additional elements of the discourse. Thus, at the core of negotiation is a conversational structure used to achieve a range of "reasonable" decisions.

Chapter 5 argues, contrary to many ethnographic treatments of plea bargaining, that lawyers do not necessarily settle the facts of the case and determine the moral character of the defendant before deciding upon a disposition. In fact, they may entirely disagree about those things and still arrive at a mutually acceptable means of disposition.

The topic of "character assessment" is pursued in Chapter 6. It is a phenomenon that has received much attention in the sociology of deviance. Here it is related to how persons are *described* in conversation. In plea bargaining, where a major activity is mustering arguments for defense and prosecution positions on charge or sentence, person-descriptions are employed as *justifications* for those positions. The systematics of this use are shown by reference to the contextual locations in which person-descriptions appear in plea bargaining discourse.

The analysis of person-descriptions and character assessment is used in Chapter 7 to address the widespread sociological interest in the fairness of charging and sentencing decisions. Much study has been devoted to ascertaining the relative influence of legal attributes (seriousness of offense, prior record) and extralegal attributes (race, class, etc.) on these decisions. But in the discussion of any given case, the defendant characteristics that are relevant to disposition represent a selection from an array of possible attributes. They are not "descriptively adequate" in any objective sense, but they are fitted to the "facts" of a case in a contextual manner as arguments are made. The relation of defendant attributes to dispositions is therefore mediated by methodic negotiating practices, and these are not captured in models of the decision-making process utilized in sentencing research. As a result, those models may be seriously misspecified, and the problem of a large amount of unexplained variance will not yield to traditional means for resolving it. Chapter 7 suggests a different kind of modeling process, one based on the idea of a Gestalt contexture. This allows investigation of commonsense reasoning practices and typifications involved in decision making. The question of whether all defendants receive equal treatment before the law is related to the kinds of typifications that lawyers and judges employ. Finally, the chapter argues that prior research has used a standard of formal rationality to measure how well the courts administer justice, whereas both formal and *substantive* rationality are displayed in plea bargaining. This means that the issue of equal treatment is more difficult to assess than is ordinarily thought.

In Chapter 8, we return to the structure of negotiation *per se* to examine the perennial question of why so many guilty pleas, as opposed to trials, occur in United States courts. Theories that plea bargaining results from concern for efficient processing, substantive justice, or obtaining a fair exchange are reviewed and shown not to accommodate known facts about the practice. Empirical analysis demonstrates a discourse system of negotiation, displayed in three decision-making patterns and their interrelations. This system exerts a pressure for here-and-now resolution of cases and thus induces guilty pleas as opposed to trials. The description of this system not only makes sense of some of the known facts about plea bargaining; it also makes possible an appreciation of how outcomes, including decisions on charges, sentences, continuances and trial, are related to specific patterns by which they are achieved. This reveals a previously neglected heterogeneity of such outcomes.

Finally, Chapter 9 looks at the advantages of an "inside" approach to the study of criminal-justice operations. While questions regarding the fairness and justness of the courts cannot be fully addressed in this sort of study, explicating the social organization of direct interaction leads to a better knowledge of what actually happens in the criminal-justice process. Thus, future research can ask questions appropriate to the phenomena.

CHAPTER 2

The Courtroom Context of Plea Bargaining

In Garden City, misdemeanor plea bargaining is conducted in a busy public courtroom where, simultaneously, defendants enter pleas, defense attorneys talk with clients, and a host of other conversations and activities take place. On the surface, the courtroom appears disorganized. In fact, there is an underlying order to the many and diverse engagements.

Studies of complex organizations have largely neglected face-to-face interaction, even in "people processing" agencies like the court.[1] We have scant understanding of how officials conduct their everyday tasks in direct interaction with clients; conversely, we know little about the contribution that clients make to the structure of people-processing settings. How does a particular social order occur in a courtroom setting in which a variety of official and unofficial activities take place concurrently? Why do defendants contribute to the management of this order even though they tend to be disenchanted with its routines and results?

BUREAUCRACY AND SOCIAL ORGANIZATION

Persons who have studied plea bargaining seem to agree on two major points. First, bargaining dialogues remain hidden from the de-

[1]Hasenfeld (1972: 256) defines "people processing" organizations as those

> whose explicit function is not to change the behavior of people directly but to process them and confer public statuses on them . . . these organizations shape a person's life by controlling his access to a wide range of social settings through the public status they confer; and they may define and confirm the individual's social position when his current status is questioned.

The definition fits the criminal court well.

29

fendants under discussion, from victims, probation officers, judges (sometimes), other officers of the court, and the wider public—any of whom might be likely candidates to scrutinize the proceedings if it were possible (e.g., Alschuler, 1975; Davis, 1970; Newman, 1966). Second, in Grosman's (1969: 50) terms, "persons become objects and products which must be processed through the system." This is due to the "organizational imperative" to presume guilt and dispose of cases efficiently (Littrell, 1979: 153). These two notions converge in the succinct remarks of a public defender interviewed for the present research:

> In plea bargaining, the client is in a sense the victim, he is being "done unto" in plea bargaining. The p.d. and d.a. go behind closed doors and decide his fate.

The upshot of these characterizations is that the courtroom context of plea bargaining is said to be a *bureaucratic* one wherein large numbers of cases, whose features are indistinguishable to the judge and other participants, are processed (e.g., Mileski, 1971: 481, 517–18; Rosett and Cressey, 1976: 8).

The characterizations of plea bargaining as a hidden activity and defendants as objects in assembly-line process may be warranted, but they need explication in structural terms. The strategy here is to treat such characterizations as situated "accounts," meaning that they are embedded in a particular social organization (Bittner, 1974; Sacks, 1975; Zimmerman and Wieder, 1977). As an interactional accomplishment of all participants, including defendants,[2] this social organization is described by such characterizations at the same time as it renders them sensible.

The important task, from this standpoint, is not to use an abstract

---

[2]In language used by Perrow (1979: 246), my approach puts "an emphasis upon the daily construction and reproduction of basic social patterns by all actors in the system." Defendants have rarely been treated for what they are—active participants in the courtroom process. For example, the study by Nardulli (1978: 110) defines defendants as "reactive agents" who are "inputs" to the court, but not fundamental to its organization or its analysis. Other studies that examine defendants include Bottoms and McClean (1976: Chapter 3), Carlen (1976), Emerson (1969: Chapter 7), Feeley (1979c), and Rosett and Cressey (1976). With the exception of Emerson, however, the studies attempt to assess the defendants' perspective, and they do not analyze defendants' actual behavioral contribution to courtroom structure. The most recent recommendations for analyzing the courts as organizations continue to emphasize the importance of professionals while ignoring defendants and other nonofficial participants (see Clynch and Neubauer, 1981; Burstein, 1980).

theory of organization as an aid in deciding whether the court is bureaucratic. Students of the criminal-justice process have already given much time and attention to the question of which model of complex organizations makes sense of the court (Burstein, 1980; Clynch and Neubauer, 1981; Feeley, 1973; Hagan, Hewitt, and Alwin, 1979; Mohr, 1976; Nardulli, 1978), and they have had little success in answering it.[3] A more fruitful procedure, given that observers and insiders experience the plea bargaining process as bureaucratic, is to discover what social organization lies behind their descriptions of a particular courtroom setting in which plea bargaining and related activities are salient occurrences. By *social organization* I refer to the "participation framework" of the courtroom, as constituted by systematic deployment of standard practices that effect order in a variety of everyday public settings (Goffman, 1963; 1981).[4]

INTERACTIONAL PRACTICES IN THE COURTROOM

Misdemeanor plea bargaining occurs in the Garden City municipal court at semiweekly pretrial and settlement conferences. Prior to this stage in the adjudication of cases, defendants have been arrested for some offense, have had cases reviewed by a filing officer in the district attorney's office, have been arraigned, and have pleaded not guilty. At the pretrial conference, defense attorneys, prosecutors, and sometimes judges, discuss levels of offense to be charged and sentences to be

[3]One problem with treating the court as a type of complex organization is that it is a "loosely coupled system" (Hagan et al., 1979), wherein a number of agencies daily come together for the purpose of administering justice. Each of these institutions—police, district attorneys, public defenders, judges, probation officers, parole boards—when taken separately may have an internal organization that resembles any of various organizational models. But the criminal justice process as a whole, as Mohr (1976: 625) has suggested, does not seem capable of being "comprehended by the dominant strains of existing organization theory." By dominant strains, Mohr (1976) refers to the Weberian (1946) ideal typical bureaucracy; Dalton's (1959) political approach; Cohen, March, and Olsen's (1972) "organized anarchies"; and the organization-as-firm framework of Cyert and March (1963). On this point, see also Burstein (1980), Clynch and Neubauer (1981), Feeley (1973), and Nardulli (1978).

[4]Other interactional studies of courtroom settings have treated social organization as being comprised of contextually bound, sequentially placed cues of legal officials, used to accomplish such courtroom features as "shared attentiveness" (Atkinson, 1979), or the appearance of "competency," "consistency," and other ideals of justice (Pollner, 1979).

administered in individual cases. Although defendants do not directly participate in negotiations (cf. Heinz and Kerstetter, 1979), they are required to be present in order to accept or reject the negotiated dispositions, and accordingly, change or reassert their prior not-guilty plea. Also present at these sessions are relatives or friends of defendants, two clerks, a probation officer, a court reporter, and the bailiff.

To step into the courtroom in the middle of the pretrial conference is to be confronted by numbers of people moving about, talking, and engaging in a variety of activities, all of which, at first glance, give the appearance of a bazaar rather than a formal judicial setting. A number of investigators (Feeley, 1979c; Heumann, 1978; Eisenstein and Jacob, 1977: 19) describe scenes similar to these pretrial and settlement conferences. For example:

> Naive visitors will be bewildered by the throngs in criminal courtrooms where they expected dignified decorum. . . . the observer will hear one case called after another and disposed of within a few seconds or minutes. . . . he will see attorneys come in and out, transacting business with the court clerk and sometimes disappearing into an unmarked door, which the observer learns takes one to the judge's chambers. He may see the judge emerge for a ceremony when several attorneys are in the courtroom. (Eisenstein and Jacob, 1977: 19)

But what seems chaotic at first glance exhibits particular forms of order on closer inspection.

Typically, an afternoon of pretrial conferences begins with numerous defendants, family, and friends sitting, standing, and milling around in the hallway outside the courtroom. At 1:30 P.M., a bailiff unlocks the doors, and defendants and their companions enter the courtroom and sit down. The two district attorneys assigned to misdemeanor cases may be seated already. Defense attorneys may be there already as well, or they may arrive shortly, and, like the district attorneys, are laden with clients' files.

A total of five or six public defenders (three full-time and two or three part-time) are assigned to misdemeanor cases. Only two are able to talk to the district attorneys at any given time. The others are free to visit with their clients and with each other, or to stand and wait their turn with the district attorney, busying themselves in a variety of self-absorbing activities such as daydreaming, reading files, and so on.

The activities of the lawyers are disrupted only momentarily or not at all when the judge enters the room. The judge's arrival is announced first by a buzzer and then by the bailiff saying, "Please remain seated and come to order; this court is again in session." As the judge enters, so does a retinue of two clerks, a probation officer, and a court-reporter. While plea bargaining and other discussions continue unabated, public defenders who have reached agreements with district attorneys in particular cases may then approach the bench and have these cases called for disposition, dismissal, or continuance for consideration at a later date.

Defendants spend but a matter of minutes conversing with courtroom officials. This occurs when their defense attorneys speak to them briefly to advise or to present an offered disposition and also when the judge calls the defendants' cases for entry of the plea. Otherwise, they may be observed talking to each other or their friends. If not engaged, they may daydream, scan the courtroom and observe various activities, read, doodle, take notes, wring hands, or even mutter to themselves.

In summary, a variety of activities, including plea bargaining discussions, disposition transactions, lawyer–client conferences, and defendants and others' waiting behaviors, occur during a pretrial settlement conference. Often, all of them are happening at once; yet they are neither random activities nor, in any strong sense, competing activities. Rather, they are made to coexist within two major kinds of limits, including (1) a precedence order and (2) an ecological order.

Precedence Order

The term *precedence order* refers to the way in which participants in the pretrial and settlement conference accord their activities a certain ranking, with respect to three kinds of encounters: (1) the judicial encounter, (2) the negotiational encounter between public defender and district attorney, and (3) encounters between public defenders and clients.

The Judicial Encounter

The judicial encounter, where involved parties officially dispense of individual cases, is the dominant activity in the courtroom. On the afternoon of the pretrial conference, when the judge first enters the room, there may be a number of defense attorneys ready to call their cases. One will step forward and address the judge.[5]

---

[5]In the examples, individual public defenders are designated by the initials "PD" and a number. District attorneys are designated by "DA" and a number. The judge is denoted by a "J." All names (including geographic names) are fictitious.

PD4 is standing behind the lawyers' table, facing the judge, when
the latter walks into the court and sits down.

PD4: Your Honor, in the matter of George Smith, we would continue
   that case by agreement for two weeks. That would be April 13.

J: Is that acceptable with the people?

DA2: Yes your honor, with a fifteen-day time waiver.[6]

J: Does the defendant waive time to the thirteenth and fifteen
   days beyond?

PD4: Yes.

J: So continued.

(Notes, 3/30)

The defense attorney or judge may also call defendants whose cases
have been settled, and the judge will accept pleas and assign sentences:

PD4: Larry Steiner, would you come forward, please?

Def: Yes, sir

PD4: Mr. Steiner understands that the complaint will be amended to add
   22350 of the Vehicle Code, unsafe speed, and he would plead guilty
   to that, and the other charge [drunk driving] will be dismissed

J: Is it now your wish to plead guilty to the infraction of simple
   speed, 22350

Def: Yes, sir

J: All right. And the DA has recommended a fine?

DA2: Yes, your honor. Thirty-five dollars

J: I will impose the recommended sentence

(Court Recorder, 3/30)

The encounter in which the judge takes defendants' pleas and hears
attorneys' recommendations for continuances or dismissals is maintained as the dominating courtroom activity by a number of means. The
first is architectural and technological. The judge sits on a platform
behind the bench, and his voice is projected over the court from a
microphone atop his desk. Both visually and aurally his behavior is easily
the focal part of the court. A second means is the practice of voice
modulation. Participants in other encounters keep their voices at a very
low level, insuring that the judicial encounter will not be "jammed out
of operation" (Goffman, 1963: 162). Finally, when a case is called, the
defendant and lawyers responsible for the case are required to drop
what they are doing and give their attention to the judge. Thus, at the

---

[6]This refers to the defendant giving up the right to a speedy trial.

time the defendants may be talking with their family in the audience section or watching their lawyers talk with defense attorneys. When an individual's name is spoken, however, that person promptly walks to the judge's bench, dropping whatever activity was occupying him or her. For example:

The judge has returned from chambers after a short recess. PD6 is
standing to the right of the lawyers' table.
   J: All right, I understand we have at least one more disposition
PD6: Yes, would the court call Miss Ellen Steward.
   J: Ellen Steward.
A woman gets up from her seat in the audience section and moves
forward along with PD6 into the space before the judge's bench.

(Notes, 6/24)

Whatever the state of an individual's current involvement within the courtroom, a constant readiness for the dispositional encounter is maintained.

Similarly, when the judge calls a case assigned to a district attorney who might be deep in negotiations with a defense lawyer, the DA drops the latter discussion and attends to the judicial encounter.

DA3 is conferring with PD4 when PD2 steps before the judge.
PD2: (to judge) I'd like to call the Robinson case and put that
       on for Wednesday morning.[7]
   J: Mr. Revell, what is your recommendation?
DA3: (looks up from conversation with PD4) No objection, your
       honor.

(Notes, 2/1)

If the judge does not succeed in obtaining an attorney's attention, that is a matter for remedy. In the following, a private attorney has called his client's name.

PA: I would like to move for a continuance in this case, your
     honor.
  J: Is that acceptable with the people?
               (silence)
  J: Jeffrey?

---

[7]"Put that on for Wednesday morning" means put it on the arraignment calendar. The case is being continued to a more convenient time for entering the plea.

DA3: (turns away from public defender he is talking to) I'm sorry.
  J: Is a two-week continuance acceptable with the people in the
        case of John Smith?
DA3: No objection, your honor.

(Notes, 4/8)

The DA's apology, "I'm sorry," is a device with which a situational offender can disassociate himself from an offense and thereby display an allegiance to some interactional rule (Goffman, 1971: 113). In this instance, the obligation to be accessible for the dispositional encounter is clearly exhibited.

The Negotiational Encounter

Whenever a district attorney and a defense lawyer converge to discuss the disposition of cases, another delicately managed interactional phenomenon appears in the courtroom setting. The two parties do not sit down and systematically run through a discussion of all their cases one by one and then present their conclusions to the judge. Rather, negotiations occur in spurts and starts. There are reasons for this.

For one, there are but two district attorneys to five or six public defenders. This means that some of the public defenders must wait their turn while others sit down to talk with the prosecutors.

For another, duties are allocated differently in the respective organizations of the district attorney and the public defender. Each district attorney is responsible for handling distinct classes of offenses. One handles drunk and reckless driving cases and the other takes care of most other misdemeanors, such as petty theft and assault cases. Caseloads in the Garden County public defender's office, on the other hand, are determined on the basis of ensuring that each attorney has an equal number of cases, regardless of what kind they may be. The result is that the PD's caseload is diversified, and he may need to see one district attorney for drunk-driving cases, and the other DA for petty theft, assault, and residual cases.

A final reason that a DA and PD do not complete their negotiations in one encounter is that they have to attend to competing activities. The district attorneys' time is divided two ways, between the judicial encounter and the negotiational encounter. The defense attorneys' time is spent among three official responsibilities: representing clients before the judge, negotiating with the district attorneys, and attending to their clients directly—advising them, obtaining needed information, presenting offers that the district attorneys have made regarding disposition.

These factors contribute to a situation in which negotiations proceed in a syncopated fashion. There is constant movement in and out of negotiations by both district attorneys and public defenders. Nevertheless, such encounters are well-managed interactions within the courtroom, and the work of plea bargaining is done expeditiously within them. Again, specific interactional practices achieve this feature of the pretrial conference.

Judges, we have seen, legitimately disrupt negotiations between lawyers. While the summoned party participates in the judicial encounter, the other awaits his return. Soon, the involved party regularly turns back to negotiation with the lawyer with whom he had been talking before the disruption. The bargaining discussion is thus displayed as a matter of importance in its own right.

Unlike the judge, others wanting to talk to the DA or PD involved in negotiations exert no interruptive rights. The few intrusions that do occur are by fellow lawyers and are accompanied by remedial exchanges. In the following, PD2 and DA3 were negotiating a particular case when PD4 stepped up to the pair.

1. PD4: Could I interrupt you jus' one second?
2. PD2: Sure, go ahead.
3. PD4: I've got a guy named Tapping out there, I gotta tell 'im I'm gonna continue his case.

(Transcript, 2/11)

As Goffman (1971) suggests, line 1 is a remedy; it is a ritual way of anticipating a possible affront. Line 2 is a relief; it affirms the appropriateness of the remedy of the associated action. In line 3, PD4 also offers an account (Scott and Lyman, 1968) that further provides a warrant for the intrusion. The function of the interchange is to allow an interruption even while respecting the integrity of the ongoing conversation between PD2 and DA3.

For the most part, however, public defenders waiting to talk to a district attorney, or clients wanting to talk with their defense attorney, extend "civil inattention" (Goffman, 1963: 196) to negotiational encounters: not looking directly at the participants, spacing themselves so as not to intrude aurally on the discussion, and presenting themselves for engagement with one of the participants at calculated moments. They notice when the conversation stops, when one member gets up from his chair, turns away, or otherwise leaves the scene. Sometimes they await a head nod or other invitation from the person with whom they desire an audience. Thus, the regard accorded negotiational encounters is carefully orchestrated, requiring bystanders simultaneously to disattend the encounter's inner workings and yet keep themselves sufficiently apprised of its contours so as to obtain involvement at the right moment with the person whose attention is desired.

Practices intrinsic to the negotiational encounter also maintain its integrity. We have already noted that participants modulate their voices, at once allowing other engagements to proceed concurrently and protecting the encounter from outside contamination. Consistently, mutually involved participants sit next to one another and turn their torsos and heads toward each other while talking, thereby creating a boundary between their interaction and the various activities around them.

Although negotiational encounters are episodic happenings rather than continuous events for pairs of district attorneys and public defenders, they articulate in an orderly way with other courtroom activities, being subordinated only to the judicial encounter while otherwise being protected by standard practices for internally and externally regulating encounters in social settings.

The Public Defender–Client Encounter

Discussions of public defenders and their clients are accorded the same respect as mutual involvements between DAs and PDs. The only intrusions are by judges. There is a difference, however, between negotiational and public defender–client encounters; this concerns the different rights of involved parties. On the one hand, negotiational encounters are started through the mutual availability and readiness of the two participants for talk. For example:

PD5 has been monitoring the interaction between PD4 and DA3. When they stop talking, he steps up to DA3.
1. PD5:   I don't know if these are your cases or not, how do I know
2.   if they're your cases?
3. DA3:   I'll tell you if they're my cases
4. PD5:   Do you have an Oswald?

5. DA3: Yes
6. PD5: Um
7. DA3: Oswald ((looks through files for the Oswald folder))
8. PD5: That's a- I'm surprised he didn't file a search on it,
9.　　　　it's a bad search . . .

(Transcript, 2/18)

The determination that the DA is responsible for the Oswald case (lines 4–5) serves as a warrant for PD5 to begin negotiating the case (lines 8–9).

Public defender–client encounters of any substance, on the other hand, occur largely at the behest of the public defender. This is shown in a number of ways. Clients must maintain the same kind of readiness for conferences with their attorneys as they do for the judicial encounter. Defense attorneys may call upon them at any time to inquire about facts, to relay a district attorney's offer, or to otherwise inform them of the state of their cases. Thus:

PD6 stands at the front of the room near the railing.
PD6: Mister Allen.
Def.: Yes.
PD6: Step to the back of the room, please.
The defendant gets up and walks to a corner at the back of the room.
PD6 walks to the same corner and they begin talking.

(Notes, 6/10)

Clients, however, regularly await the disengagement of their lawyers from dispositional or negotiational encounters before seeking their attention.

When defendants are summoned by their lawyers, not only must they demonstrate readiness for the encounter; they also must talk at length if the lawyer so desires. But lawyers may rapidly close down an encounter opened by a defendant if they are, for whatever reason, not ready to talk.

Client walks up to PD2.
PD2: What do you want? Do you have a defense to this thing?
Def.: No. That's what I want to talk to you about.
PD2: Okay, I'll be back.
PD2 walks away to talk to another defendant, and the client sits down again.

(Notes, 6/24)

Thus, the public defender–client encounter is given less ritual regard than either the judicial or negotiational encounter. While clients are required to participate fully when public defenders want them to, the defense attorneys themselves do not view these engagements as obligatory in the way they do judicial or negotiational discussions. A final point is that the least ritually important activities in the courtroom are the face-engagements and self-involvements of defendants and audience members, insofar as their activities are subject to interruption by judges and lawyers at any time.

The Ecology of the Courtroom

The courtroom in which the pretrial and settlement conference is held resembles other courtrooms in its physical structure, and it is divided into three distinct regions. The first is the *audience section*, where there is seating for 130 persons. Two aisles run through the audience section to the second area, a *lawyers' region*, which is separated from the audience section by a three-foot railing. It contains a long, conference-type table with six chairs on the audience side, facing the judge's bench. Six or eight chairs are placed against the three-foot railing, also facing the judge's bench. The jury box, on the right of the room as one faces the bench, is considered part of the lawyer's region because prosecuting and defense attorneys may use it to conduct their negotiations and conferences. The third area is the *judge's region*, with a five-foot-high bench, a raised platform behind the bench, and a witness stand (unused during pretrial and settlement). In front of the bench is a three-foot-high table. At the left side of this region, two court clerks and a probation officer sit at a desk. The court recorder is situated at the right side of the area.

Although, in part, these regions are designated by physical objects (railings, bench, etc.), they are also maintained through members' orientations to them (cf. Goffman, 1963: 152). For example, there is a barrier that bounds the audience section in front, but it is not continuous; the aisles on either side of the room cut through the barrier. Even though the forward parts of the courtroom are thereby readily accessible to members of the audience, and although there are ample seats in the jury box, on the front side of the railing, and at the lawyers' table, the defendants and their companions never move up and occupy them unless invited. Furthermore, just as clients do not sit in the lawyers'

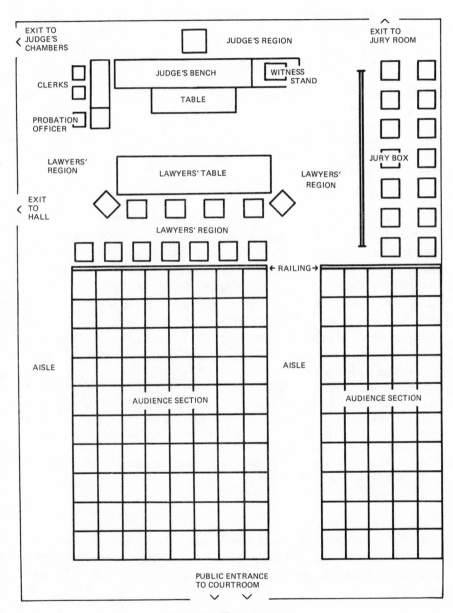

Figure 1. The courtroom.

region, neither they nor the lawyers traverse the area behind the judge's bench.

There are exceptions that nevertheless fit the general pattern.[8] First, clients may legitimately enter the lawyers' region or judge's area if summoned. Second, clients may approach their defense attorneys in the lawyers' region by gaining permission to enter it.

A private attorney is sitting in one of the chairs at the railing, next to the aisle. A defendant walks up to him.
Defendant: Are you Mr. Carson?
 Attorney: No, that's him up here (motioning toward the lawyers' table).
Defendant: Would it be possible for me to talk to him?
 Attorney: Go ask him.

(Notes, 3/1)

Third, court clerks and attorneys may be seen behind the judge's bench depositing a file or other papers on the bench when the judge is out of the room. In all breaches of geographic boundaries, then, the intruder has business and carefully exhibits that fact when entering a restricted region. It is not, for example, idle wandering, curiosity, or desire for more comfortable seating (the chairs in the lawyers' region are wider and more padded than those in the audience section) that prompts clients to enter the forward parts of the courtroom. They only do so to talk to their lawyers. Lawyers, clients, and bailiffs all seem oriented to such matters.

A defendant is standing next to the lawyers' region, just near the railing. He is talking to his public defender, who is standing near him, but who has momentarily shifted his attention to reading some papers while the defendant waits. The bailiff notices the defendant and walks over to him.
Bailiff: You should go out and sit in the audience until your name is called.
 PD1:   Oh, I'm talking to him.
Bailiff: Oh, okay.

(Notes 6/17)

Here, the bailiff takes the client's presence in the lawyers' region as an unwarranted intrusion. But the public defender's statement is permitted as an account for why the person's presence is not in violation of courtroom order.

[8]Clients may legitimately enter the lawyers' region or judge's area if summoned. And lawyers may enter the bench slot, too, when they have called a case. But by "exceptions" here I am referring to gaining informal access to these areas.

In summary, participants engage in a number of practices, such as voluntarily avoiding certain regions, entering them only for reasons of business, and asking permission—all of which simultaneously demonstrate a respect for, and produce social boundaries within, the courtroom.

This examination of the ecology of the courtroom directly bears on its dominant and subordinate encounters. As one moves from the back of the courtroom to the front, there is a transition from a free-access area (the audience section), to limited access (the lawyers' region), to very restricted access (the judge's region). The same move from the back to the front involves a change from an area of most subordinate involvements (those of the client with himself and his others) to encounters of secondary importance (negotiational) to the dominant encounter (the judicial one). Public defender–client discussions take place in the rear of the courtroom, in the audience section, in the jury box and jury room, outside in the hall, and so forth. In short, they occur anywhere but the judge's area, and their in-between status is thus exhibited by the fact that there is no specifically designated area where they can take place.

Discussion

We noted earlier that many activities occur simultaneously during pretrial conferences. The courtroom initially gives one an impression of constant movement, talking, and interaction rather than of stability, quietude, and a step-by-step processing of individual cases. Nevertheless, all the encounters and events are made to happen in an orderly fashion. In fact, a hierarchy is assigned to the various courtroom activities, not by pre-established organizational directives, but by everyday ritual practices of courtroom members. The judicial encounter appears as the matter of dominant concern in the way that it exerts strong claims on the interactional attention of lawyers, defendants, and audience members alike, and in that it is conducted in an area where courtroom participants most stringently restrict their access.[9] The negotiational encounter follows the judicial one in importance; it is accorded an integrity that is violable only by the judge's incursions and occurs in an area of

[9]In discussing the hierarchy of the courtroom in terms of not only a precedence order but an ecological one as well, the attempt is to incorporate a conception of *space* into the analysis of social interaction. On this topic, see Giddens (1979: 209), who observes, "Weber's characterization of modern bureaucracies as involving hierarchies of offices applies to the differentiation of physical space as well as the differentiation of authority."

limited access. Public defender–client encounters are of tertiary significance. Though clients must participate fully in these encounters when
the defense attorney wants them to do so, there is not a symmetrical
obligation for the attorneys. And, they are done in a variety of locales
within the courtroom, which further makes visible their unceremon-
iousness relative to judicial and negotiational encounters. Finally, defendants' auto- and mutual involvements are of least significance in the
court, as evidenced in the way that their activities are both subject to
interruption by judge and lawyers at any time and are conducted in an
area subject to contamination because of its free access to any professional or lay person.

These observations cast light on the descriptions of plea bargaining
as an aspect of a bureaucratic court wherein bargaining dialogues are
kept private and persons are processed like objects. Such phenomena
are usually accounted for by referring to the large number of cases that
must be processed each day. For example, in a study of municipal court,
Mileski (1971: 479) noted that 72 percent of the cases were handled in
one minute or less. "In the bureaucratized court," she concludes, "encounters of short duration along with mass processing are two means
that mitigate some of the case-load pressures." The Garden City municipal court and pretrial conference appear to be not unlike the courtroom Mileski observed. The time each defendant spends with the judge
is short, and between 60 and 130 cases are handled in one afternoon
session.

However, the notion that a large quantity of cases necessitates speedy
handling and covert negotiations is misguided. It is part of the idea that
plea bargaining itself has arisen in recent years because urban courts are
so overcrowded that "compromise" in the form of "bargain justice" is
necessary. Yet students of the criminal-justice process have shown that
nontrial methods of disposing of cases have been prevalent historically
in the United States, particularly since the late 1800s (Alschuler, 1979),[10]
and are present now in both rural and urban jurisdictions (Buckle and
Buckle, 1977; Feeley, 1979c; Heumann, 1978; Moley, 1929).[11]

[10]For example, Heumann (1978: 28–29) shows that, at least as far back as 1880, in Connecticut the courts were sending an average of only 8.7 percent of their cases to trial,
so that nontrial dispositions have been the overwhelming means of case adjudication
for a hundred years in that state, whether for high-volume or low-volume courts.

[11]For a study of a *small town* court in Connecticut, see Feeley (1979c: Chapter 8). Buckle
and Buckle (1977: 63) examined an uncrowded *urban* court in Massachusetts. Plea bargaining and bureaucratization were intrinsic parts of each.

The argument here is that specific bureaucratic features of the court-room are surface phenomena whose underlying structure is in the participation framework of the court. First, it is true that bargaining dialogues are mostly hidden from the involved defendants and other persons who might be interested in their details. In this setting, however, it is clear that these discussions do not literally take place behind closed doors. Instead, negotiational encounters are closed off by standard practices that accord integrity to focused interactions in any social setting.

Second, if defendants are objects being routinely processed at the pretrial conference, this is rooted in their insulation from plea negotiations, the expectation that they will await dispositions agreed to by the legal professionals, and the necessity to be accessible to accept or reject them. If they reject an offer, they must await further negotiations. If they accept, they must then maintain readiness to go before the judge at some time in the afternoon and have the disposition officially ratified.

Third, if individual defendants are then indistinguishable to the judge, this is not simply a matter of sheer numbers and their rapid processing, but it is connected with the protection of the judge from ordinary interaction with defendants by layers of hierarchy intrinsic to the courtroom. The overall implication is that small-town courtrooms and uncrowded city courtrooms will be as bureaucratized as heavily populated courts to the extent that they evidence these patterns of social interaction and this type of participation framework.[12] As with the practice of plea bargaining, the framework of the courtroom can accommodate any necessity to process large quantities of cases, but it is not explained by that necessity.

A final point is a methodological one. In this study, no attempt was made to assess whether the court is or is not a "bureaucracy." That is, the research was conducted by treating accounts of the court's bureaucratic features, particularly the hiddenness of plea negotiations and the cursory treatment of defendants, as situated descriptions whose sense is provided by the social organization exhibited in the concrete inter-

---

[12]Atkinson (1982) has argued that, in various institutional settings, an "appearance of formality" may be due to specific departures from ordinary conversational practices. Turns may be preallocated, rather than participant controlled, ratified speakers may be announced and given platforms from which to talk, utterances may be short and largely consist of question–answer sequences, and so on. In the trial court (where only one case is viewed at a time), caseload or overcrowding is clearly not the issue. Rather, attaining a focus of attention for participants and spectators, achieving ease in understanding parties' speech, and other problems endemic to similar multiparty settings are resolved by the above-mentioned *patterns of interaction.*

actional practices of courtroom participants. According to Garfinkel (1967: Chapter 1), any given setting is so organized as to provide methodic displays of its accountable features. What this suggests is that accounts of the bureaucratic nature of modern organizations, in general, can be treated as features of those organizations, not as abstract or ostensive definitions with which empirical phenomena are compared.[13]

SOCIAL ORDER IN THE COURTROOM

We have addressed the question of how a courtroom social order is accomplished. But in describing the order of the court and how it is rooted in the interactional practices of the courtroom participants, a motif left implicit was the fragility of the order so produced and accomplished. Goffman (1974: 238–333) has argued at length about how public order depends on members' confidence and trust that surface appearances in social situations will not be exploited for the nefarious purposes of those who manage them.

Now it may be that the judges, defense attorneys, prosecutors, probation officers, clerks, and court reporters who are part of the pretrial conference are not likely candidates for pursuing its subversion. Court personnel evidently regard most defendants as guilty and believe that they are dispensing justice in the most expeditious manner possible; thus, these personnel realize both the immediate organizational goals of clearing the docket and dispensing justice and their own personal and professional interests, such as maintaining professional respect and the dignity of the court.[14]

Yet, if we are to incorporate either a specific understanding of defendant behavior in an analysis of the court or a general understanding

[13]The approach to studying bureaucracy as an account may be consistent with Weber's use of the ideal type, in the following sense. Rather than hypothesizing universal features of bureaucracy, the ideal type was meant to capture historically and culturally specific characteristics of bureaucratic authority (Burger, 1976). An alternative to the use of the ideal type in capturing its historical and cultural specificity is to locate "bureaucracy" as an occasioned achievement of practices that make it a plausible, member-recognizable characterization of given social settings. This view is related to that expressed in Wilson and Zimmerman (1980), who locate ethnomethodology within a "minority" tradition in sociology that regards sociological concepts as historically and culturally situated.

[14]See Buckle and Buckle (1977: 150–154), Feeley (1979c: 283–84), Heumann (1978: 153–157), Nardulli (1978: 52–53), and Rosett and Cressey (1976: 173).

of client behavior in relation to any people-processing agency, it will benefit us to examine the basis for the contributions of defendants or clients to public decorum in settings where officials are in close contact with them. The specific question here, as earlier presented, is *why* do defendants help to manage the courtroom social structure when they may be disenchanted with its routines and results? One reason for pursuing this question is that it will lead us naturally into the discussion of negotiation practices investigated in later chapters. A second reason is that we can see how these negotiation practices are a reflexive part of the setting in which they occur. That is, plea bargaining is allowed to happen in this setting because participants engage in the patterned production of certain routines and ritual skills. And those skills may be employed, by defendants at least, because of specific methods through which defense and prosecuting attorneys arrange dispositions for them in the plea discussions.

The problem of why defendants participate in the management of courtroom order needs to be thrown into greater relief. In the courtroom where pretrial and settlement conferences are held, officials are highly dependent on defendants suppressing the noisiness of their self-absorbing activities and their talk with others, maintaining interactional availability, answering when summoned, civilly disattending interaction among lawyers and between lawyers and clients, producing remedial exchanges when wanting to talk to their lawyers, and so on. These practices display the defendants' harmlessness and accomplish the "normal appearance" of the courtroom that its officials rely on, trust, and take for granted. But they also represent points of vulnerability, the very ways in which courtroom decorum could be shattered. When summoned by judges or by lawyers, defendants could refuse to answer; when wanting to talk to their lawyers, they could hover threateningly on the edges of the lawyers' focused interactions; they could interrupt these proceedings and the judicial encounters with solicitations, obscenities, and importunities. These are, in fact, strategies employed in some political trials (Antonio, 1972; Barkan, 1977).

In the second place, there is ample evidence that criminal defendants are disenchanted with, and degraded by, the legal process. Two anecdotes will illustrate the point. On one occasion, I overheard the following comment from a defendant awaiting his attorney in the hall outside the courtroom; the lawyer had passed by the client on his way into the courtroom and told him to stand there until he (the attorney) returned.

Defendant: (to person standing beside him) It's so incredible, the shifting around. It's
            so inefficient.

On another occasion, I was sitting in the audience section of the courtroom. The judge had been in chambers for ten minutes; he returned to
the bench to accept a plea and then promptly recessed again. I heard
this from two persons sitting nearby:

Defendant: Jesus Christ
    Friend: I don't understand this recess business. How can anyone sit there for just
             two fucking minutes and then recess? This is absurd!

Such discontent is not idiosyncratic. A study of a traffic court (Brickey
and Miller, 1975: 695) noted that defendants were similarly dismayed
by "the apparent manipulation of pleas, the studied intolerance of the
judge, and the rapid speed of the proceedings." Interviews with prisoners (Alpert and Hicks, 1977; Arcuri, 1976) reveal widespread frustra-
tion and feelings of cursory treatment from defense attorneys, prosecutors, and judges. Defendants often see their own public defenders as
employees or agents of the state rather than as advocates of defendants'
rights (Casper, 1972: 69, 96). These negative evaluations should not be
sociologically surprising, given the structural ways that courtroom ritual
is status degrading for defendants (Carlen, 1976; Eisenstein and Jacob,
1977; Emerson, 1969; Hetzler and Kanter, 1974; McBarnet, 1979). For
example, Schwartz (1974) suggests that *waiting,* while it expresses def-
erence toward courtroom officials, is also a mortifying experience for
those who do it.

Finally, then, we can restate the problem. Given the tenuousness
of the social arrangements that enable the pretrial conference to occur
and the alienation of its bottom-rung participants, why do those arrangements persist day after day and week after week with such stability? Goffman (1971: 288), after quoting a description of a 1968 student
occupation of the Columbia University's president's office, remarks,

> The great sociological question, of course, is not how could it be that human
> beings would do a thing like this, but rather how is it that human beings do
> this sort of thing so rarely?

To paraphrase Goffman, the question here is not why would defendants
disrupt proceedings, but why disruptions occur seldom or not at all.

This question assumes greater interest when we recall Merton's

(1968: 252) assertion that for a bureaucracy "to operate successfully," there must be a high degree of reliability of behavior, something that we have observed in the courtroom.[15] Such patterns, according to Merton (1968: 262) must be supported by strong attitudes and sentiments such as the devotion to duty. But here, if defendants are lacking in such supportive attitudes and sentiments, how are we to account for their routine contribution to social order in the courtroom?

Negotiational Pattern and Public Order

Now, one answer to this question might be that defendants, their friends and family, and other courtroom observers are cowed by the formal authority of the judge, who has the power to sanction them by directing the bailiff to take care of troublemakers, by issuing contempt citations, and so forth. Although this explanation seems to make sense, it is nevertheless inadequate. First, we know that even though the judge does have formal authority, there is room for behavior that is disruptive of courtroom decorum without being formally sanctionable. Insolence could be displayed through subtle gestures, glances, hesitations, and so forth (Werthman, 1963), but it is not. Second, judges' exercise of their formal pattern is limited. They know that if they infringe on defendants' behavior too much, they may create "reversible error," or may appear to be unfairly harassing the defendant (Barkan, 1977: 331). Finally, recall that during pretrial proceedings, the judge (and his bailiff) are out of the courtroom much of the time. Lawyers confer among themselves, defense attorneys talk to their clients, and clients behave, all in the same atmosphere that prevails when the judge is present.

These considerations are not to suggest that official power is without importance in the courtroom. Nor should we neglect other matters, such as the way in which symbolism is manipulated to impress clients and elicit their cooperation (Edelman, 1964: 95). For example, Kessler (1962) discusses the judicial robe as a symbol of justice; Hetzler and Kanter (1974) compare the judicial robe to the dress of lawyers and defendants; and Hazard (1962) shows how furniture arrangements signify different judicial, prosecutional, and defense roles in various Western countries and in the Soviet Union. But emphasis on such symbolism, or even

---

[15]Merton was, of course, talking about the bureaucratic official, but that only underscores the need to assess the behavior of the bureaucratic client.

official power, depicts individuals as passive respondents to external stimuli and overlooks order-producing activities intrinsic to specific settings of interaction. In courtrooms, one such activity is *character assessment*.

At least since Newman's (1966) pioneering examination of plea bargaining, students of the court have stressed the importance of a defendant's background in adjudication of their cases.[16] As Newman has noted,

> It is difficult, in many instances, to separate the circumstances of the crime from the personal characteristics of the defendant, with the result that respectability or lack of it, for example, may be considered along with the particular conditions of the offense. (p. 125)

More specifically, the argument has been made that *any* of a defendant's attributes, *including public demeanor*, may be used when court officials make decisions regarding their cases (cf. Emerson, 1969). The following is an example. A judge, a public defender, and a district attorney had retired to the judge's chambers to discuss a few cases that the two attorneys had been unable to resolve in their courtroom negotiations. One of the cases involved "Frank Bryan," a man charged with disorderly conduct and resisting arrest.[17]

1.	J1:	And now that brings us to Frank Bryan. Is he the poor chap
2.		sitting out there all by himself?
3.	PD2:	Yeah, he's the sweet man with the nice smile . . . See he's
4.		drunk and he comes home to his own house where he had a fight
5.		with his family, and he's out in front in his own front yard
6.		apparently having such a fight or at least—
7.	DA3:	His mother having called the police
8.	PD2:	Mother having ca(h)ll(h)ed the (h) co(h)ps. It's a family thing,
9.		he's screaming and saying fuck and all that kind of stuff . . . And
10.		this is, I mean, the same very happy go lucky good natured
11.		guy, as you can tell, he's sitting out in the courtroom and when
12.		the police come into his own home, his castle, he decides he
13.		ain't going without making some trouble

---

[16]See, for example, Buckle and Buckle (1977), Cicourel (1968), Emerson (1969), Mather (1974), Rosett and Cressey (1976), Skolnick (1966), and Sudnow (1965), and Chapters 6 and 7 of this book. For discussions of the relevance of "demeanor evidence" in trials rather than informal discussions see John M. Conley's "The Law" in O'Barr (1982: 41–49), Dane and Wrightsman (1982), and Kalven and Zeisel (1966: 203–206).

[17]The full transcript of negotiations in the Frank Bryan case is in Appendix 2. The negotiations are subject to further analysis in Chapters 3 and 5.

The defense attorney attempts here to draw a clear distinction between the private and public behavior of his client. Although the defendant is acknowledged to have been drunk, fighting, and cursing (lines 3–9), these activities occurred at his home as part of a "family thing" (line 8). While the DA reminds the PD that the mother called the police (line 7), PD2 treats the matter lightly by inserting laughter tokens (the *h*'s in parentheses) in the utterance that acknowledges the DA's reminder (line 8; cf. Jefferson, 1979). PD2 subsequently depicts the police as coming "into" the defendant's "home" and "castle" (line 12) and the defendant's resistive behavior as being precipitated by their intrusiveness (lines 12–13). But if the defendant was combative at home, in the courtroom he can be described as a "sweet man with the nice smile" (line 3) who has been sitting happily during the pretrial conference (lines 1–2, 10–11).

The contrast exhibited here draws on cultural conceptions of a natural separation between public and private life, a distinction that is recognized in the law (Stinchcombe, 1963). As Flacks (1975: 265) has stated, one's private sphere, in American society, is regarded as being "immune from the intrusions and controls of unwanted others," including police. What one does in public, on the other hand, is and should be subject to social convention; this is where interference by authorities, if needed, is properly done. According to this conception, the defendant can be depicted as acting according to his *rights* at home and his *obligations* in public. In the preceding example, the effect of the argument in the negotiations was to diminish the defendant's culpability and solicit a dismissal of the resisting arrest charge. (Eventually, in fact, the DA did agree to such a proposal and the defendant pleaded guilty only to the disorderly conduct charge.)

Thus, while research has stressed the importance of "personal characteristics" for case disposition, it is ill-appreciated that a subject's character need not be all of one piece. That is, there may be a radical disjunction between defendants' illegal, destructive behavior outside the courtroom and their carefully articulated conformity within it (cf. Piliavin and Briar, 1964). This returns us to the question of why disruptive behavior so seldom occurs in court.

The example suggests that the answer must involve motivation *at the level of interaction.* Blum and McHugh argue that motives help to establish links between particular acts and a person's biography, both for the actor involved and for those who observe him:

> Most fundamentally . . . whatever a motivated actor does will show his methods for affirming himself as a person. . . . For any member to ascribe a motive is thus to do no less than generate a person. (Blum and McHugh, 1971: 108)

In this view, "Frank Bryan" was not merely intimidated by the presence of official authority and symbolism. He was in fact "affirming himself as a person" by producing pleasant behavior in the courtroom and thus actively constituting its social structure. This behavior was then used by the public defender as evidence to generate, in conversational negotiations, a type of person who would be inculpable of the resisting arrest charge. Insofar as defendants retain interest in receiving the minimum sanction from the courts[18]—having charges dropped, being charged with lesser offenses, and reducing jail time, fines, and other penalties—they are strongly motivated to contribute to the reproduction of the courtroom's social order. And the "deep structure" of that motivation is sociological (Blum and McHugh, 1971).

CONCLUSION

A profitable topic of inquiry in the study of organizations, especially of the people-processing type, is the structure of direct interaction. It is that structure which invests accounts of these organizations with their particular sense. In the plea bargaining process, hidden decision making and rapid processing of cases are accomplishments of participants' specific interactional skills and orientations and are not the natural or necessary outcome of overloaded courts, urbanization, or other macrosociological processes stamping their imprint on particular settings of interaction.

Examining direct relations among courtroom members makes disciplined behavior understandable even among those who lack the usual "attitudes and sentiments" (including the "devotion to one's duties") thought to motivate most bureaucratic personnel (Merton, 1968: 252–253). For defendants in court and, possibly, clients of other people-processing bureaucracies, one basis for social control is the orientation of clients to the ways in which one's demeanor can be used to assess one's character

---

[18]As Barkan (1977) argues, the transforming of a defendant's interest in the specific goal of the courts (being convicted or being discharged) is one feature of political trials.

by agents who determine the clients' access to external punishments (fines, imprisonment) or rewards (food stamps, medical care, dismissals).[19] Thus, the discretionary decision-making responsibilities allocated to people-processing agencies, however they influence the later fate of clients, also have a profound effect on the orderly ways in which those responsibilities are discharged in immediate interaction with those clients. Coercion, as an organizational means for inducing situated compliance (Etzioni, 1961) need not be direct or formally sanctioned.[20] It can be quite oblique and circuitous.

[19]For a relevant discussion of the moral evaluation of hospital clients in relation to the services they receive, see Roth (1972) and Sudnow (1967). For a general treatment of the issue with reference to "street-level bureaucracies," see Lipsky (1980: 57–58).

[20]The discussion of coercion here is consistent with the framework developed by Luckenbill (1979: 107) for the study of power, defined as a collective event in which interaction is assymmetrical and compliance is produced intentionally. Moreover, the use of power can be distinguished from authority, which involves a subject's exerting choice and consenting to outside control over one's behavior (Luckenbill, 1979: 103).

CHAPTER 3

Frame Analysis of Plea Bargaining

Structural aspects of plea bargaining will later be examined from a conversational analysis perspective. As a prelude, a problem with this perspective must be noted. Within conversational analysis research there is a focal concern with structures of talk that are invariant to particular settings of interaction, while little analytic attention is given to those settings *per se.*

The model of turn-taking in conversation is a good example. It is through the turn-taking system described by Sacks et al. (1974) that speaker change and one party talking at a time are maintained as invariant features of conversation. That is, these features do not change in different settings, even if the number of parties, their identities, and the type of occasion (party, picnic, business conference, luncheon date, etc.) do vary (Sacks et al., 1974: 698–700). Moreover, turn order and turn size are negotiated on an utterance-by-utterance basis as participants respond to the topical content of the conversation, to rules governing word selection, to the relevance of opening and closing sequences, and so on (Sacks et al., 1974: 43). This responsiveness shows that turn-taking is locally managed and under participant control, meaning that conversation is recipiently designed or oriented and sensitive to parties who are co-participants.

Thus, the analytic thrust is on the uniformity of turn-taking as a transituational system. In fact, the power of conversational analysis is its capacity to identify conversational patterns and systems of talk having this sort of invariance—cross-cultural research tends to corroborate how effective conversational analysis is in describing transsituational patterns of talk (e.g., Boden, 1981; Moerman, 1977). And even though the patterns and systems are sensitive to a host of contextual matters—including the kind of setting, the participants, and their topics—the trouble is that these matters have been slighted. The neglect is of little importance to students of everyday conversation, who usually examine interaction that is somewhat insulated from the world outside its auspices.[1] But with other types of discourse, such as plea bargaining, the talk that occurs is distributed systematically within work routines which relate its primary participants to a series of activities occuring both before and after any particular episode of negotiation. That is, plea bargaining is only one aspect of the work routines and relationships in which lawyers participate, a fact which is visible in the different *alignments* participants take in regard to the speech they produce and hear. Goffman (1974, 1979) has discussed these alignments as "footings," and he has used "frame analysis" as an approach to studying them.

THE STRUCTURAL SITUATIONS OF DEFENSE AND PROSECUTING ATTORNEYS

In frame analysis of spoken discourse, the general argument is that *speaker* and *hearer* are terms too gross for dealing with the way parties orient to the discourse. For instance, a speaker may employ a variety of *production formats* so that different footings are exhibited with respect to the talk the person emits. Similarly, hearers of the utterance may take on different *participation statuses*, such as ratified recipient, overhearer, eavesdropper, and the like.

With respect to production formats, a distinction can be made be-

---

[1]Sacks et al. (1974) recognize that there is a wide variety of discourse activities within any society, and refer to other "speech exchange systems" besides conversation, such as meetings, interviews, debates, and ceremonies. Their suggestion is that these other systems may be partly discriminated by the sorts of turn-taking organizations they employ. Such an orientation may perpetuate a concern with sequential organization in diverse types of discourse, rather than a concern with the types themselves. For example, as Atkinson and Drew (1979) discuss the management of accusations and denials during courtroom examination, they initially define this discourse by referring to how it departs from ordinary conversation in two main ways: (1) turn order is fixed (attorneys speak "first" and witnesses "second"); (2) turns at talk are allocated to just two speakers, who are constrained as to what should be done in their turns (lawyers ask questions; witnesses answer). In ordinary conversation, turn order and the allocation of turns are subject to local management. Fortunately, Atkinson and Drew (1979) go beyond this concern with how courtroom examination is different from the conversational process to discuss how it is organized as an entity in its own right. See the discussion in Chapter 1.

tween *principal*, the party whose position is represented, and *animator*, the one who simply speaks some set of words. In plea bargaining, principal and animator often coincide, as when a PD or DA exhibits a position to which he officially adheres:[2]

(1)

DA1: I've got an offer that I'll make at this time
PD2: Sure shoot
DA1: I'd offer, if the defendant pled guilty to the one forty eight, dismiss the other court, thirty days suspended for a period of one year on condition he do two weekends

(2)

PD2: I think a fine would settle the case

However, animator and principal need not coincide:

(3)

PD3: ((addressing the judge)) The district attorney was asking for a two forty three conviction for a guilty plea with thirty days.

In this last example, three matters are important. First, with respect to *referencing*, the PD uses a title ("district attorney") from a family of categories appearing in this discourse that invoke the official roles of the involved parties.[3] Second, the reference to the DA precedes an "embedded" utterance, where PD3 animates speech previously emitted by the DA, who is the principal. Finally, if a distinction can be made between principal and animator, there is a further contrast between principal and the *originator* of a position, as is clear in the next example, which involves a case of drunk driving:

---

[2]In the transcript segments, personnel are labeled with abbreviations and numbers: J1 = Judge #1, PD2 = Public Defender #2, DA2 = Assistant District Attorney #2, PA1 = Private Defense Attorney #1, etc. Explanatory notes are in double parentheses.

[3]And obviously I am using those categories (district attorney, public defender, judge) for referring to the parties. Other terms used in the discourse, as the following three examples show, include "people," "defense," and "the court," respectively.

(a)   J2:   People feel this is as far as they can go, is just the reckless?

(b)   J1:   And what's the defense position at this point?

(c)   PD2:   Would the court consider less?

(4)

1.	DA3:	What are you proposing we do with this
2.	PD2:	If you want a reckless and a hundred and eighty dollar fine, he'll
3.		do it
4.		((silence as DA3 looks through file))
5.	DA3:	Should do at least one weekend nothing less, it's what it says
6.		here
7.	PD3:	Well, in that case you get to try it
8.	DA3:	Okay
9.	PD2:	You refuse his offer
10.	DA3:	Yes
11.	PD2:	Okay

In this exchange, the DA animates a position (line 5), and acts as principal, that is, according to his official role. However, the position was originally established by someone else in the DA's office. And this makes for an ambiguity in the DA's commitment to the position he animates. In line 9, PD2 produces a candidate statement that asks the DA to verify whether his quoting from the file constitutes a refusal of the defense offer.

Thus, parties in these negotiations make a distinction between the person-in-role and the "office" they represent. This raises a referencing issue concerning the use of "you" (see lines 1, 7, 9 above). When one party refers to another as "you," the capacity that is addressed and then spoken from may be subject to on-the-spot negotiation. The equivocal usage may evoke a bit of humor:

(5)

DA3:	Why couldn't you plead him to petty theft
PD2:	Mm hmm. False.
DA3:	You want to try it
PD2:	You can't win it! . . . Now when I say you can't win it, I don't
	mean that you PERsonally can't win it[4]
DA3:	I might come out of retirement

If negotiators refer to one another in their official capacities, they also designate themselves that way, by the use of "we" and other terms (Goffman, 1979: 17).

---

[4]Capital letters denote emphasis.

(6)

PA1:   Our position is one, he didn't steal it, and two, he received it
        but not as stolen property

(7)

PD1:   So we feel like that she certainly wasn't acting within her
        normal characteristics

(8)

DA2:   In all cases where there are at least two convictions
PD2:   Okay
DA2:   Two prior convictions, we would urge that they be referred for a
        probation and sentencing report

When the DA speaks this way, it is "the people," abstractly considered, whose interests are expressed. More concretely, the stance of an individual prosecutor belongs to the *office* of district attorney, and it reflects the policies and priorities established by various persons within that office,[5] in accord with laws established by parties even further removed from the courtroom situation. That is, legislatures provide broad sentencing limits for some crimes, and with reference to these, the DA animates positions that reflect his office's "standard" penalties. For example, where California law allowed petty theft crimes such as shop-

[5]There is a framing issue with respect to whether a position established by a district attorney in plea bargaining represents one that will be respected by the judge when the guilty plea is entered. Because there has been a blurring of prosecutorial and judicial functions in criminal courts (McDonald, 1979), however, this problem is not acute. In most jurisdictions, judges essentially "rubber stamp" recommendations made by district attorneys on the basis of their negotiations with defense attorneys (Alschuler, 1976; Feeley, 1979c; Neubauer, 1974; Nimmer, 1974). Therefore, when prosecutors make proposals, they speak on behalf of both the district attorney's office and the judge. But consider this:

> In a misdemeanor case that I observed in surburban Cook County, Illinois, a prosecutor had secured a defendant's guilty plea and his testimony against three alleged accomplices by promising a short sentence that the defendant could serve concurrently with another sentence that he had already received. The defendant performed his part of the bargain, and the prosecutor described the defendant's cooperation in detail at the time that he made his recommendation to the court. Without a word of explanation, the judge sentenced the defendant to a substantial jail term, to begin after the expiration of his current sentence. (Alschuler, 1976: 1067)

Since such mishaps are always possible, a base problem in plea negotiations is how to frame some suggested disposition so that the originator is clear. Lack of attention to that can have real consequences, first for the defendant, who may be misled, and second for the state, insofar as defendants may be entitled to relief if "promises" of a DA are not kept (Alschuler, 1976: 1068).

lifting to be punished by fines up to $500 and/or imprisonment in the county jail for up to six months, the district attorney's office, in the jurisdiction studied, established a 24-hour jail sentence as the usual sentence for "ordinary" shoplifting cases.

(9)

    J: Well what kind of offer are you making
DA3: Minimum disposition . . .
PD2: What's the minimum mean?
DA3: Twenty-four hours

(10)

DA3: What the twenty-four hour rule is, is that in the ordinary,
       average mickey mouse petty theft, which is what they usually
       are . . . I understand the rule to apply not to items of sub-
       stantial loss but to an average petty theft . . .

When a defense attorney takes a position, it is more in accord with his client's wishes or stand than with the policies of his office or penal code statutes. Sometimes the PD simply lifts words out of prior encounters with the defendant for reportage in a particular plea bargaining session.

(11)

PD2: He says he can live without the (driving) license, he could sur-
       vive, he could still work on his job without the license, but the
       jail time is going to change his whole life

(12)

PD3: He says I was not doing anything wrong, said I didn't feel
       the alcohol, I wasn't under the influence

Of course, the defendant must assent to, and may have veto power over, anything the PD may negotiate.[6]

---

[6]Defense attorneys have been known to misrepresent offers of a district attorney, persuading defendants to plead guilty on the basis of a promise never made by the DA. The very possibility of that strategy occurs because of framing practices in talk, where a coparticipant can quote sayings of a party whose nonpresence prevents *in situ* crediting or discrediting of the animated version of his position. The consequences of a defense attorney's misrepresentation to a defendant appear worse than the situation where a DA has made an unfulfillable promise, for, according to Alschuler (1975: 1195), most courts have upheld guilty pleas even if obtained by a defense attorney's fabrication.

(13)

PD2: Now do you want to settle the case without a trial?
DA3: Yeah
PD2: Or do you want everything you could get if you won
DA3: For a fine and restitution
PD2: Well I'll discuss it with him and I'll see what he says

(14)

J1: Arright so we've got guilty and seventy-five dollars right
PD2: If he wants it yes

(15)

PD2: Is there an offer in the case?
DA1: One day credit for one day
PD2: I've already told him that he could have one day credit for one
      day, and he turned it down

In these ways, then, both prosecutor and defender appear as go-betweens, persons who must take into account parties outside the immediate situation. This should not imply that they operate mechanically according to others' dictates, but that the negotiators are each in a particular structural situation, defined as much by their relations to those whom they officially represent as by their associations with bargaining co-participants. Moreover, such structural situations present characteristic problems as the parties negotiate with one another. These problems are both visible in, and managed by, various framing practices or strategic devices through which the negotiators can pursue reasonable outcomes in particular cases. By *reasonable,* I mean the outcomes are in accord with the normative orientations of involved lawyers (Feeley, 1979c: 25), as partly articulated in terms provided by other persons or groups to whom negotiators refer.

FRAMING PRACTICES AS STRATEGIC ACTION

The central task in plea bargaining, for both defense attorney and district attorney, is to arrive at some mutually acceptable outcome for every case.[7] That task takes on a different texture for both parties, according to their structural perspectives.

[7]Practices and decision-making patterns by which outcomes are achieved are the topic of Chapter 8.

The Defense Attorney

Sometimes defense attorneys believe strongly in a client's inculpability, but for them to uniformly adopt a stance of "innocent until proven guilty" would be out of keeping with what they know, and what they know others know, about the bulk of defendants. Simply put, attorneys come to regard most of their clients as guilty in varying degrees and believe that they are dispensing justice in the most expeditious manner possible by arranging guilty pleas.[8] If defense attorneys took what might be a preferred line for clients, proclaiming their innocence or holding out for the least possible penalty, every case might end up in trial. The cooperative arrangement necessary to obtain appropriate responses from the prosecution would be nullified (Heumann, 1978; Skolnick, 1967).

As a practical matter, a defense attorney may support a client's protestations of innocence but nevertheless align with the prosecutor or take a stance somewhere between the client and district attorney. The basic point is not that defense attorneys adopt one or the other of these logically possible stances willy-nilly; rather, it is that PDs carefully demonstrate an orientation to what their words may be projecting about the rationality of an exhibited position in terms that invoke the variety of organizational forms in which the attorneys are embedded.

We have already noted the defense attorney's capacity for simply lifting a client's words out of a prior encounter and quoting them in some present negotiation. By portraying a defendant as author of some position, the defense attorney can then strategically align with or against that position. For example, if they have developed sufficient trust with district attorneys, PDs may obtain leniency by expressing belief in a defendant's claim of innocence or remorse (Alschuler, 1975: 1221). In a case of hit-and-run driving involving a Chicano defendant, the PD replayed the following story to the DA.

(16)

PD1:   Lemme tell ya what he said. Uh he said that after the hit and run he said that he
       did get scared, 'cause he didn't know what was happening and he says that he
       didn't know how to speak to the people that were there, and he thought about

---

[8]See the discussion in Chapter 2, and Buckle and Buckle (1977: 150–154), Feeley (1979c: 283–84), Heumann (1978: 153–157), Nardulli (1978: 52–53), and Rosett and Cressey (1976: 173).

his friend that lived close by. He went over to his friend's house, uh apparently it was late at night, and the friend took him back to the area. The car was gone and he stayed that night with his friend. The next morning he had the friend take him up to his house and the CHP ((California Highway Patrol)) had already been there and left a note telling him to contact them on the nineteenth.

In the next segment, PD1 provides an assessment of the truth value of his client's story,[9] and then solicits an eventual dismissal.

(17)

PD1:   What I would like to see—you know this guy is really, I think he's just strictly honest, I think he's telling me the truth. What I'd like to see happen is just have us continue the thing for like thirty days, let him make restitution on his own and if he does it, then dismiss the case.

DA3:   I'll do that if I can verify from the officers who left the note, if they said uh call us on the nineteenth.

Just as a defense attorney can align with the defendant, he can also set himself apart from his client, as in the next example. As the PD told it, the defendant was working at a local department store where there had been some thefts from employees' purses. One afternoon, she went into the cloak room where the thefts had been occurring, ostensibly to make some phone calls.

(18)

PD3:   . . . and she sees a strange purse and she's looking in it and the store detective comes in and she gets busted. And she says no, I wasn't going through that purse to steal. I had no intention of stealing anything, I didn't recognize the purse, I knew there'd been thefts, I lost some money and I wasn't trying to steal anything. The store detective says she was trying to hide some money. She says that's not true.

Here, there is little hint of the PD's attitude toward his client's story. But after the judge evaluates the case, PD3 articulates a stance he would prefer, and it is opposite that of the defendant:

[9] Legal and ethical problems are raised by the defense lawyer's ability not only to represent a client's position in plea bargaining, but, by changes of footing, also to evaluate the client's position (whether positively or negatively). When he does so, Alschuler (1975: 1721) suggests, "he inserts himself into the state's administrative criminal justice machinery and becomes a judge."

(19)

    J1:   Seems to me no defense that a jury's really going to buy, so
            maybe uh-
  PD3:   Well it's not- from my standpoint I'd much rather be sitting in
            Mister Severt's ((the DA's)) seat, you know
    J1:   Yeah on this one
  PD3:   From an advocacy point of view

PD3's "standpoint" involves a change of footing that invokes a self with commitments other than to the role of public defender; that is, his framing activity exhibits a *professional* self capable of evaluating the case[10] and agreeing with the judge's assessment. By way of contrast, speaking on behalf of his client appears as an obligation performed as part of his public defender job, perhaps as part of the "disinterested service" (Rosenthal, 1974: 22) that he is supposed to provide.

A further consequence of reporting talk in which the PD and the defendant take contrapositions is that the PD may project an advisory aspect of defender's role, a self that is fully attuned to the "reality" of the client's situation. As Skolnick (1967: 62) remarks, the defense attorney may, at times, be more of a "coach" than an advocate for his client. This does not necessitate an alignment with the prosecutor's position, as in the last example. The next excerpt concerns a defendant named Richard Sanders, who was drinking at his sister's house and, according to the PD, had an "alcoholic blackout" during which he began breaking furniture and other household items, getting hurt in the process. The police were called, one of whom was also injured while taking the defendant to a hospital. Sanders was charged with battery against a police officer ("two forty three"). In earlier talk, the DA suggested that if Sanders would plead guilty to the offense, he would get 30 days in jail. The PD had counterproposed a guilty plea to disturbing the peace ("four fifteen") with 15 days in jail.[11]

(20)

  1.   J1:   Now with Sanders, uh you're offering thirty days and what kind of
  2.   probation?
  3.   DA1:   Uh I would say two years probation of sixty suspended over,
  4.   ninety days on condition he do thirty.

---

[10]In Sacks' (1972a) terms, taking an abstract "advocacy point of view" and positing one's hypothetical "rather's" is an activity bound to "professional" as a membership category.

[11]The 243 offense is considered more serious than the 415, because it carries a maximum penalty of a $1000 fine and six months in jail as compared to a maximum $200 and 90 days in jail.

```
 5.  PD3:  Sanders was talking to me in terms of a fine which I KNEW, I
 6.        said Dick, wait a second, this is the real world. I knew that
 7.        that was really off the wall so I don't even know that he would
 8.        go for fifteen days and a four fifteen. I know that he's NOT
 9.        going at ALL for a two forty three and he's not going for thirty
10.        days.
```

In his turn (lines 5–10), PD3 accomplishes a rejection of the DA's proposal (lines 3–4) with stepwise changes of footing. First, he *replays* a prior encounter between the defendant and himself, animating the defendant's position and his own skeptical attitude toward it (lines 5–7). Second, PD3 exhibits his uncertainty about the defendant's position (lines 7–8). Finally, he *preplays* what his client's attitude would be were he informed of the DA's offer (lines 8–9).[12] Thus, through a series of differently framed positions, the PD presents himself as one who aligns neither with the defendant nor the DA. Rather, he articulates a middle position, both in the substantive sense of holding to a median charge and penalty *vis à vis* the defendant and prosecutor and in the sequential sense of presenting that stance midway in the series of animated positions.

One expert on plea bargaining has characterized the prosecutor as being "relatively passive" during the negotiation process (Feeley, 1979c: 177). It is defense attorneys who take the more active role, arguing that the law or some policy of the district attorney's office is not applicable to a given case, and bringing up mitigating circumstances that might elicit a more lenient treatment for their clients. The artfulness of this task is apparent in framing practices by which defense attorneys animate a variety of postures so as to display allegiances to defendants, to the prosecutors and others in their "workgroup" (Eisenstein and Jacob, 1977), to their profession, and to different aspects of their principal capacity.

The Prosecuting Attorney

If defense attorneys are to succeed in their endeavors, district attorneys must relinquish viewing cases according to strict legal mandates or official policies. Framing practices are particularly apparent when a DA dismisses a case or agrees to a defense proposal, in that such practices work to establish and preserve the reasonableness of the decision.

Earlier, we noted that negotiators may invoke their official capacities by the use of *we*. This term enables a party to portray some actions as

---

[12]Replays and preplays are discussed in Goffman (1974: 504–505).

not necessarily willful, but as duty, however delightful or onerous it may be in particular cases. Consider Rodney Tapping, a defendant charged with petty theft:

(21)

1. DA3: You know it's a humdrum case in the abstract, it's made comic
2.   when you consider the cast of characters. Uh Rodney Tapping, who
3.   is the sometimes investigator of Billy Cunningham, he was the
4.   snitch in this case. And uh Leonard Allen, a self-proclaimed
5.   chaplain of the marine corps, who it turns out is a baby
6.   molester . . .
7. PD4: These are the people's witnesses?
8. DA3: We don't make cases, we just file 'em

DA3's turn from lines 1–5 appears as a keying[13] of a melodramatic framework onto the introduction of the persons involved in the case, the keying being at least partly accomplished by calling the parties a "cast of characters" (line 2). By this framing, and by employing descriptions of the parties that are clearly discrediting, the DA makes visible a self who views the case skeptically. In addition, by denying involvement in making such cases (line 8), he may be registering a complaint against those who do (e.g., police). And, he portrays his acting on the case as his official duty ("we just file 'em"), not his choice. In short, the DA projects something larger than what his role implicates. Behind that which he must do is a self with thoughts, attitudes, and feelings about the must-do activity (Goffman, 1974: 540–541).

This talk by the DA serves as a prelude to a suggestion for dismissing the case:

(22)

DA3: . . . I'm going to be most forthcoming in this case
PD4: Arright. Going to dismiss it?
DA3: Yeah we're suggesting probation in this case, probation to the
      district attorney's office
PD4: Yeah
DA3: Uh rather than a three week continuance can I suggest a six months
      continuance
PD4: And if there're no problems you'll dismiss it?

---

[13]A "key," according to Goffman (1974: 43–44), refers to "the set of conventions by which a given activity, one already meaningful in terms of some primary framework, is transformed into something patterned on this activity but seen by the participants to be something quite else."

DA3:   Yes
PD4:   Okay let me run out and talk to Mister Tapping.

That disposition, then, appears not to be capricious or arbitrary. Rather, DA3's framing practices construct the decision as dictated by the trivial nature of the case.

The DA's offer to dismiss a case, as in the above example, is an infrequent happening. More usual is a granting of a defense attorney's request for leniency in charging or sentencing. This is illustrated in the following case of petty theft, where the defendant had taken a parking sticker at his college. During negotiations, the PD reminded the DA that the college's dean of students had written a letter on the student's behalf.

(23)

PD2:   The court's file would have a letter from the dean of students
       asking for a possible courtesy in this case . . . I think the dean of
       student's position is that the guy should not have a criminal
       record

While the DA at first held to a legalistic interpretation of the offense (i.e., that appropriating found property "is a variation on the theme of theft"), he eventually yielded:

(24)

DA3:   Well maybe I can make an exception in this case on the theory
       that if the dean of students doesn't care enough for the enforcement
       of the college's own rules, why should we . . .

While DA3's change in footing represents a departure from his original, principaled stance, it is depicted as consistent with the attitude of an educational authority. The device might be termed "diffusion of responsibility."[14]

Another method for yielding to a defense attorney is for a DA to portray an original position as technically correct but perhaps not substantially justified, as in the following segment. These negotiations concern Frank Bryan, the defendant whose courtroom presentation of self was discussed in Chapter 2 (see Appendix 2). Recall that Bryan was charged with resisting arrest (section 148 of the penal code) and disorderly conduct (section 647f). The usual manner of handling such cases

---

[14]The term is taken from Darley and Latane (1973), who use it in a different context.

is to drop one of the charges in exchange for a guilty plea to the other. Because in this case the 148 charge carried a maximum penalty of one year in jail and a $1000 fine, while the 647 offense had a maximum of six months and a $500 fine, the 148 offense was considered the more serious of the two. And it is over which charge is appropriate that the DA and the PD contend.

(25)[15]

1.	DA3:	Uh- I think it's a case that oughta be uh settled, it's uh
2.	PD2:	Okay
3.	DA3:	strikes me as a dandy one forty eight, probably a better one
4.		forty eight than a six forty seven "f" if you want to be very
5.		strict about it.
6.	PD2:	Well I see it as a six forty seven "f", uh he didn't lay hands
7.		on any officers, if he hadn't been so drunk I assume nothing-
8.		none of this would of happened. Well I don't think it's
9.		worth any jail time no matter what it is
10.	DA3:	I was being academic when I said that uh
11.	PD2:	Oh
12.	DA3:	I think technically it's a better one forty eight than it is a
13.		six forty seven, he put the officers through their mettle.
14.		In collaring him they had to pursue him through the house
15.		and all that sort of stuff.
16.	PD2:	And they did a very fine job of it, I have to- I wanted
17.		to add the officer's uh conduct was highly commendable, and if
18.		my client accidentally tripped and conked his head, I am sure
19.		that justice was done.
20.	DA3:	On the other hand, I don't know that the substantial interests
21.		of justice require any more than a plea to six forty seven "f"

In indicating a preference for the 148 charge, DA3 first displays an "academic" self (line 10) concerned with technical legal issues. Yet, in a change of footing, he aligns with the position favored by PD2 (line 6) which is for the 647f charge. The agreement is made reasonable, however, by DA3 appealing to the "substantial interests of justice," thus drawing on professionally learned distinctions between the formal law and its intent.[16]

---

[15]This segment of negotiations is given more detailed attention in Chapter 5.

[16]In frame analytic terms, the point would be that a co-participant's "frame space," or set of footing options (Goffman, 1981: 230) in face-to-face interaction, is normatively controlled by organizational forms both indigenous and exogenous to the setting of that interaction. See Carlin's (1966) and Handler's (1967) discussions of how lawyers learn professional norms and practices for dealing with individuals and cases.

Discussion

A defense attorney may represent the interests of a client, and even animate the latter's strict position in plea bargaining. By various framing practices, however, the defender also projects alignments that go with or against the defendant's stance in particular cases. This does not mean the attorney acts independently in any simple sense. Rather, it suggests that the lawyer may take a position consistent with that of the prosecutor (and judge) with whom the case is discussed or may assume a posture exhibiting elements of a professional identity. Thus, the defense attorney pays attention to a variety of experiences and relationships intrinsic and extrinsic to the setting when and where negotiations are conducted. The district attorney, on the other hand, often takes an initial position that is legally and officially proper, speaking for those who establish laws and policies regarding how criminal offenses should be treated. That the DA concedes an initial position in favor of a more viable posture does not convey an air of arbitrariness, but it displays an allegiance to a professional identity and a sensitivity to institutional forms (such as an educational setting) with interests that may be relevant to the case at hand.

There are similarities, then, between the framing practices of defense and district attorneys, even if the two parties face different structural situations. Both orient to proprieties established by relationships with each other, their offices, their professions, and representatives of other institutions in the society. When a position is taken or a posture is shifted, it reflects more than the direct relations between defense attorney, prosecutor, and judge. A participant's stance is taken in ways that appear rational and reasonable in the setting by way of what the person's inside *and* outside affiliations provide as sensible to say.

DRAMATURGY IN PLEA BARGAINING

We have examined talk that primarily indicates the importance of *prior* relationships and allegiances of the negotiating parties. But *subsequent* relationships and activities may also thus influence present negotiations. For example, much of what is considered the process of establishing an information base in plea bargaining is really the display of a scene that could be enacted at a trial before a jury. The latter, then, is a relevant audience, if only in a hypothetical sense, for everything said during negotiations.

The prior talk or writing of a number of outside persons, including victims, police, and witnesses, is regularly introduced in the discourse between attorneys, and this material is often counterposed to the claims of the defendant.

(26)

PD3:   The store detective says she was trying to hide some money, she ((the defendant)) says that's not true

(27)

DA1:   I think I've come down on a seventy five dollar fine, I really do. I mean here's a guy that's actually at the door, trying to get it in

PD2:   Well his recollection was that he was dead drunk laying on the ground . . .

DA1:   We got an officer's report saying-

J1:   Uh the report observed Bush attempting to open the locked sliding door

(28)

PD2:   Detective Jones says that he feels that the defendant committed the crime out of a petty jealousy

Quotes of this sort might be viewed as efforts to improve the information base on which plea bargaining decisions are made. That plea bargaining is an information processing venture is the presumption particularly evident in research based on simulations, quasi-experiments, and interviews with prosecutors and defense attorneys (Lagoy, Senna, and Siegel, 1976; Miller et al., 1978; Rossman, McDonald, and Cramer, 1980). It is also a view expressed in ethnographic and participant observation studies (e.g., Feeley, 1979c; Rosett and Cressey, 1976; Utz, 1978). By considering not only what offenders say, but what witnesses, victims, police, and others say, negotiators may be able to agree on "what happened" and better determine appropriate charges and sentences in given cases (Miller et al., 1978: 64–73; Rosett and Cressey, 1976: 105–109; Utz, 1978: 135–36).[17] But a dramaturgical approach makes better

[17]For a treatment of negotiation in general as an information exchange process, see Gulliver (1979: 83–88), who provides an insightful discussion of the complexities of "messages" conveyed during negotiation, but who does not get beyond the basic exchange model.

sense of the practice of animating the talk of these others within the discourse because the central aim appears not to be providing information but rehearsing a scenario before the animator's audience (Goffman, 1974: 508).[18]

Consider again the case of Richard Sanders, the defendant who, according to the PD, had an alcoholic blackout (segment 20 above). During the episode of violence at his home, which included an altercation with police officers when they arrived, Sanders was injured. The police took him to the hospital.

(29)

PD3: . . . and the police report says that Sanders slugged Officer Smith,
      hit him in the lip and bruised his lip, which Sanders can't deny
      because he doesn't remember. However
J1:   Yeah
PD3: Sanders also came out of the hospital with a lot of bruises that
      he didn't have on him when he went in

Here, PD3 raises the possibility that (as he says later) the officer "got his licks in" and had "a chance to retaliate" while the defendant was being taken from the hospital. An investigator in the public defender's office, Dick Blinn, interviewed a male nurse at the hospital named Johnson, who suggested that what happened to Sanders may have been written into the hospital records.

(30)

PD3: And Johnson says somebody changed the records that were in the
      file. There were some changes made in Sander's medical file from
      the night before, so the next day the file didn't read the same
      as it read when Sanders had left
J1:   Is that right, he's going to say- testify
PD3: That's what Johnson told Dick Blinn

The key item here is the judge's query about Johnson; the correction from what Johnson might "say" to what he would "testify" signifies that, in plea bargaining, importance is attached not just to what police, witnesses, and victims might have said, but to what they can be arguably expected to testify if the case goes to trial.

---

[18]Some plea bargaining studies have recognized the way "facts" of a case are assessed by trial standards (Neubauer, 1974: 200–201; Eisenstein and Jacob, 1977: 32–34), but they have not explored the *staging* that is involved in the presentation of those facts during negotiations.

Three points follow from this. First, as much attention may be focused on the background and demeanor of those who would testify as on the content of their testimony (Stanko, 1981: 229). In the Sanders case there were two officers involved, Smith and Blackwell, and each came under scrutiny during the plea discussions (Smith was the officer allegedly hit by Sanders).

(31)

PD3: I did a Pitchess motion[19] and I got back some complaints on . . .
        Smith. Blinn went out and turned up three people who would be
        willing to testify concerning incidents they had with Smith . . .

  J1:   That's sort of my impression, Bill ((the DA)), that—just as a
        judge—that Smith is getting involved in a little bit too many
        of these . . . I get the feeling that Smith's maybe got too heavy a
        hand. And just for what that's worth with you, now that doesn't
        mean you got a lousy case here. I don't know. I haven't read
        the report. And uh, it may be a perfectly good case, but at
        least for what that's worth.

DA1: Well I got Sargeant Blackwell, uh you know Blackwell . . . you've
        heard him testify before

  J1:   Yeah he's good

DA1: And he's going to say I was just standing there and this guy came
        off the table and BAM

PD3: He didn't hit Blackwell

DA1: No he didn't hit Blackwell

  J1:   No I know but if he's a good witness

PD3: Yeah

The assessment of witnesses' talk in plea bargaining, then, is very much concerned with how it can be presented at trial. Defendants are also evaluated with respect to how well they will hold up under cross-examination (Alschuler, 1975: 1311). It is as though witnesses and defendants were required to audition for the trial performance. But, unlike a play, if an auditioned person is regarded as deficient, the trial may not be staged at all, for there is usually no possibility of selecting another party for any particular role.

A second point about rehearsed scenarios is that it is not just the PD's or DA's present audience that is the target of the animated words. It is partly with a hypothetical, but potentially real, group of eventual hearers in mind that certain words are spoken and various stances are

---

[19]A "Pitchess motion" is a discovery procedure, listed in the California Misdemeanor Bench Book, that allows counsel to secure records of a sheriff's department regarding aspects of its internal actions (such as disciplinary proceedings against officers).

taken in plea bargaining.[20] Thus, in a case where a woman defendant had taken a mixture of pain-killing and sedative drugs before removing some clothes from a department store, the PD animated the talk of a number of involved parties, including character witnesses.

(32)

PD1:   I have about half of Hillside ((defendant's home town)) is going
       to come down and testify what a tremendous reputation she has,
       what a sweet person she is

There are also "experts" on the issue of what kind of effects drugs can have:

(33)

PD1:   I had Ron Stout check with County pathology and with a pharmacist.
       And they both say that if she took what she said she took,
       that they can very well understand that her mind would be so
       befuddled that she could have done something like that without
       realizing that she did it.

While the talk of these witnesses is clearly reproduced for the DA and the judge who are present, the PD also projects the reaction of a jury who would hear the case.

(34)

PD1:   I don't think a jury in the world will convict her

Thus, the PD has enacted a scene by animating the positions of a variety of real others (witnesses) and potential others (jury) who have been or might be involved in the case.[21] Discourse is produced, offering a world

---

[20]Bennett (1978, 1979) has examined various storytelling and rhetorical devices for ways in which they structure jurors' response to, and judgement of, the "facts" of a case. Such devices are important in plea bargaining to the extent that the process embodies rehearsals of trial testimony.

[21]Other potential audiences that influence stances taken in plea bargaining include (1) the appeals court and (2) the public. The issue of whether defendants who proclaim innocence should be allowed to plead guilty (because of inducements to do so) when they are regarded by both prosecution and defense as guilty is often resolved by letting the defendant go to trial, but not necessarily because this is the fair and just thing to do. Rather, defense attorneys are concerned about postconviction proceedings in which defendants may assert ineffective assistance of counsel. As well, defense attorneys may be concerned about the public relations of a policy that allows defendants to plead guilty when they assert innocence. See Alschuler (1975: 1283–1285) and Graham and Letwin (1969: 531).

for recipients to get caught up in (Goffman, 1974: 6), however much they differ on whether that the world is capable of later realization.

(35)

DA3:   It's a triable case
PD1:   Well it may be a triable case but you're not going to win it
DA3:   Okay. Let's put it down as a go

DA3, in assessing the case as "triable," offers a quite different inference regarding what testimony may be presented and what the jury might make of it. Still, there is an orientation to a future scene, even if the details of who will say what and how it will be heard depart from those pictured by the PD.

The jury speaks in plea bargaining only in a contingent and hypothetical sense when negotiators animate its suppositious reaction. This is a point not to be taken lightly, for it implies that a modicum of the local community's voice is heard during negotiations. For instance, lawyers considered the Garden City community to have a harsher punitive orientation than other localities, particularly Los Angeles.[22] This alleged orientation was brought up in a discussion of whether a defendant from Los Angeles, who had been apprehended for drunk driving while in Garden City, should go to trial.

(36)

J1:   When you get defendants from the LA area that come here, they're
       not used to the sophistication of Garden City juries, and they're
       not used to the punishments. I mean the defendant doesn't know
       about the juries, compared to what punishments are like there.
PD2:   That's right. Juries here are pushovers compared to some places.
       The punishments are very unusual compared to LA I should think
J1:   Yeah

If the jury speaks in this way during plea bargaining, a further lesson is that we need more of a relational and dramaturgical view of the negotiations. Clearly, when a defense attorney or prosecutor quotes defendants, witnesses, victims, and investigators, there is a fine line between what these persons have said and what they will say before a

---

[22]The "punitiveness" of a jury has long been recognized to vary by jurisdiction and to influence its response to "extra-legal" factors surrounding a particular case. See, for example, Kalven and Zeisel (1966: 293–312).

jury. Consider this from discussion of a defendant charged with impersonating a police officer:

(37)

PA3: There was one thing to keep in mind and that is that the victims
state that he identified himself as being an officer of the
County foot patrol. Now there is no such thing as the County
foot patrol, there's a Woodenville foot patrol. But what my
client will say is that if you don't leave I'm going to call a
member of the county sheriff's or the Woodenville foot patrol,
and somehow the victims testify that they stated to the police
that the window was rolled up, and maybe they just misunderstood
what he said.

What *was* said by an involved party, then, takes its meaning in part from what those in the present situation argue will be said, and what will be made of that saying in a future context, and this imputation reflexively informs what is made of it now, during negotiations.

A third and final point is that plea bargaining needs to be considered less for its information-exchange properties—although those are important—and more for the rehearsing, posturing, and attempted conning that occur within it. We may then appreciate the kind of flourishes accompanying one negotiator's projected scenario that are designed to contain and even dupe the other participant. At the extreme, for example, "Prosecutors sometimes go to the point of empanelling a jury before dismissing a hopeless case, hoping all the while to exact a plea of guilty" (Alschuler, 1968: 66).

CONCLUSION

Plea bargaining is one kind of "speech exchange system" or discourse to be placed alongside others, including everyday conversation. It is a unique type of discourse because it occurs in a single setting, the criminal-justice process, where participants are embedded in work routines that relate them to other persons and activities that influence how negotiations may be conducted. Later sequential analyses of plea-bargaining discourse deemphasize the importance of these other parties and activities surrounding the discourse. The focus will be on basic structures underlying wide surface variations in plea bargaining. But it is also important to obtain a sense of the aspects of the setting to which such structures are sensitive. Stated positively, when one is engaged in researching the talk within a singular setting, it may be desirable to involve the setting analytically.

Frame analysis of plea bargaining discourse shows that what is said is not just a product of those doing the face-to-face negotiations. By frequent changes of footing, practitioners take up different alignments that attest to the variety of organizational forms in which they are embedded, including their relationships with other persons, such as defendants and witnesses, their own offices and professions, other agencies (such as the police), and the court and its activities, such as trial.

The temptation might be to employ Merton's (1968) framework of status and role to account for the stances exhibited during negotiations, where each stance marks the different relations the occupant of a status position (district attorney or public defender) has with members of a role set. But this approach invokes the vocabulary of role "expectations" to account for performance, an approach too mechanical for dealing with actual behavior.[23] Better than an image of actors performing according to role expectations is a model of them acting strategically. Changes of footing are devices by which these strategists meet the contingencies of their respective structural situations and adduce dramaturgical arguments for particular positions. In so doing, they display their decisions as being attuned to a variety of social organizations transcending their immediate interaction.

---

[23]See for example, Gibson (1980) and Rosenthal (1974: 95). I follow the comprehensive critique by Hilbert (1981) who suggests that the most tenable approach to the sociological analysis of role is not to treat it as an explanatory concept. Rather, role should be regarded as an organizing concept for *members*, who use it, when required, as a sense-making procedure in practical situations.

CHAPTER 4

The Structure of Bargaining Sequences

Researchers agree that plea bargaining refers to courtroom transactions in which there is an *exchange* between the prosecution and defense in criminal cases. A consistent and common observation is that defendants who plead guilty receive some dispositional "consideration" from the state, which, in turn, gets sure convictions with less expenditure of time and money than going to trial (Alschuler, 1968: 50; Baldwin and McConville, 1977: 23; Bottoms and McClean, 1976: 123; Feeley, 1979c: 185; Grosman, 1969: Chapter 7; Klein, 1976: Chapter 1; Miller et al., 1978: xii).[1] However, such a definition does not cover the gamut of activities that actually occur as part of plea bargaining (Feeley, 1979a: 199–200). For example, the definition covers situations in which charges and/or sentences are reduced in exchange for guilty pleas. But district attorneys and defense lawyers also use the term to refer to negotiating charge dismissals, continuances, and trials, where a consideration or concession is not traded for a guilty plea (McDonald, 1979: 289; Feeley, 1979b: 462). The definition also fails to capture distinctions between (a) perfunctory discussions in which there is an exchange that is standard or routine procedure but where no overt discussion of the offense and the offender occurs (Feeley, 1979c: 190), and (b) protracted negotiations in which seemingly adversarial sides are taken on these issues before an agreement is reached (e.g., Buckle and Buckle, 1977: 86; Eisenstein and Jacob,

[1]Note that the studies cited include two Canadian ones (Grosman, 1969; Klein, 1976) and two English ones (Baldwin and McConville, 1977; Bottoms and McClean, 1976) in addition to those conducted in the United States, so that there appears to be some consensus among researchers in different countries.

1977: 32). In summary, as Feeley (1979a: 200) has observed, "If plea bargaining is the generic term for negotiation in the criminal process, then we need a richer vocabulary for generating typologies and exploring in greater detail the process of nontrial."

Conversational analysis provides a social organizational perspective that, applied to the 52 cases in our study, orders the range of practices subsumed by the plea bargaining term. Examination of "bargaining sequences" shows a two-part structure that can be systematically elaborated to achieve various features said to be characteristic of bargaining, including "routine processing" and "adversary conflict." Moreover, where others have argued that agreeing on the facts of the case and the character of a defendant are necessary features of negotiated decisions, my analysis shows that the defining characteristic of these decisions is simply the bargaining sequence. It is manipulated to achieve a mutually satisfactory outcome even when lawyers disagree about facts and character.

THE BARGAINING SEQUENCE

Recall that when the defense and prosecution meet at the pretrial and settlement conference, a list of misdemeanor cases has been scheduled for official action. For each one, defense and prosecution must decide on some disposition (which may be anything from a dismissal to a jail sentence), agree on a trial date, or agree to continue the case for reconsideration at a later time.[2] This is not done haphazardly, but in an orderly fashion by means of bargaining sequences consisting of (1) a turn in which speaker exhibits a position, and (2) a next turn where recipient displays alignment or nonalignment with the initially exhibited position. Two principal devices are used to initiate most bargaining sequences: the proposal, and the position-report.

---

[2]Plea bargaining is thus an officially recognized and scheduled occurrence in this court. This may be a qualitative difference from the Canadian "discovery" and "disclosure" sessions Lynch (1982) has studied, where plea bargaining within those sessions is a delicately managed phenomenon. Still, "discovery" and "disclosure" appear to be salient issues in the conferences reported on here, where plea bargaining is officially recognized, so that "bargaining sequences" are delayed until those issues are settled. See the discussion below regarding how bargaining sequences are "locally occasioned."

Proposals

Negotiators characterize some of the utterances in which they make a position visible as "offers," "suggestions," "asking-fors," and "proposals," the latter being an umbrella term.

(1)[3] [Disorderly Conduct]

1. PD2: Is there a offer in that case
2. DA1: I would say in this case uh a fine, seventy five dollars
3. PD1: Arright

In this example, PD2 solicits an "offer" from DA1, who provides it in line 2. Proposals like this are also defined by the replies they obtain, which are acceptances or rejections. In the above, PD2 accepts the DA's offer, in line 3, with "arright." Following are other examples of proposal sequences. In some, the proposal is accepted, in others, it is rejected.

(2) [Burglary]

PD2: Well, tell you what, how 'bout the very short jail sentence
DA3: Arright

(3) [Breaking or removing vehicle parts]

DA3: How 'bout three months
PD1: Naw, that's too much

(4) [Breaking or removing vehicle parts]

DA3: I'll give ya ninety days
PD1: Naw that's no good

(5) [Shoplifting]

DA1: How about a four eight four[4] and a referral to probation
PD1: No

---

[3]Beginning here, transcripts will be displayed more formally than before. They are numbered according to their order of appearance in this chapter, such as (1), (2), etc. In square brackets next to this number is the offense charged (if it is not mentioned in the text). When transcript segments are from a case in an Appendix, line numbers from the Appendix will be in square brackets. Personnel are labeled with abbreviations and numbers. As noted earlier, the tapes were originally transcribed in detail according to the system devised by Gail Jefferson (see Appendix 1). Where details are unnecessary to the analysis, they have been omitted. All examples should thus be considered as "simplified" transcripts. If actual talk is omitted, however, it is noted by the use of elipses.
[4]"Four eight four" refers to the section of the California penal code regarding theft.

(6) [Carrying a switch-blade]

PD5:   Let's continue it two weeks
DA3:   Arright uh, will be continued

(7) [Petty theft]

DA3:   Let's put this down for a go
PD2:   Arright go it is

An initial observation about these examples is that there is variation in the kinds of actions that are proposed via the sequences. Examples (2), (3), and (4) contain specific proposals for sentence, and example (5) embodies an offer on the charge *and* sentence. In contrast, examples (6) and (7) contain suggestions for courses of action that would delay the dispositional decision by way of a continuance and trial, respectively. The point is that there do not seem to be distinctive ways of exhibiting different *kinds* of positions on how to handle a case. Proposals are used to suggest a wide variety of actions.

Another feature of the above proposals is that they are often prefaced with items that make acceptance or rejection a relevant action in the next turn. Examples (2), (3), and (5) employ a prototypical suggestion-preface ("how about . . ."), while (6) and (7) utilize an invitational device ("let's"), and (4) is formulated as a possible "gift" (I'll give ya . . ."). However, not too heavy an analytical load should be placed on such prefaces—for the simple reason that proposals are as much defined by what precedes and what follows them (replies) as by what is intrinsic to the proposal utterance itself.

(8) [Vandalism]

1.   PD2:   Okay uh is there an offer in Delaney
2.   DA3:   Yeah plea to Mal Mish[5] and uh uhm modest fine and uh restitution
3.   PD2:   Okay
4.   (0.8)
5.   PD2:   Fifty dollars?
6.   DA3:   Yes

The utterance in line 2 can be characterized as a proposal because it follows an utterance in which an "offer" has been specifically solicited. And, in line 5, "fifty dollars" can be heard as a proposal regarding the

---

[5]"Mal Mish" refers to "malicious mischief," the title of the penal code section under which vandalism falls.

amount of the penalty in that it follows the *sequence* in which a "modest fine" has been suggested and accepted.[6]

Position-Reports

A second way that negotiators assert their positions is by forming them as *reports*, marking the utterances with prefaces such as "I'd like," "I want," "I think," and the like, which indicate that the position taken is a private or personal idea, preference, or desire. Reports may also be ways of performing a "mitigated" or downgraded version of the proposal (cf. Labov and Fanshel, 1977: 845).

(9) [Petty theft]

PA2:   I'd like ta see it kept off his record

(10) [Drunken driving]

PD2:   We wanta plead 'im to a first time deuce[7]

---

[6]More precisely, the "fifty dollars" (line 5), following the "okay" (line 3), helps to accomplish the latter's visibility as an acceptance. As a comparison, in the following, a judge exhibits a position (lines 1–2). That "report" (position reports are discussed in the next subsection) is similarly followed by an "okay" (line 3). In this instance it does not at all indicate acceptance, but rather a mere acknowledgment of the judge's position, since what follows it is PD4's statement of nonalignment (lines 5–6).

[Assault with deadly weapon]

```
1.   J2:   My inclination is that he- you know I think he should spend
2.         some more time in
3. PD4:   Okay
4.                               (0.2)
5. PD4:   My- my problem with that judge is uh their case doesn't
6.         look that good to me
```

To return to example (8), just as the "okay" (line 3) is partly constituted as an "acceptance" by what follows it, that "okay" is also an "acceptance" because it is positioned after a proposal-utterance. Moreover, it is involved in accomplishing DA3's utterance in line 2 as a proposal, in that proposals are followed by acceptances/rejections. Thus, characterization of an utterance as a "proposal" or "acceptance" is profoundly dependent on how the utterance is heard in relation to what precedes and follows it and how what precedes and follows it is heard in relation to the given utterance. In other words, any utterance's status as a characterizable entity is an achievement of its reflexive relation to the retrospective-prospective sequential context of its production. (See the discussion on how utterances "derive their character as actions" in Schegloff and Sacks, 1974: 241–242.) In what follows, terms such as "proposal" and "reply" should be understood as glosses for the work involved in their ongoing constitution.

[7]"Deuce" refers to drunken driving.

(11) [Drunk driving]

PA4:   I'd be willing to take two movings[8]

(12) [Petty theft]

DA1:   I think she should be placed on probation and do jail time

Reports, like proposals, exhibit varied sorts of positions. In example (9), the utterance indicates a preference for dismissing the case; in (10) and (11), the positions reported concern charges; and in (12), the issue is sentencing.

As with proposals, we should not place too much emphasis on the prefacing items in position-reports, because the sequential context in which these utterances occur is crucial to their constitution. Take, for example, the following two segments, where the discussion involves a defendant named Kevin Castle. DA2 asks for, and gets, a statement of an unequivocal *want* from PD2.

(13) [Disorderly conduct]

1.   DA2:   What do you want on it
2.   PD2:   I want you to dismiss it

Following this, there is discussion regarding the police report, and then the talk is interrupted when another DA enters the room. After he leaves, PD2 takes up the case again.

(13a)

3.   PD2:   What about Castle
4.   (1.8)
5.   DA2:   I'll dismiss that
6.   PD2:   Arright

DA2, in line 5, aligns with PD2's position by indicating his willingness to take the course of action that PD2 "wanted." But DA2's utterance thereby seems to be more of an acceptance of a proposal rather than a reply to a position-report. This is a matter that requires some argument.

What may be distinctive about utterances in which some personal state descriptor prefaces a possible course of action for a case is that—

---

[8]"Two movings" means two moving violations, which are infractions rather than misdemeanors.

in comparison with proposals—different foci and response options are thereby presented to recipient. An acceptance (or rejection) can be achieved by focusing exclusively on the "course of action" part of the utterance. To focus also on the preface by producing a parallel one is to preserve the visibility of speaker's and recipient's similarities, differences, or gradations in perspective regarding the posed course of action.

These issues become clearer in the next segment. This is another petty theft case, in which the woman defendant is described by the PD as "middle-aged" and as someone who would not "fit in well with the jail population." In line 1, DA3 produces a candidate statement of PD2's position, which is ratified in the first part of line 2 by his report, "I don't want her to have to do time."

(14)

1. DA3: Eh so ya wanta plead her but ya don't want to have 'er do time
2. PD2: I don't want her to have to do time
3.   (0.1)
4. PD2: I wonder if uh probation however might not be in order
5. DA3: I think probation IS in order. I think time susPENded is in order
6. PD2: Arright

After that, PD2 produces another position-report regarding the possibility of probation (line 4). The utterance is prefaced by "I wonder" and contains the hypothetical "if" and the auxiliary "might," all of which indicate hesitancy regarding the course of action posed. In his following move, DA3 utilizes a number of devices that contrast with those of the PD: "I think" (line 5) displays a firmer attitude toward the probation possibility than "I wonder"; the hypothetical construction is dropped; and "is" runs counter with "might not be" (a countering that is emphasized by the stress placed on "is"). DA2 then exhibits, in a similar utterance (second part of line 5), a position for "time suspended." In line 6, PD2 replies to DA3's reports with an "arright" that displays (and, in subsequent talk, is treated as) an alignment with the position that probation and time suspended are "in order."

Thus, we see two sorts of second moves in this segment. First, DA3's response[9] (line 5) to PD2's line 4 utterance focuses on both the preface and course of action part of that utterance, and thereby makes

---

[9]"Responses," and their relation to "replies," are discussed in the section on elaborating the bargaining sequence.

observable a strong preference for what PD2 regards less surely (probation) and for another item (time suspended) not broached by PD2.
Second, when PD2 replies with the "arright" (line 6) to these utterances
by DA3, he hearably focuses off of the perspectival issue and proffers
to treat the probation and suspended sentence actions not just as *posed*,
but as *pro*-posed, and accepted. The distinction between proposals and
position-reports cannot be made on the basis of the utterances alone,
then, but is a contingent achievement of the way the positions are presented and reacted to.

Bargaining Openers

Proposals and reports are two forms by which negotiators display
their positions on what course of action should be taken on a criminal
case. A proposal or report, together with (and as partly accomplished
by) its reply, constitutes a *sequence* that is basic to the production of plea
bargaining as a coherent discourse activity. Proposals include offers,
suggestions, etc., by which some possible course of action is exhibited
to be accepted or rejected by recipient. Position-reports employ personal
state prefaces or descriptors that allow the utterance of which they are
a part to be treated as either a perspectival statement or a proposal. But
proposals and position-reports are only bargaining sequence *openers*.

BARGAINING SEQUENCES IN RELATION TO OTHER
ASPECTS OF PRESENT NEGOTIATIONS

Bargaining sequences are used to exhibit positions on a variety of
possible actions, including charges to be made, sentences, dismissals,
continuances, and trials. The bargaining sequence also accommodates
variations in the kinds of discussions in which negotiators engage, rang-
ing from routine, perfunctory ones, to extended negotiations over the
character of the defendant, what the person did, who the witnesses and
victims were, and so forth. Ultimately, we will see that the difference
between proposals and position-reports is important to the distinction
often made between routine and "adversarial" justice. To do this, we
first need to look at ways in which the bargaining sequence articulates
with the rest of negotiations, and to further investigate the internal
organization of the sequence.

Entering into, and Exiting from, the Bargaining Sequence

That bargaining sequences articulate with the rest of negotiations means that they are locally occasioned and sequentially implicative.[10] *Local occasioning* refers to regular ways that the sequence is introduced into turn-by-turn talk. *Sequential implicativeness* means that, once completed, a bargaining sequence has consequences for the talk and actions that follow.

Bargaining openers are often occasioned by forms that either *solicit* or *announce* them. Solicits are designed to obtain a proposal or position-report from a specific *other*. That is, if the PD produces a solicit, it is directed to the DA, and vice versa:

(15) [Drunk driving]

PD2: Is there an offer in that case
DA2: Yeah a reckless with a deuce ((drunk driving)) dispo

(16) [Disorderly conduct]

PD2: Is there an offer in the case
DA1: I would say in this case a fine, seventy five dollars

(17) [Disorderly conduct]

DA2: What do you want
PD2: I want you to dismiss it

(18) [Drunk driving]

DA3: What are you proposing we do with this
PD4: If you want a reckless and a hundred and eight dollar fine he'll
        do it

In the three-party situation, it is often the judge who solicits a bargaining opener from one of the other parties.

(19) [Battery]

J1:   What do you want out of it Steve ((the DA))
DA6: We want him on probation, I feel that he should be on probation
        and supervised on probation

---

[10]See Jefferson's (1978) discussion of how *stories* are locally occasioned and sequentially implicative in ordinary conversation.

(20) [Shoplifting]

J1: What do you want
PD1: Want it dismissed

Rather than requesting an opener from "other," an attorney may indicate that "self" is willing to produce one, by using an *announcement* (lines 1 in the examples below). Announcements are usually followed by "go-ahead" signals (lines 2) that permit speaker to make the proposal (lines 3ff.).

(21) [Resisting police officers]

1. DA1: I think I've got an offer that I'll make at this time
2. PD2: Sure shoot
3. DA1: Um I'd offer, if the defendant uh he pled guilty to the one
4.   forty eight, dismiss the other count, thirty days suspended for
5.   a period of one year on condition he do two weekends

(22) [Battery; driving without a license]

1. PD2: I'll propose a deal to ya
2. DA3: Tell me what deal ya got
3. PD2: If ya dismiss the two forty two, I might be able to arrange a plea
4.   to fourteen six oh one for a fine

Solicits and announcements are examples of a generic category of "pre-sequences," or devices that project an upcoming discourse action.[11] In that those considered here specifically prefigure the first part of a bargaining sequence, an appropriate term is *pre-opener*. Although pre-openers are most often followed by the projected action, they do allow recipient to forestall its production. A solicit can be turned down (and a reason will be given for the turn-down):

(23) [Drunk driving]

PD2: Is there any offer in this case
DA2: No

---

[11]Sacks (1967, lecture 8; 1972, lecture 1) discusses pre-sequences as preliminary to particular types of "adjacency pairs" (which I discuss below). A prototypical pre-sequence is that which comes before an invitation:

Pre-sequence		A: What are you doing on Friday	
		B: Nothing	
Adjacency pair	Invitation	A: Want to have dinner?	
	Acceptance	B: Okay	

PD2: Very well
DA2: Not without a probation report, the law requires a probation report

And announcements can be handled in ways that indicate a recipient is not fully knowledgeable and ready to hear a proposal. This may implicate work that identifies the case.

(24) [Petty theft]

PD2: Let me offer you a deal on Gage
DA3: Gage
                    (12.0) ((DA3 looks through file))
DA3: That a petty theft?
PD2: Mm hmm
DA3: It was grand theft actually
PD2: Mm hmm
DA3: Filed as a misdemeanor
PD2: You should probably talk to Severts ((DA1)) about that one, see
        the problem is they don't know how much money was in there . . .

Thus, pre-openers allow systematic movement into a bargaining sequence in such a way as to preserve the opportunity for discussion of other relevant items before the sequence is started. With an exception to be noted later, in all negotiations where the bargaining sequence is done as a "first topic" in negotiations,[12] it is preceded by a solicit or announcement. When a bargaining opener occurs without a pre-sequence, it occurs after a PD or DA (or both) has told "what happened" or has characterized the defendant in such a way as to justify a position-report or proposal.[13] Consider the next case, in which the PD and DA first established that the defendant's blood alcohol level was barely above the statutory limit for drunk driving. The DA reports the state's position after the PD and he discuss other items as well:

(25) [Drunk driving]

PD: Um his girlfriend was in the car up to about five or ten minutes before the detention.
       He'd had something to drink seven, seven thirty at night, he had three beers and
       uh he had a little whiskey earlier in the day. He went to sleep, woke up to take
       her to work, drops her off at work. He's got his kid with him and he's driving

---

[12]Sacks (Winter 1971: lecture 1) explores "first topics" and the special status they may have in conversation. For example, a first topic often serves as a "reason" for a conversation to have occurred. For a published treatment of the issue, see Schegloff and Sacks (1974: 242–243).

[13]Chapter 6 examines ways that "person-descriptions" justify proposals.

home. And uh he says I was not doing anything wrong, said I didn't feel the
alcohol, I wasn't under the influence, and she says well I was in the car with him,
he was driving perfectly and I wouldn't have went with him, I would've taken the
car myself, if I thought he couldn't drive . . .

DA2: What we've got here is a- for driving, we've got a couple of unsafe lane changes,
he's weaving at least three times within a single lane, he's outside of the lane, he's
on ((highway)) one fifteen, least a couple of times. He's steaming along, you know
at sixty. He really doesn't do very well on the field sobriety. It's a triable drunk
driving. We're obviously offering a reckless

The general maxim seems to be that initial bargaining sequences
must be preceeded by relevant discussion, or by solicits and announcements that allow such discussion to happen if needed. The apparent
exception to this maxim serves to confirm it.

(26) [Driving a motor vehicle while under the influence of drugs]

J1:   Next is Jerry Romney, which is a two three one oh nine bee
PD2: Yeah we haven't discussed that yet but if you'll take a speeding
      and a thirty five dollars

When the judge marks a transition from negotiations regarding another
defendant to the Romney case, PD2 produces a proposal almost immediately. It is, however, prefaced by PD2 specifically mentioning an
absence of discussion. That statement proffers a remedy for any possible
offensiveness that his act might cause, thereby exhibiting an orientation
to the "discuss first" maxim even while it is breached (Goffman, 1971:
109).

If remedies of this sort perform ritual work, so may pre-openers
produced in the beginning stages of negotiation. They allow movement
into a bargaining sequence as a first topic in a situation where that
otherwise might be offensive behavior. In addition, that an opener is
produced emerges as a collaborative, synchronized achievement, as if
the bargaining sequence required "coordinated entry" as much as a
conversation itself (Schegloff, 1968). The key issue is not the general
interactive availability of participants, however, because that is established at the outset of their encounter. The issue is practitioners' dual
consent to parley about a dispositional action for a given case at the
current moment. A solicit indicates the solicitor's willingness to entertain
a proposal, and, in issuing it, the proposer simultaneously agrees to the
propriety of its timing. With an announcement, proposer signifies read-

iness to make an offer, and with a go-ahead move, recipient ratifies the appropriateness of the offer being made now. Conversely, when an offer is forestalled, it is not that the offer will necessarily be improper, but that its present occurrence is. Thus, in the following, before DA1's offer is completed, PD4 interjects a preface to an "explanation" of his own position, mentions the timing of the DA's offer, and proceeds with the explanation.

(27) [Assault with a deadly weapon]

J2: What can ya do with Mister Gordon
            (2.4)
DA1: I've offered uh
            (0.4)[14]
PD4: Why don't I explain uh- I might as well explain my position,
     there's no use discussing their offer at this time. Uh Gordon
     is nutty, we've had problems with him before. Uh the thing
     about his case is, is uh the guy he got in a fight with is uh is
     crazy if not crazier than he is . . .

A further clue that pre-openers are sensitive to the proper timing of a bargaining sequence derives from their placement not at the beginning of negotiations but after participants have discussed a case at length. Then, their work is observably retrospective *and* prospective in character. That is, an announcement or solicit later in negotiations suggests that enough has been said regarding facts and circumstances, and it is time to put ideas and proposals regarding disposition on the table. In one case of petty theft, the PD began negotiations by describing his client in positive, if not glowing, terms. He then told the story of her taking clothes from a department store and explained that she did not know what she was doing because she had ingested two different prescription drugs. After the PD and judge both discussed the effects of the drugs, the judge questioned whether the defendant had a prior record of any kind. The PD answered, "she's had nothing," and repeated the list of descriptions regarding her character that he had produced earlier. The judge immediately asked, "What do you want?"[15] While this solicit provided for the relevance of a bargaining opener in next utterance, it

---

[14]Note that DA1's hesitation, as marked by the "uh" and four-tenths of a second silence, may *invite* PD4's talk.

[15]See example (35) in this chapter, and the full transcript of negotiations in Appendix 3. See also Chapter 6, segments (7) and (8) and discussion.

also clearly operated as a *terminal boundary* to the prior discussion of what had happened, why it had happened, and what kind of person the defendant was. Used at the very beginning of negotiations, therefore, pre-openers may *fictitiously* submit that enough discussion has taken place or may imply that such discussion is not necessary and that it is already time to perform the real business of bargaining.

Bargaining sequences are occasioned in regular, organized ways, and they are also sequentially implicative. The kind of consequences a sequence has for subsequent talk is dependent on whether the recipient of an opener does or does not align with the position exhibited in it. If recipient does not, that results in further proposals that may be accompanied by discussion, argument, appeals, and other negotiational work. Because this matter is fully explored in Chapter 8, it needs only be mentioned here.

When a recipient does align with the displayed position, that occasions specific next activities that bring about the close of negotiations on the particular case. For example, recall the case in which the defendant had stolen a parking sticker at a local college and the DA acceded to the PD's request to reduce the charge from petty theft to a parking infraction, in part because the dean of students had written a letter on the defendant's behalf.[16]

(28) [Petty theft]

1.	DA3:	Well uh maybe I can make an exception in this case on the
2.		theory that if the dean of students doesn't care enough for
3.		the enforcement of the college's own rules, why should we
4.		feel all that uh- what was the section found uh
5.	PD4:	Twenty one, uh two one one one three ay
6.	DA3:	Hm
7.	PD4:	I'm almost sure it is, I can show you
8.	DA3:	What do you want in a fine
9.	PD2:	Mm what's reasonable. Fifty dollars
10.	DA3:	Fifty's fine
11.	PD2:	Fifteen dollar penalty assessment
12.	DA3:	Mm hmm
13.	PD2:	Total sixty five dollars
14.	PD2:	Mm hmm
15.	PD2:	Arright. Uh Delaney

---

[16]Also see Appendix 5, and the discussion of example (2) in Chapter 7.

After accepting the PD's proposal in terms of "making an exception" (line 1), DA3 checks out the traffic code section number (line 4), which PD4 provides (line 5). Then, by way of a solicit (line 8), and further bargaining sequences (lines 9–12), the sentence is decided. And after the "total" is checked and ratified (lines 13–14), PD2 initiates negotiations on the next case ("Delaney," line 15).

Elaborating the Bargaining Sequence

Bargaining sequences are related to other aspects of negotiational discourse *externally* in that they are locally occasioned and sequentially implicative. As well, they can be elaborated *internally* by various practices that raise relevant bargaining issues. Exploring the internal elaboration of bargaining sequences raises a technical matter. Many proposals or position-reports and their replies take on the appearance of adjacency pairs,[17] as examples (1)–(8) show. To recall just one of these:

(29) [Burglary]

PD2:   Well, tell you what, how 'bout the very short jail sentence
DA3:   Arright

According to Schegloff and Sacks (1974: 238), an adjacency pair sequence is characterized by five features: (1) it consists of two parts, (2) adjacently positioned, (3) with different speakers producing each utterance; furthermore, (4) the parts are "relatively" ordered (i.e., first pair parts precede second pair parts), and (5) they are "discriminatively" related (i.e., the pair type of which the first is a member is relevant to the selection among second pair parts).

Bargaining sequences regularly consist of two parts (a proposal or position-report plus reply) that are relatively ordered (an opener precedes the reply) and discriminatively related (proposals and reports implicate distinctive reply possibilities). However, these sequences are often elaborated in systematic ways so that their parts are not necessarily adjacently positioned and produced by different speakers.

---

[17]Adjacency pairs have been discussed extensively by Sacks (e.g., 1967, 1972) in his unpublished lectures as well as in published papers (Sacks et al., 1974; Schegloff and Sacks, 1974).

Direct Responses

One ordinary way in which this happens is the placement of an "insertion sequence" between an opening and its reply. The following involves "Jim Helwig," who took part in a fight in an alley. When his case is brought up in the judge's chambers by the district attorney, the public defender is not sure if the case is his, and he leaves the room momentarily to check. When he returns, the following takes place:

(30) [Disorderly Conduct]

1.	PD2:	I'm sorry, I recognize mister Helwig. Uh yeah this is mine, is
2.		there an offer in that case
3.	DA1:	I would say in this case uh, a fine. Seventy five dollars
4.	PD2:	Arright, well, why don't you put it aside for a minute because uh
5.		the amount o' the fine is something we're taking issue with. Is
6.		there- did mister Helwig- was he arrested on that, did he go to
7.		jail
8.		(12.0) ((DA1 leafs through report))
9.	DA1:	I don't think so. No we sent 'im a letter
10.	PD2:	Arright uh I'll convey that to 'im

In line 3, DA1 proposes a "seventy five dollar" fine, which obtains a candidate acceptance (line 10), subject to the defendant's approval. Between those two utterances is an insertion sequence that operates to obtain information relevant to the production of the proposal's reply (cf. Sacks, 1972: lecture 1; Schegloff, 1972: 109–110). If we look closely at the turn in lines 4–7, however, it consists of several pieces of work by which the "relevant information" is obtained. First is a trouble-marker, when the PD suggests that the DA put the proposal "aside for a minute" (line 4). Next, PD2 locates the trouble as being the "amount of the fine" (line 5). And then comes the informational question as to whether Mr. Helwig was arrested and went to jail (lines 6–7), a matter relevant to the "amount of the fine" because it is a standard practice to offset "time served" against any prescribed fine in determining a sentence. So within the turn that initiates the insertion sequence some step-by-step work is done.

This turn can be considered as a *response* to the proposal it follows, to distinguish it from the occasioned reply (acceptance or rejection). Responses, in general, are next moves by which a recipient of a proposal or position-report speaks to other aspects of the prior move instead of addressing what it directly implicates.[18] And responses can be classified as *direct* or *indirect*. Direct ones, such as an insertion sequence-initiator, are those in which *recipient* provides material that formulates some trouble source preventing the production of a reply. Indirect responses, including silences and tokens like "well," "uh," etc., occasion attempts by *speaker* to locate a source of the trouble and to remedy it in order to obtain a positive reply.

Another characteristic direct response is the counterreport or counterproposal. Generally, these are devices by which a recipient arrogates production of the first part of a bargaining sequence and occasions the relevance of a reply from the person who originally opened. Recall example (14):

(31)

1. DA3: Eh so ya wanta plead her but ya don't want to have 'er do time
2. PD2: I don't want her to have her do time
3.   (0.1)
4. PD2: I wonder if uh probation however might not be in order
5. DA3: I think probation IS in order. I think time susPENded is in order
6. PD2: Arright

In line 5, DA3 counters PD2's position report with one of his own in which, it was argued, he displays a firmer attitude than PD2 toward probation as a means of handling the case and also poses "time suspended." That, then, occasions the relevance of a reply from PD2, which he provides in line 6 ("arright").

A counter to a position-report or proposal makes visible a contrasting position of the one who speaks it and simultaneously suggests what trouble exists with respect to the opposed position. Counterproposals regarding fines, for example, can indicate that the prior is asking too little or too much.

(32)

1. PD2: Okay uh, twenty five dollar fine
    . . .

---

[18]The distinction is related to one made by Goffman (1981: 43).

> Although a *reply* is addressed to meaningful elements of whole statements, *responses* can break frame and address aspects of a statement which would ordinarily be "out of frame," ordinarily part of transmission, not content—for example, the statement's duration, tactfulness, style, origin and so forth.

2. DA3: Seventy five dollar fine
3. PD2: Why don't we compromise and make it fifty
4. DA3: It's done
5. PD2: Arright

Here, DA3's counter ("seventy five dollar fine," line 2) to PD2's offer ("twenty five dollar fine," line 1) signifies that the latter is too little. PD2's "compromise" (line 3) suggests that DA3's proposal asks too much. Clearly, any counterproposal itself can be countered so that there can be a *round* (Goffman, 1971: 147) of such devices, each co-participant alternatively occasioning an opportunity for the other to move off of a last-exhibited position.

This example can be compared with segments (1), (8), (13), (14), and (30). In these, decisions are reached by standard use of the adjacency pair sequence. That is, an action for some case is determined by one party exhibiting a position in a bargaining opener and the other party simply aligning with the position. Thus, example (1) again:

(33) [Disorderly Conduct]

1. PD2: Is there a offer in that case
2. DA1: I would say in this case uh a fine, seventy five dollars
3. PD1: Arright

In segments like this, the standard adjacency pair format is clearly displayed, with second pair parts following first parts. The variant presented by counterproposals is that a first part follows another first pair part, as in riddle sequences where an initial question is followed by a question (Sacks, 1972: lecture 1). Such variants do not violate adjacency pair organization so much as they accomplish observable and reportable features of interaction. Compromise, for instance, is clearly not a deviant form of bargaining discourse; rather, it is a contingent outcome, achieved by systematic manipulation of bargaining sequence parts.

Indirect Responses

Indirect responses, it was said, are moves after a proposal or position report which involve little or no talk by recipient. They regularly occasion work by which speaker attempts to make his position acceptable to recipient. The next segment is from a discussion in which the defense attorney (Private Attorney #2) has argued that the defendant, "who does want to become a school teacher," is afraid of having a criminal conviction "go on his record." He had taken a bottle of eye-wash from a drug store.

(34) [Shoplifting]

```
 1.  PA2:  I know there's a policy there where he'd be put on probation for
 2.        six months, uh with no similar violations, after six months he'd
 3.        come in and he could drop the plea
 4.                              (1.4)
 5.  PA2:  An' for administrative reasons (0.4) for administrative purposes,
 6.        he doesn't have to- when he's asked if he's ever- if he's ever been
 7.        convicted of a misdemeanor, he can reply with a NO on application
 8.        form
 9.                              (3.0)
10.  PA2:  The other thing that I would be asking for is that in lieu of the
11.        twenty four hour uh mandatory jailtime, that this is one of those
12.        cases where I don't think it merits twenty four hours in jail, and
13.        I'll be willing to uh have another disposition such as ten days
14.        suspended for the six month probationary period
```

The standard penalty for shoplifting is 24 hours in jail (lines 11–12), so, in rough terms, PA2 is attempting to head off this sentence. In lines 1–2, he reports his knowledge of a "policy" that would have the consequence of keeping the defendant's record clean—the "probation" PA2 refers to is a practice in the district attorney's office whereby the case would be continued for the "six months" at which time, if there were "no similar violations," the case would be dismissed.[19] In line 4, there is a "withhold," a recognizable absence of an occasioned reply to the posed course of action.

A characteristic form of talk after such a response is an utterance in which speaker assesses or formulates the defendant, the proposal, or the case in general, in a way that *justifies* the suggested course of action. In lines 5–8, PA2 makes the action appear relevant for "administrative reasons" and "purposes" of applying for a job. Again, however, there is no talk by the district attorney (line 9). Next, PA2 gives up the issue of "dropping the plea" and focuses on the sentence (lines 10–14). Instead of the "twenty four hour mandatory jail time" (line 11), he indicates a "willingness" to have a ten-day jail sentence "suspended for the six

[19]This practice is not unique to the Garden City jurisdiction. Feeley (1979c: 176) notes a similar preadjudication sanctioning method in Connecticut. There the arrangement is also called "prosecutor's probation."

month probationary period" (line 14; this means the defendant would only serve the ten days if he were arrested for another offense while on probation). Because a suspended jail sentence necessitates a guilty plea, PA2 thus offers an account of the DA's prior withhold as displaying trouble with a proposal for something other than the guilty plea.[20] PA2's utterance is an instance of how the *speaker* of a position can volunteer that it is "asking too much," as contrasted with the counterproposal in which it is implicitly suggested by the *recipient* of an offer that it is out of line.

Given the sort of work that a speaker may do after an opener is dealt with by a silence or minimal response, the withhold is clearly a device that can be strategically employed by recipient for various ends. In the last example, successive silences occasioned (1) a rationalization, and (2) a modification of the PA's position in a direction potentially more acceptable to the prosecutor. In the next example, withhold responses to a defense attorney's position-report also obtain rationalizing utterances. These are then used by the district attorneys to construct disagreement turns and to accountably exhibit nonalignment with the PD's position. In earlier discussion, the PD depicted the woman defendant in this shoplifting case as being under some pain-killing drugs when she took several clothing items from a department store, being in a "state of confusion, delirium, in a dream world," and not knowing "what in the world" she was doing.[21]

(35) [Shoplifting]

1.	J1:	What do you want
2.	PD1:	Want it dismissed
3.		(2.2)
4.	PD1:	Wasn'- she was obviously not acting on 'er own free will
5.		(1.0)
6.	J1:	Well
7.		(3.0)
8.	PD1:	They'll never- you'll- they'll never get a conviction
9.		(0.8)
10.	DA2:	₁Do you understand how much manual dexterity it takes to₁
11.	DA1:	₁Maybe we won't but uh:::::: ₁

---

[20]As Pomerantz (forthcoming: 5) has observed, a remedying utterance proposes "an order of trouble it purportedly remedies."

[21]This case is mentioned in the section on "Entering into and Exiting from the Bargaining Sequence" above. See footnote 15. The negotiations are analyzed further in Chapter 6.

12. DA2: ₁operate a booster operation   ₁
13. DA1: ⌈I just can't believe that the drug⌉ is- (1.4) if the drug affects
14.   you that badly you gonna do something bizarre
15.   (0.4)
16. PD1: Well that's w₁hy don't you- ₁
17. DA1:   ⌈In other words⌉ you're gonna walk out swinging
18.   around your arm or carrying out bananas in your ear or something
19.   crazy. Here she was extremely sophisticated. Go into the dressing
20.   room, pin it up underneath her coat, um her uh dress like that.
21.   Extremely sophisticated. Uh I just can't buy it.

In line 1, the judge solicits a position-report from PD1, which he provides
in line 2 ("want it dismissed"). Then, following minimal responses on
the part of the two district attorneys present and the judge (lines 3, 5,
and 6) PD1 produces successive justifications of his position. The first
one is a "person description" (Chapter 5) characterizing the woman as
"not acting on her own free will." It is fitted to earlier remarks about
the effects of the drugs she took and is related to the legal issue of
"intent." If it can be established that intent is missing from an act, then
it is not criminal (Hall, 1960: 70–77; Sigler, 1981: 56–59), and this is
grounds for dismissing the case. PD1's second justification is an assessment of the trial potential of the case and is hearably linked with
earlier discussion regarding the good character of the woman and the
number of witnesses who would testify to it.

After the latter utterance, turn transition is achieved, as each DA
uses PD1's justifying utterances in constructing disagreement turns. DA2,
in lines 10 and 12, produces an utterance that can be heard as directed
to PD1's description of the defendant, in that having "manual dexterity"
and performing "a booster operation" are contrast activities to "not
acting on her own free will." DA1, in overlap with DA2, and in a standard disagreement format, acknowledges PD1's assessment that the state
will not get a conviction ("maybe we won't," line 11), produces a contrast
marker ("but," line 11), and constructs his own disagreement item. He
starts up with the hypothetical statement, "if the drug affects you that
badly," utilizing PD1's earlier characterization of the drug's influence,
and suggests how "you" might act: "bizarre," "swinging around your
arm," "crazy," etc. (cutting off PD1's utterance at line 16). The descriptions of the defendant ("extremely sophisticated," line 19) and of her
activity ("go into the dressing room, pin it up . . .," lines 19–20) are the

converse of those predicated of the hypothetical person who takes drugs. This comparison of the defendant to the abstract "you" provides the accountability of DA1's last utterance ("I just can't buy it," line 21), which summarizes his disagreement with the PD's argument and indicates his unwillingness to align with the course of action originally posed (to dismiss the case).

In this example, then, "indirect responses" to a defense attorney's bargaining opener result in justifying work by the attorney. That work occasions disagreement utterances by each of the prosecutors, one of whom shapes his turn to exhibit nonalignment with the position posed in the opener. That is, if "want it dismissed" (line 2) and "I just can't buy it" (line 21) can be considered as two parts of a bargaining sequence, it is one systematically elaborated by withholds, justifications, and disagreements.

Three-Party Negotiation

In the two-party situation with only a defense attorney and prosecutor talking, silences and minimal utterances after bargaining openers engender various sorts of rationalizing or revising work on the part of speaker. In the three-party situation, the attorneys negotiate before the judge, who may simply provide a type of minimal response after one attorney produces a position report or proposal (example 35, line 6). However, the judge may take the opportunity to urge a particular resolution. In one case a defendant was charged with falsely representing himself as a public officer, and "using offensive words inherently likely to produce a violent reaction." The defense attorney argued that what the two complainants in the case thought they heard was not what his client said. The DA's response focused on the victim's uncertainty.

(36) [Impersonation of police officer; challenging to fight]

```
1.   DA3:  So I suggest we might do- uh resolve it in this fashion. Uh I could
2.         contact each of the two uh witnesses and uh determine so far as I
3.         can what their best recollection is 'n how specific they are. If
4.         they're very specific you've got yourself a lawsuit to try and if
5.         they are not or if they confess to confusion on the point or the
6.         possibility that they could be confused, that maybe his account of
7.         what he said is incorrect, then I'd be willing to dismiss the case
8.                                        (8.0)
9.   J1:   That sounds fair I assume
10.  PA3:  Yes
```

After the DA has produced a bargaining opener, a long silence occurs (line 8). The judge bids for PA3's alignment with the district attorney's position by means of an assessment of the proposal ("that sounds fair") that could reflect his own view; by appending "I assume" he transforms it into a candidate statement which invites agreement from the Private Attorney. PA3 provides it in line 10.

Here, the judge aided the district attorney. In the Romney case (example 26), the judge did work on behalf of the defense attorney. This occurs after the PD's proposal meets with a silence (line 3 below).

(37) [Driving a motor vehicle while under the influence of drugs]

```
1.   PD2:  We haven't discussed that yet, but if you'll take a speeding and
2.         a thirty five dollars
3.                              (0.6)
4.   J1:   Oh I'm sure the people'll do that, right
5.                              (0.4)
6.   J1:   Looks like ₁it's just₁ breaking traction
7.   DA3:             ⌈Sure  ⌉
8.   DA3:  Sure.
```

J1 requests a response from the DA (in line 4) by utilizing a device that specifically selects DA3 as next speaker (Sacks et al., 1974); "the people" refers to the DA, and the utterance is a candidate statement of his position, with an appended request for a positive response.[22] However, another silence appears (line 5), after which the judge produces a characterization of the case minimizing its importance (line 6). That utterance is overlapped by the DA's delayed response ("sure," line 7), which is repeated by DA3 in line 8. This achieves agreement with the judge and acceptance of the PD's proposal.

Thus, it appears that one important means for elaborating the bargaining sequence is through the use of characteristic forms of talk by which some third party can display and accomplish his "judiciousness"—assessing the fairness of bargaining positions, urging resolution, and so on.[23]

---

[22]Syntactically, the sentence is modally marked to obtain agreement, with the verb form "will" ("people'll do that") and the tag question "right" (cf. Lyons, 1968: 308).

[23]An adjacency pair first part not only occasions a next move, but can also be a "basic component" in selecting next speaker in talk (Sacks et al., 1974: 717). When a nonselected party speaks after the first part of an adjacency pair, he regularly preserves as *next* speaker the one who was selected in the first pair part (cf. Sacks, 1967: lecture 6). This pattern seems operative in example (36) and (37), in that the judge's utterances retain the relevance of recipient replying to bargaining sequence openers.

Summary

A bargaining sequence consists of two basic parts—an opener and its reply. Differing from usual characteristics of adjacency pairs, the two parts are not necessarily adjacently positioned nor produced by different parties. The reply can be delayed by various direct and indirect responses.[24] Direct ones, such as insertion-sequence initiators and counterproposals, immediately make visible the source of trouble that prevents production of a reply, while indirect ones, such as silences and token utterances, occasion moves by speaker that infer a trouble source, or utterances in which a third party to the negotiations can perform mediation. Stated differently, the bargaining sequence may consist of two relatively ordered, discriminatively related utterances. But after a bargaining opener, the provision of a reply, which party ends up producing each part, and whether the sequence is completed in simple or elaborated fashion, all remain contingent upon how a variety of other methodic negotiating practices are utilized. Direct and indirect responses, and the talk they initiate and implicate, however, should not be construed as *alternatives* to a reply. Rather, they are a means of *delaying* the occasioned reply while on the way to its performance (Jefferson and Schenkein, 1977: 90).

BARGAINING SEQUENCES IN RELATION TO SUBSEQUENT NEGOTIATIONS

In the strict adjacency-pair format of the bargaining sequence, we have seen that one party produces an opener and the other (recipient) a reply, although that may be modified by systematic elaboration of the sequence. A further complication is that when an episode of negotiation is completed without a specific disposition, an opener can be reported or quoted in subsequent encounters.

(38) [Drunk driving]

DA2:   I offered ya a reckless with a fine

---

[24]In an educational setting, Mehan (1979: 54–77) has described how instructional sequences, consisting of teacher elicitations and student replies, can be "extended" by various prompts, repeats, specifications, and other devices.

(39) [Assault with a deadly weapon]

PD4: When I started out talking with Bill ((DA1)), I told him that I
thought it was a four fifteen. I don't really care so much
whether it's a four fifteen or a two forty two, and uh I think I
suggested what fifteen days suspended

Here, the party who makes a prior offer is the one now reporting it, but
quoting can be done by the person who was recipient of the original
opener.

(40) [Drunk driving]

PD3: Well the last offer was a deuce with a reckless disposition

(41) [Petty theft]

PD2: The original offer in this case was uh if he'd make restitution, ya'd
dismiss it

In frame analytic terms, phrases such as "the last offer was . . ." and
"I offered . . ." are keying mechanisms that transmit the accompanying
proposals or position-reports from past negotiations to present ones.

Quoted openers still operate as do the originals on which they are
fashioned. The recipient, after reporting an opener, can align with the
position exhibited in it:

(42) [Drunk driving]

J2: All right what are ya going to do in Rodriguez
PD2: Well the DA has suggested a pre-plea report and we're gonna go along
with their suggestion as soon as we can get him inta court. The
only reason I was going by that way is this guy has got a drinking
problem and it looks like people who just plead straight up don't
really get involved in rehabilitation

The PD's concern here was to obtain some help for his client, which he
thought could be done by involving the probation department—the
agency responsible for "pre-plea reports." He was willing to go along
with the DA's suggestion if he could be assured that the help for his
client would also be forthcoming. More often than displays of alignment,
openers reported to a judge are accompanied by a discussion of mitigating circumstances:

(43) [Drunk driving]

PD2:   Seventy five days is what they offered and the guy's got
       two priors and he lives in South Beach, he's got a
       good job, well least he's working, he supports his family,
       wife and kids, and it's his third drunk driving offense.
       And uh, if he does seventy-five days straight time he's
       going to lose his job, his wife's going to be on- kids,
       you know, family's going to be on welfare

Or quoted offers may be followed by displays of non-alignment, such as reported counterproposals:

(44) [Battery]

PD3:   The district attorney was asking for a two forty three conviction
       for a guilty plea with thirty days. Um the guy was crocked, and
       I came back and I said what about a four fifteen with fifteen days
                                    (0.6)
  J1: Oh gee that sounds very fair gosh
                                    (0.4)
DA1:   Uh I can't do this judge, I've talked to the officers about it.
       The guy was on the table at that time and he just reared off and
       just whacked Solomon

Here, the judge handles the reported counterproposal by assessing it in positive terms. The DA, however, supplies a reason for not going along with it, and this results in further talk regarding "what happened" and what kinds of persons were involved.[25]

Thus, discussions subsequent to initial negotiations provide initial evidence regarding participants' orientation to the bargaining sequence as the fundamental component of plea negotiations. By being reported or quoted, prior sequences form the starting point for later haggling and may occasion further statements, assessments, and arguments for and against the positions displayed within those sequences.

---

[25]See examples (29)–(31) in Chapter 3, where the conduct and character of the police are probed.

CHAPTER 5

Routine and Adversarial Justice

"Plea bargaining" discourse can be approached sociologically by exploring how an interactionally achieved structure is at the root of various phenomena covered by the term. The bargaining sequence is a fundamental unit of social organization[1] involved in arranging charges, sentences, dismissals, continuances, and trials for misdemeanor cases. Systematic procedures for leading into, elaborating, and exiting from the sequence relate it to other components of negotiation, such as discussion, argument, justification, counterproposing, third-party participation, and so on.

We have noted in a preliminary way that experts on plea bargaining make a distinction between "routine" determinations of case disposition and negotiations in which some "adversariness" is evident. It is now time to investigate this distinction more deeply. Careful scrutiny of plea-bargaining talk reveals that the bargaining sequence is an organizational foundation for both routine and adversary discourse. During perfunctory negotiations, resolution of "what to do" may be reached with minimal talk about the offense, the character of the defendant, or other matters. Proposals and related devices are nonetheless used to achieve a decision. When negotiations include more extensive segments of talk and adversary stances regarding the character of defendants and the nature of their offenses, these stances also articulate with bargaining sequences. This latter fact is particularly important in controverting the

---

[1]Schegloff (1980: 151) addresses how the study of conversational turns and sequences is fundamentally an inquiry into social organization. Sociologists, traditionally concerned with abstractions such as unit acts, roles, groups, and aggretates, have neglected "actual particular, social actions, and organized sequences of them."

received motion that negotiators must agree on facts and character before reaching a decision.

ROUTINE PROCESSING

A common perspective on plea bargaining, represented by Mather (1979: 57–58), is that when prosecution and defense "converge" in their assessments of how strong (in terms of evidence) and serious (in terms of charge) a case is, they do not "really negotiate." In particular, with cases that are strong but not very serious, settling "what should be done" is considered to be a routine matter that does not necessitate overt haggling.

The trouble with this characterization is that it makes the negotiation process appear to be more automatic and less contingent than it actually is. Certainly it is possible for some cases to be handled perfunctorily; examples (8), (13), and (30) in Chapter 4 each represent nearly the entire discussion of a particular case.[2] Yet the lesson from foregoing analysis is that a bargaining opener can be initiated in different ways and, once produced, can be handled through diverse responses and replies, so that a routine outcome or final decision still reflects strategic and systematic negotiational efforts.

In the Romney case, for example, the PD, DA, and judge talked only briefly. However, a bargaining sequence preceded by a remedial statement about the absence of discussion and elaborated by indirect responses plus the judge's assessments was at the core of the decision process:

(1) [Speed contest]

1.	J1:	Next is Jerry Romney, which is a two three one oh nine bee
2.	PD2:	Ya we haven't discussed that yet but if you'll take a speeding
3.		and a thirty five dollars
4.		(0.6)
5.	J1:	Oh I'm sure the people'll do that, right
6.		(0.4)
7.	J1:	Looks like ₁it's just₁ breaking traction
8.	DA3:	⌈Sure ⌉
9.	DA3:	Sure
10.	PD2:	Okay, we'll do that

---

[2]See the discussion of implicit bargaining in Chapter 8.

11.   J1:   Okay so that's gonna be-
12.   PD2: Yeah
13.   J1:   Two two three five oh and thirty five
14.   PD2: Yes
15.   J1:   Okay
16.   PD2: Including penalty assessment?
17.   J1:   Yeah
18.   PD2: Okay
19.   J1:   And there's no victim on it
20.   PD2: No
21.   J1:   And the last case is Lloyd Fridley

After the DA (in line 9) accepted the PD's proposal, PD2 acknowledged the acceptance and ratified the decision (line 10). Then, movement toward discussing the "last case" (line 21) was rapidly accomplished by the judge checking out the correct penal code number (lines 11, 13), the PD inquiring whether the fine included a penalty fee (line 16), and the judge querying about victim compensation (line 19).

Consider also the following example of routine processing, a case in which the defendant was charged with a misdemeanor speeding violation:

(2) [Speed contest]

1.   PD2: Okay. Ya wanna make an offer in that case
2.   (2.6)
3.   DA3: I have so little use for these uh, dumb uh (9.0) ((DA3 reads file))
4.   I can't intelligently make an offer in that case cause I have no
5.   idea whether it's a bankrupt uh, you know, sometimes they hear
6.   the scratch uh y'know, little squealer
7.   PD2: Forty five in a twenty five, I mean you know what are we
8.   doin' here
9.   DA3: I'll be happy uh- would you give me forty five in a twenty
10.   five on that?
11. PD2: Twenty five dollar fine
12. DA3: How 'bout a fifty dollar fine
13. PD2: How 'bout a twenty five dollar heh fine heh real misdemeanors
14.   go for fifty dollars
15. DA3: How 'bout thirty five including p.a.
16. PD2: Eh yeah, I think that's not a bad deal

PD2, in line 1, solicits a bargaining opener from DA3, who initially says nothing while reading the file, and then formulates the case as "dumb" (line 3) and as possibly "bankrupt" (line 5). These characterizations suggest that he considered the case, in Mather's (1979) words, as light (in terms of seriousness) and weak (in terms of evidence). DA3's turn implicates further discussion of the offense, but PD2 himself produces an opener (line 7) with an appended phrase from a class of items that urge, in a sense, "let's get on with it" (lines 7–8). Subsequently, the bargaining sequence opened by PD2 is skillfully elaborated to produce a mutually benefical decision.

In detail: PD2's proposal (line 7) is for an excessive speed *infraction*, a lesser violation than the original misdemeanor charge. In line 9, DA3 starts an utterance, "I'll be happy uh," that may have been an acceptance. But it is cut off, and, in lines 9–10, DA3 produces a "questioning repeat" (Pomerantz, 1975: 72–73) that returns the "forty five in a twenty five" proposal to PD2 for a reply.

A "questioning repeat" is a means by which a recipient can, among other things, check a hearing or call attention to a speaker's mistake. The device here appears to be testing the "seriousness" of PD2's position. Rather than replying to the return-proposal, however, PD2 responds with a suggestion for a "twenty five dollar fine" (line 11), thereby focusing off of the *charge* ("forty five in a twenty five") and dealing with the *sentence*. Note the apparent strategy. DA3 has already described the case as being perhaps "bankrupt," has implied that he would be happy with the infraction charge, and has characterized it as something PD2 would "give" him. Reading these cues as an indication that the prosecutor is unsure of the case but still wanting a conviction, PD2 can make agreement to the charge conditional on obtaining a favorable sentence.

However, the sentence proposal ("twenty five dollar fine," line 11) itself is followed by three instances of counterproposing (in lines 12, 13, and 15). First, DA3 suggests "a fifty dollar fine" (line 12). Second, PD2 reasserts his "twenty five dollar" offer (line 13). By holding to this position, and characterizing the "fifty dollars" as appropriate to "real misdemeanors" (lines 13–14), PD2 may be appealing to DA3's earlier acknowledged uncertainty regarding the worth of the case as a way of further inducing some concession from him. Third, then, DA3 proposes a compromise of "thirty five including p.a." (line 15; the initials mean "penalty assessment," a fee attached to some fines), which PD2 accepts (line 16).

If PD2's acceptance of DA3's $35 proposal can be considered agreement to the charge suggestion (lines 7–8) as well as the sentence, then three issues are dramatically brought to a close here, in such a way that the "not a bad deal" (line 16) character of the negotiation is made assessable. It is resolved whether PD2 was "serious" about his original offer, whether DA3 will exchange sentence concessions for a guilty plea, and whether the fine would represent a median between the positions that PD2 and DA3 first take up on the sentencing issue.

This episode of negotiation, like the last, is notable for its brevity. Largely unappreciated among those who study the process is how such brevity can be, and is, an organized, collaborative achievement. Two things are prominent. First, the PD issued a pre-opener that, as has been argued, may suggest that "discussion" is not necessary and bargaining over charge and sentence is immediately relevant. When the DA declined to open a bargaining sequence by reading the file and characterizing the case in a way that implicated "discussion," the PD pressed the issue by making a proposal himself. This ultimately engaged the DA's participation in an elaborated bargaining sequence. Second, a distinction has been made between "proposals" and "position reports"; the former straightforwardly occasion an acceptance or rejection, while the latter permit an exhibit of perspective regarding a stated position. Proposals thereby suppress "personal state" talk regarding a case. In this example, the series of proposals and counterproposals clearly detopicalized the question of what kind of case it was, with the result that little talk was spent on the offense, the defendant's biography, or other possibly connected items. Nonetheless, an artfully elaborated bargaining sequence was used to decide an action for the case, and "negotiation" was therefore a salient phenomenon. In conclusion, the "routineness" of a case does not mean there is an absence of negotiation, but only that it is conducted so as to focus on *what* should be done and focus off *why* it should be done and *how* prosecution and defense view the case.

ADVERSARIAL DISCOURSE

Negotiational discourse can involve disagreement and extended argument over how and why an offense is perceived in different ways. But, opposing stances taken by prosecution and defense still articulate with bargaining sequences. And these sequences, not adversariness and resolution of disagreement, are what remain basic to the determination of a course of action in the case.

This point needs to be stressed, because a number of ethnographic studies of plea bargaining argue that when negotiation is "explicit," two stages of talk precede the actual determination of a disposition. These are (1) settling the facts of the case and (2) resolving what the moral character of the defendant is. Based on these determinations, lawyers are said to (3) make a decision as to what charge, sentence, or other course of action is appropriate (e.g., see Buckle and Buckle, 1977: 120; Eisenstein and Jacob, 1977: 32; Miller et al., 1978: 118–120; Rosett and Cressey, 1976: 105–109; Utz, 1978: 135). It has already been evident that while these stages may be involved in the discussion of some cases, they are not present in all decisions.[3] Plea negotiations in the last two examples and others (see 1, 8, 13, and 30 in Chapter 4) consist of bargainings sequences that directly address charging and sentencing; and they are without conversational consideration of "facts" and "character." An additional finding is that even when these items *are* discussed, prosecutors and defenders can remain at odds over them and still reach agreement on disposition.

It is true that disagreement between lawyers may result in trial. A typical case involves a woman charged with drunk driving. The district attorney offered to suspend $200 from the standard $315 fine if the defendant would plead guilty. The PD turned down the offer, reminding the DA that, although the defendant's blood alcohol level was over the statutory limit for intoxication, "there was nothing wrong with her driving." Then he raised the question of her drinking habits:

(3) [Drunk driving]

PD3:   She's basically not a drinker, um might have a couple of beers once
        in a while, but she's not really a- she doesn't really drink
DA6:   She did on the day in question your honor. She went to a liquor
        store and bought two cans of these COCKtails that are pre-made ⌊and ⌋
PD3:   ⌈Yeah⌉
PD3:   they're not much alco⌊hol ⌋
DA6:   ⌈Okay⌉
DA6:   But you know, somebody who's not a drinker doesn't just go to a
        liquor store and buy uh pre-made uh cocktails. I think that she
        is a drinker
 J1:   Maybe you ought to run that by her, just for your own protection

Not only do the PD and DA exhibit opposing views regarding whether the defendant is or is not a "drinker," but the discrepancy is left un-

---

[3]Part of the argument here is that plea bargaining discourse concerning individual cases displays a heterogeneity not susceptible to glosses of the sort attempted by the cited sources. On this point, see Lynch (1979: 315).

resolved as the judge urges the PD to "run" the DA's offer by the defendant. After the PD left the room and checked with her, he came back in and said, "I guess we're gonna try this one." (The case did go to trial, and the defendant was acquitted.)

That disagreements may result in trial does not mean that they necessarily do. We return to the case of Frank Bryan, the defendant charged with a "148" offense (resisting public officers) and a "647f" (disorderly conduct). Three points can summarize our earlier discussion of the case (the analysis is given in the last part of Chapter 2). First, the PD had described the defendant as a "sweet man with a nice smile," at least with respect to his *public* demeanor in court. Second, PD2 characterized the offense as a "family" affair: the defendant's drunkenness, fighting, cursing, and "taking a menacing stance" toward an officer all occurred at his home, his *private* domicile. Third, immanent within PD2's talk were cultural conceptions of a natural separation between public and private life, which he drew upon to depict the defendant as one who behaves reasonably in public, according to his *obligations*. If he acts badly at home, especially when intruded upon, this is according to his rights in the *private* sphere.

Following this initial talk was further discussion of the offense, in which PD2 admitted that Bryan did "take a menacing stance" (line 013, Appendix 2) and DA3 suggested that the defendant "did resist being handcuffed and resisted walking from the residence" (022). PD2 and DA3 agreed that the defendant had a laceration on his head which, according to the police report, resulted from "collapsing on the floor and striking his head" (023–024). Then:

(4a) [029]

1. DA3: One senses that um uh other than that it was a lotta talk
2.   of uh assuming fighting stances and then running away
3. PD2: Yeah it's a verbal uh one forty eight and a real six forty
4.   seven ef. Now I would like to settle this case
5. DA3: Well I'd like to settle it

At this point, DA3 and PD2 appear to converge in their assessments of the case. Moreover, each party indicates a willingness to "settle" the case. However, we will see that disagreement ensues over the appropriate charge.

In Chapter 3 it was mentioned that the 148 charge had a maximum penalty of one year in jail and a $1000 fine, while the 647 offense carried a maximum six months and a $500 fine. Thus, the 148 offense would be considered the more serious of the two. The following segment is repeated from Chapter 3, so that we may pay more attention to certain details.

(4b) [035]

1. DA3: Uh- I think it's a case that oughta be uh settled, it's uh-
2. PD2: Okay
3. DA3: strikes me as a dandy one forty eight uh b- probably a better
4.   one forty eight than a six forty seven ef if you want to
5.   be very strict about it
6. PD2: Well I see it as a six forty seven ef, uh he didn't lay hands
7.   on any officers, if he hadn't been so drunk I assume nothing-
8.   none o' this would of happened. Well I don't think it's
9.   worth any jail time no matter what it is
10. DA3: I was being academic when I said that uh
11. PD2: Oh
12. DA3: I think technically it's a better one forty eight than it is a
13.   six forty seven, he put the officers through their uh mettle.
14.   In- in uh collaring 'im they hadta pursue 'im through the house
15.   and all that sorta stuff
16. PD2: And they did a very fine job of it, I have to- I wanted
17.   to add the officer's uh conduct was highly commendable, and
18.   if my client accidentally tripped and conk(h)ed his head, heh I
19.   am su(h)re tha(h)t-
20. DA3: On the other ha⌊nd ⌋
21. PD2:   ⌊jus⌋tice was done
22. DA3: I don't know that the substantial interests of justice require
23.   any more than a plea to six forty seven ef

In line 1, DA3 produces a pre-opener. Then, following PD2's go-ahead (line 2), he reports a position regarding the charge (it's a "dandy," "better" 148 "if you want to be very strict," lines 3–5) that offers a contrast with PD2's characterization of the case (4a). The contrast in positions is actively pursued in PD2's response (line 6) to DA3's opener, when he produces a counterreport that asserts he "sees it" as the 647f. This is followed by his characterization of the offense in a way that justifies the lesser charge (lines 6–8). Next, PD2 displays a position that the offense is not "worth any jail time" (lines 8–9).

This utterance bears some attention because it may be instrumental in obtaining a "backdown" from the DA regarding the charging issue. Although the PD suggests the case is not "worth any jail time," that utterance hearably invokes that it might, then, be worth a *fine*, since jail time and fines are co-members of the *class* of sentences appropriate in such cases. Thus, in a manner more subtle than, but related to, a device we saw employed in example (2), the utterance may signal the DA that if some concession is made on the charge, at least he will get a guilty plea and a fine from the defendant.

The "backdown" is accomplished by DA3 formulating his earlier position-report as "being academic" (line 10), invoking the "technical" correctness of the 148 charge, and supplying a "reason" for its correctness (lines 13–15). However, DA3's talk regarding the officers' pursuit of the defendant occasions a turn by PD2 in which he acknowledges the "commendable" conduct of the officers, and reminds the DA of the injury the defendant apparently suffered (lines 16–19). While the laughter tokens (lines 18–19) lighten PD3's treatment of the event, he may be bringing up the possibility of "police brutality." Whatever the exact issue, it appears to be a touchy one in that if the laughter tokens constitute an invitation to laugh (cf. Jefferson, 1979), DA3 does not accept it and his interruptive utterance (lines 20, 22–23) returns to the charge.[4] At lines 22–23, he aligns with the position that a 647f charge is appropriate in the case.

Thus, in this segment, agreement on the charge for defendant Bryan is achieved through an artful concession by the DA in which a specific attitude is preserved regarding what the "real" nature of the offense is. Where the PD sees it as disorderly conduct, the DA can "think technically" it is resisting arrest. "Substantial interests of justice" contrast with "technical correctness" in a manner that justifies assenting to the charge.[5]

While agreement is reached on the charge in this segment, then, different positions on certain facts of the case are displayed. In subsequent talk, DA3 and PD2 do not return to the particulars of the offense, and the disparate characterizations of the defendant's behavior remain conversationally unresolved. After some joking by the participants (059–062), the question of sentencing, first broached in lines 8–9 above (4b), is reintroduced.

[4]A more technical analysis would reveal that DA3's utterance in lines 20, 22–23, is fitted, in a variety of ways, with his turn at lines 12–15 and thus attempts to delete the "sequential implicativeness" (Schegloff and Sacks, 1974: 239) of PD2's utterance at lines 16–19.
[5]That is, "technical correctness" and "substantial interests of justice" correspond to professionally learned distinctions between the formal law and its intent, as argued in Chapter 3.

(4c) [063]

PD2:   Okay uh, twenty five dollar fine . . .

Before the DA can reply to PD2's proposal, the judge raises the issue of how much time the defendant has already spent in jail (076). PD2 leaves the room to find out, returns, and reports that the defendant has been in jail 10 to 12 hours (083). Then:

(4d) [084]

 1. DA3:   He has uh one prior conviction in this jurisdiction with
 2.   the um sheriff's office of, interestingly enough, uh striking
 3.   a public officer and uh disturbing the peace
 4. PD2:   Will you knock it off, you wanna make a federal case out
 5.   of this
 6. DA3:   No, I- I just think that it's not uh this uh happy go lucky
 7.   chap's uh first encounter with uh (the law)
 8. PD2:   Statistically if you got black skin you are highly likely
 9.   to contact the police, uh substantially more likely than
10.   if you're white, now c'mon, what do you want from him. He's
11.   got a prior
12. J1:   Well we know he spent ten hours and uh maybe (   ) some
13.   more. And what do you think would be reasonable, Jeffrey
14.   ((DA3 looks through files))
15. DA3:   Seventy five dollar fine
16. PD2:   Why don't we compromise and make it fifty
17. DA3:   Its done
18. PD2:   Arright

Here, DA3 brings up the defendant's "prior conviction" (line 1), which is acknowledged by PD2 ("He's got a prior," lines 10–11). Between those two utterances, there is a dispute over the meaning of the prior record. DA3 notes the similarity of the prior to the present charge (lines 2–3), while PD2 devaluates that topic ("Will you knock it off," etc., lines 4–5). Next, DA3 undercuts PD2's earlier description of the defendant ("happy go lucky chap") by juxtaposing it with the fact that the present charge is not the defendant's "first encounter" (line 7). But PD2 produces an utterance minimizing the importance of the prior offense by invoking the defendant's race and its effect on contacts with the police (lines 8–10).

Then, PD2 solicits a display of position in an utterance that is latched to his last one (i.e., there is no gap between ". . . if you're white" and "now c'mon . . ." line 10). That topic change may work to prevent a

"rejoinder" by DA3 on the issue of prior record.[6] J1 collaborates in
soliciting a proposal or report from "Jeffrey," the DA (lines 12–13). Given
PD2's earlier suggestion of a $25 fine, DA3 counterproposes "seventy
five dollars" (line 15), which itself is countered by PD2's offer of a "compromise" fine (line 16). After DA3 accepts that suggestion (line 17), PD2
acknowledges the acceptance (line 18). Thus, agreement is reached on
a sentence by way of proposals and counterproposals that observably
focus away from the topic of the defendant's prior record.

In summary, over the course of this discussion a number of issues
are raised, including the moral character of the defendant, the "facts of
the case," and the significance of "prior record." Each of these topics
is constituted by prosecution and defense formulations that remain un-
reconciled. For the public defender, Frank Bryan is a nice guy whose
only offense was being drunk, fighting with his family, and cursing in
his own home. He was intruded upon there by police officers who may
have roughed him up during the arrest. He has a prior record by virtue
of being black and statistically more likely to encounter the police. For
the district attorney, the defendant is one who gave the police much
difficulty in making an arrest and who has a prior conviction for the
same kind of conduct. These different interpretations buttress or provide
the "reasonableness" of the original positions that DA3 and PD2 take
up, and their disparateness is preserved as the negotiators, through
bargaining sequences, reach agreement on both charge and sentence.
Thus, in plea bargaining, negotiators do not necessarily "decide" character and "settle" facts. Rather, considerable disagreement and "adversariness" may be maintained in the pursuit of those topics, even while
a decision is made on an action for the case, through the deployment
of bargaining sequences.

One consequence of the idea that defense and prosecution come to
agree on the character of the defendant and the facts of the case before
deciding disposition has been the depiction of these actors as overin-
volved in their situated bureaucratic identities. As Buckle and Buckle
(1977: 80) put it, "All the attorneys are, generally, motivated by their
need to conform to the culture of the court." In Eisenstein and Jacob's

---

[6]It is not that production of a rejoinder is impossible, but that PD2's utterance sequentially
implicates a report or suggestion regarding what the DA "wants" as a sentence. A
rejoinder on the "prior record" topic would take special work by PD3 to tie his utterance
to that topic, whereas producing the implicated utterance requires no special means of
accomplishing its "why that now" status. See Sacks (1972: lecture 4) and Sacks et al.
(1974).

(1977: 25) treatment, the members of the courtroom "workgroup," including judge and attorneys,

> share values and goals. These shared perspectives undermine the apparent conflicts generated by the formal roles of workgroup members—the prosecutors' push toward convictions, the defense attorneys' quest for acquittals, and judges' inclination toward neutrality.

It may be that the court culture, especially the goal of processing cases, is a major concern among workgroup members. Consistent with the discussion of framing practices, however, it is clear that bargaining sequences can articulate with descriptions of defendants, disagreements, challenges, backdowns, topic changes, and other devices whereby lawyers exhibit commitments to their clients, the "state," their offices, their professions, and so on. Perhaps as a solution to what Lipsky (1980: 73) describes as the incompatibility of advocacy and the bureaucratic perspective, it seems that negotiations can be constructed so that participants have it both ways. That is, they employ bargaining sequences to make charging, sentencing, and other decisions and thereby meet common workgroup goals, such as clearing the docket. By systematically relating such sequences to other negotiational strategies, lawyers and judges display an orientation to adversarial justice.

Another consequence of the plea-bargaining-as-agreement perspective is to neglect the importance of potential trials. Again recall the analysis of framing. It may be that the adversariness evident in disagreements over facts and character are rehearsals of scenes that participants would be willing to portray before a jury. For example, PD2's possibly sarcastic reference to the "commendable" conduct of the police and to Bryan's "accidentally" tripping and conking his head might inform the DA that the behavior of the police would be an issue at trial. Counterposed to the officer's conduct would be that of Bryan assuming a "fighting stance" (4a) and being pursued "through the house" (4b). In short, adversariness in plea bargaining refers not just to the rhetorical skills of participants but to the ways that they import trial structures into negotiational discourse (Lynch, 1982: 310–311; Mather, 1974; Utz, 1978: 30–32).

THE BASIC ORGANIZATION OF PLEA BARGAINING

Bargaining sequences in misdemeanor cases consist of two turns: one in which a given party makes a position visible by means of a proposal or position-report and a second in which the other party replies by exhibiting alignment or nonalignment with the presented position. The bargaining sequence can thus be considered as a basic unit of social organization which, in its simplest form and by way of its systematic elaboration, achieves the visible "bargaining" features of lawyers' talk at the pretrial conference.

That this sequence is basic to plea bargaining can be established in two ways. First, in examining the 52 cases in the corpus, the bargaining sequence is produced or reported on in discussion of every case,[7] with one exception, where its absence is subject to complaint and repair. In this case, the defendant was charged with a second drunk-driving ("deuce") offense, which made her a candidate for a rehabilitation program that is referred to by the fictitious acronym "drinalp"[8] in the following segment:

(5) [Drunk driving]

```
 1.   PD2:   . . . she's a hard headed young lady who has discovered
 2.            religion, okay, and she's eligible for drinalp. This is
 3.            her second deuce, eligible for drinalp and would go into
 4.            drinalp, but she says SHE has a program that she thinks is
 5.            better than drinalp. And she came to me and she said look
 6.            I want a chance to sell my program to George ((DA2)) in
 7.            the DA's office. And George and I agreed some time ago,
 8.            arright George will make some time for her. Uh I've been
 9.            in trial and I haven't had an opportunity to set up an
10.            appointment between her and George
11.                              (1.0)
12.   DA2:   I'm not gonna wait, it's been several weeks
13.   J1:    Yeah and this goes back to the start of July
14.   PD2:   Arright, well let me ask you th⌈is George      ⌉
15.   DA2:                                   ⌊We're gonna⌋ try the case
16.   PD2:   Let- w'l- wait a minute, uh you're tr- you're trying a case
17.            where the girl says she- she- she says I don't turn down
18.            drinalp I just think I have something better
19.   DA2:   She turned down back in October and here it is, y'know this
20.            is thr⌈ee months⌉                     ⌐
21.   PD2:         ⌊No no   ⌋ well you know you used the word turned down,
22.            she never turned it down. ⌈I always say-   ⌉
23.   DA2:                               ⌊She didn't want⌋ to participate
```

---

[7]A series of bargaining sequences is sometimes employed in the discussion of any one case. Example (4) shows this, and the matter is explored further in Chapter 8.

[8]"Drinalp" derives from the fictitious name, "DRiving under the INfluence of ALcohol Program." A real acronym, which needs to be disguised for purposes of anonymity, was used in the negotiations.

```
24.   DA2:  ₁So ₁
25.   PD2:  ᶦGeoˡrge
26.                                    (0.4)
27.   PD2:  Why don't you let me finish because you see if you and I are
28.         just gonna kind of obstruct each other's talking- it's the
29.         easiest thing in the world for you to do is set a calendar
30.         for trial. That's simple!
31.   DA2:  It's not gonna get-
32.   PD2:  Ya come in here to settle the case? er to- just to- er to
33.         throw 'em in my teeth
34.   J1:   Well but- but what do you want to do on it
35.   PD2:  Well. I- y'know are you saying you won't allow her inta
36.         drinalp
37.   J1:   No it's- it's-
38.   PD2:  Because if so we'll try it
39.   DA2:  Ya we'll try it
40.   PD2:  Okay here we are .hhh hh so you know, this is the kind of-
41.         this isn't plea bargai(h)ni(h)g
42.                                    (1.2)
43.   PD2:  I mean you know yer- yer ₁teaching her a lesson₁ or teaching
44.   J1:                             ᶦWell it's been a long-ᶦ
45.   PD2:  me a lesson
46.   J1:   We've had everybo₁dy work₁ing long and hard all ₁day ₁
47.   PD2:                   ᶦUh:::::  ᶦ                    ᶦyou cˡan't-
48.   DA2:  ₁Well₁
49.   J1:   ᶦWellᶦ so then what's a fair settlement of this
```

Of particular interest here is PD2's assessment at line 41: "this isn't plea bargaining." The feasibility of that complaint can be traced to a number of features in foregoing turns. Among them are the overlapping utterances at lines 14–15, 20–21, 22–23, and 24–25, which PD2 refers to as obstructing "each other's talking" (line 28), and the disagreement over whether the defendant had or had not turned down the rehabilitation program (lines 16–22). The major feature, however, appears to be the issue of going to trial. Just prior to his line 41 assessment, PD2 queried the DA as to whether his client would be allowed into "drinalp," invoking trial as the alternative (lines 35–36, 38). DA2 agreed with the alternative, a position consistent with his earlier announced intention not to "wait" (line 12) and to "try the case" (line 15).

Announcing an intention is a way of indicating an action for a case that clearly differs from what we have discussed before as bargaining-sequence openers. Position-reports and proposals implicate acceptance or rejection as a reply. If an acceptance is produced, negotiations are brought to a close. If rejection occurs, a new round of bargaining ensues (see Chapter 8). Even when a trial is the outcome, decisions are thereby achieved collaboratively. Here, in contrast, DA2's move displays a readiness to act in a forceful, unilateral way. At least that is a hearing evident in two characterizations of the DA's announcement that are provided by the PD. In lines 28–30, PD2 describes setting a case for trial as "easy" and "simple" and further associates that with "throwing" cases in his "teeth" (line 33) as a contrast to "settling" them (line 32). Later, PD2 formulates DA2's activity as "teaching" the defendant or himself "a lesson" (lines 43–45). Each of these depicts the DA as solely determining a trial action and the PD as an object in the process, not a co-participant.

Thus, it seems that the basic violation in this segment is exhibited as one of mutuality. Insofar as such mutuality is ordinarily constructed in and through the bargaining sequence, it is that sequence that is missing. Morever, the absence of the sequence is specifically made observable in the judge's two attempts at repair, each occurring after one of PD2's characterizations and consisting of a pre-opener or solicit that would introduce the sequence (lines 34, 49).[9] In conclusion, the ethnographers of plea bargaining have been correct about the importance of collaboration in negotiations. What they have missed is how that can be achieved not by agreeing on facts and character but by utilizing a unit whose interactively accomplished organization entails mutually produced dismissal, charge, sentence, continuance, or trial decisions. It is *not* plea bargaining when that organization and mutuality are absent; it *is* plea bargaining when they are present.

Connected with this point is another way of establishing how basic an organized unit may be, which is to show that it is involved in the constitution of other features of talk which are not necessarily implicated in the construction of that unit (Sacks, 1972: lecture 2). Consistently we have seen that the bargaining sequence accommodates a wide variety of bargaining practices. Some, but not all, negotiations involve discussion of charges. Some, but not all, involve consideration of sentence. Others concern dismissals, continuances, or trials. In some negotiations, one party simply aligns with an initially exhibited position of the other's, while in others "compromise" is produced as a visible feature of the discourse. In some discussions, "character" and "facts" are argued, making for "adversary" conflict. Others involve only proposals over which action should be taken in the case, and appear more "routine." Thus, while no one of these features is invariably related to the consti-

[9]The second repair attempt is preceded by a "cooling out" form (lines 44, 46).

tution of a plea bargain, it is the case that the bargaining sequence is involved in "charge bargaining," "sentence bargaining," the achieving of a dismissal, continuance, or trial, reaching a straightforward agreement, "compromising," "arguing character," "discussing facts," and so forth, when they are done.

CHAPTER 6

Descriptions and Assessments of Defendants

For both prosecution and defense, a prominent factor in the discussion of what should be done with Frank Bryan's case was their assessment of what kind of person he was. Observers of discretion in the criminal-justice process generally argue that talk about "who a defendant is" is at least as important in the determination of what should be done as are the so-called "facts" of the case.[1] This view has to be modified somewhat in light of the argument of the last chapter that many cases are settled routinely, without extensive deliberation of "character" or "facts." Yet, in cases where lawyers take strong adversary stances, they do consider background factors not legally relevant to the question of whether the defendant is guilty as charged (cf. Newman, 1966: 114–130), including the person's age, mentality, respectability, and so on.

Of the many items concerning a defendant's background that could be deliberated, however, a relative few are utilized. As Atkinson and Drew (1979: 248) put it, "a description is in principle incomplete, and hence necessarily a selection from what could have been said."[2] This is true not only of descriptions in general, but also of those pertaining to persons. In plea bargaining, negotiators select and formulate defendant attributes that support the bargaining positions they take up, a feature made apparent by the relation of descriptions of defendants to the conversational context in which they occur. Examining this specific issue means that a more general problem in "communicative competence"

[1]See other references in Chapter 2, footnote 16.
[2]See the discussion regarding this issue in Sharrock and Turner (1980), who examine a description, telephoned to police, of a *car*.

(Hymes, 1974: 527) can be addressed: In the conduct and interpretation of any spoken discourse, how are third parties described?

PERSON-REFERENCE AND PERSON-DESCRIPTION

We have a good understanding of how people *refer* to third persons in conversation. Two principles are involved.

First, parties regularly employ "membership categorization devices" to do the work of reference. Simply put, a device of this kind consists of a collection of membership categories that may be properly applied to the members of a given population (Sacks, 1972: 32). For example, male-female, man-woman, he-she, and guy-gal are all paired collections of categories deriving from the device "sex" or "gender." Such categories are often used as referential forms in conversation:

(1)

PD2:   He's in Arkansas

(2)

PD2:   She is advanced middle aged

Secondly, as Sacks and Schegloff (1979) have noted, when reference to persons is done, two preferences are operative. One is that reference should be done with a single form, and the other is that the form should be recognizable by a recipient. In the above examples, "he" and "she" are single forms, occurring in a context (not reproduced here) that makes such pronouns adequate communicators of who the referent persons are.

But talk about third parties is not just a matter of reference. Examples (1) and (2) also show that a reference form may be accompanied by a descriptive item or biographical formulation ("in Arkansas"; "advanced middle aged") regarding the referent persons. The term "person description" identifies utterances in which some person-reference form is linked with one or more formulations. Thus:[3]

---

[3]Person-descriptions are one instance of a general way in which not only *other* persons, but the *self*, ("I'm forty-five") and *nonperson* referents ("camisoles are essentially slips") are described.

person-description = reference form + descriptive item(s)

Conversational structure, not *grammar,* is the important determinant of whether an utterance is a person-description. Linguists (e.g., Lyons, 1968: 419–420) and sociolinguists (Hymes, 1974: 49, 53) have both pointed out that the construction of utterances in conversation is heavily dependent on contextual matters. By the same token, placement of an utterance within an ongoing sequence of talk is critical to its recognition as a person-description and not another sort of conversational unit. For example, the following statement regarding a defendant could be taken several ways:

(3)

PD1:　She goes into Davidson's

If PD1 were employing "goes into Davidson's" as an activity-description related to some category of person, embedded in a series of utterances working to establish the "type" of person the defendant is, then the utterance would be considered a person-description. However, as we shall see in example (7), this utterance initiates a story about the defendant's alleged shoplifting and thus primarily helps characterize the *offense* rather than the defendant.

PERSON-DESCRIPTIONS AS JUSTIFICATIONS

Because person-descriptions are recognized, in part, by their relation to the context wherein they are spoken, we should expect that they also are sensitive to, and partially constitutive of, the conversational topic or activity, as are location formulations, for example (cf. Schegloff, 1972: 104). This is because conversational terms are regularly fitted to situational particulars, such as the persons to whom an utterance is spoken, where it is spoken, and so forth, a feature referred to as recipient design.[4]

We have seen that a basic activity in plea bargaining is the exhibiting

---

[4]The "recipient design" feature of conversation was discussed in Chapter 3, and is described in Sacks et al. (1974). See also Ervin-Tripp (1972), who investigates the way in which *address* terms are sensitive to the particularities of situations in which they are used.

of positions regarding how a case should be handled. Person-descriptions justify or rationalize the positions taken by negotiators as they solicit, propose, accept, agree or disagree, and so forth. In some cases, the work of defendant descriptions is transparent in immediate sequential environments. In other cases, descriptions are not visibly related to immediate sequences. They nevertheless fit the basic pattern of providing support for some defense or prosecution position, as it is developed over long stretches of talk. This pattern is nontrivial in the sense that participants require mutual adherence to it; that is, not just anything can be said about a defendant.

Immediate Sequential Environments

Now one way that negotiating parties attempt to establish the facts of a case is by telling various versions of what happened. Lawyers typically have a police report or a police officer's testimony and the defendant's version of the event, and they may have a victim's as well. Where there are competing versions, truthfulness may be of critical concern when a person's story is repeated. For example, in one case a young man was charged with petty theft for allegedly taking some beer from a liquor store. The defendant's argument was that it was his *companion* who had taken the beer, and that he (the defendant) had actually protested the theft. So when the lawyer defending the young man tells the story to the judge, he prefaces his representation as follows:

(4) [Battery]

1. PD2: . . . my client, who- in fact who's story I-
2.   I tend to believe because of the way he tells it, eh
3.   an' for y'know subjective things like that 'n for no
4.   other reason, uh says that . . . ((story))

Between the connecting parts of the story entry ("my client," line 1, and "says that . . . .," line 4), the PD reports his own belief of the story on the basis of "subjective things."

When a defendant's story is quoted, then, a speaker may address its truth value by making visible his own attitude. In the following example, which was briefly discussed in Chapter 3, the PD does this by employing person-descriptions. The PD had been animating a Chicano defendant's version of a hit-and-run event, relayed to the PD by way of an interpreter, Bill Campbell. The defendant claimed that he had left the scene to obtain a friend who could speak English for him and that he was planning to return when he was apprehended.

(5) [Hit and run driving]

```
1.  PD1:  But uh, you know I- I was talking to 'im through Bill
2.        Campbell and uh, this is what he tells me
3.                          (0.6)
4.  PD1:  What I would like to see- you know this guy is really,
5.        I think he's jus' strict- strictly honest, I think he's
6.        telling me the truth. What I'd like to see happen
7.        is just have us continue the thing for like thirty
8.        days, make him- let him make restitution on 'is own and
9.        if he does it, then dismiss the case
```

The focal utterances are at lines 5–6; in line 4 there is a projected person-description, "this guy is really," but it is cut off and followed by two other complete ones, each with a perspectival preface:

Preface	+	reference form	+	descriptive item
A. I think	+	he's	+	jus' strictly honest
B. I think	+	he's	+	telling me the truth

Just how precisely placed these descriptions are can be appreciated by close attention to the details of segment (5). Lines 1–2 represent an ending point of the PD's retelling of the defendant's story. After the silence (line 3), PD1 produces a proposal preface (line 4, "What I would like to see"). However, the person descriptions are inserted after this preface. Following the descriptions, it is repeated with some added components (lines 6–7). The repeat of the preface may serve to delete its first occurrence so that the person-descriptions can be heard as tied to the foregoing story. Finally the proposal is made: "have us continue the thing for like thirty days," etc. (lines 7–9). Thus the person-descriptions follow the PD's relaying of the client's own story that defends him against a criminal charge, and precede the PD's proposal of eventually dismissing the charge (line 9). In short, the descriptions assess the defendant's story as truthful just after it is animated and just before the production of the proposal that the story would warrant if true.

Just as person-descriptions regarding defendants help justify proposals or position reports, they also rationalize replies to them. In discussing a shoplifting case, for example, a PD suggested that if the defendant pleaded guilty she should receive a fine rather than spend 24 hours in jail (the "standard disposition"), because the stolen item was just one jar of soap ("Mini-wash") and it was a first offense. Then the following took place:

(6) [Shoplifting]

1.		(7.6) ((DA3 reads file))
2.	DA3:	I have difficulty making this other than the standard
3.		disposition
4.		(0.8)
5.	PD4:	For a dollar and some odd cents worth of Mini-wash?
6.	DA3:	Yeah I mean I- I can BUY the logic within the limits
7.		of the- you know the items of necessity by somebody very
8.		poor, but a-
9.	PD4:	Yeah
10.	DA3:	cosmetic item by a young um lady who's just uh in too
11.		much of a hurry to go pay for it. Uh I can't buy that

After reading the case file, DA3 here reports his "difficulty making this other than the standard disposition," lines 2–3. PD4 expresses disappreciation of the DA's report by minimizing the value of the stolen item ("dollar 'n some odd cents worth o' Mini-wash," line 5) and by producing upward intonation (as signified by the question mark; see Appendix 1), so that the utterance can be heard as a questioning of the position the DA displays in the report. Moreover, that utterance (which is in a class including questioning repeats and requests for clarification) and the silence preceding it (line 4) are both disagreement implicative (Pomerantz, 1975: 72–73). That is, while not directly expressing disagreement themselves, they indicate that it may follow.

Subsequent conversation does, in fact, exhibit disagreement, but the point is that a justification of the DA's position has been sequentially occasioned by these items. The extended turn from lines 6–11 follows a position report (lines 2–3) and a question from recipient that specifically invites further talk relative to the report. And, the same turn (lines 6–11) may be spoken with reference to projected disagreement. Thus, both retrospectively and prospectively, an utterance that makes visible the propriety of the proposed standard penalty is elicited.

We can now focus on the person-description that occurs in lines 10–11. The turn (lines 6–11) of which it is a part is tightly and artfully constructed. There is an acknowledgement ("Yeah," line 6) tying this turn to the PD's question. Then DA3 produces a prefacing item "I mean I can buy the logic within the limits of . . ." (lines 6–7) that specifically contrasts with the concluding utterance, "I can't buy that" (line 11). Between the preface and the conclusion are several comparative descriptions, connected by the contrast marker "but" (line 8). First, there are two nonperson descriptions regarding stolen articles:

Nonperson reference form	+	descriptive items
A. (i) items of necessity	+	(ii) by somebody very poor
B. (i) a cosmetic item	+	(ii) by a young lady who's just in too much of a hurry to go pay for it

Second, embedded within each of these formats are person-descriptions:

Person reference form	+	descriptive items
(A,ii) somebody	+	very poor
(B,ii) a young lady	+	who's just in too much of a hurry to go pay for it

In both sets of descriptions, contrasts are exhibited between reference forms and between descriptive items. Furthermore, the comparison between person-descriptions represents a standard device for making "character assessments," which consists of contrasting descriptions of a particular person (the "young lady") with descriptions of a hypothesized person ("somebody").[5]

In sum, the activity implicated at line 6 is a justification of the DA's announced refusal to consider an alternative to a standard penalty for the defendant. The description of the defendant is fitted to this context by means of the contrastive work it does for the discrepancy claimed between the actual stolen article (in B above) and the prior version of allowable stolen items (in A above). That is, the person-description is

---

[5]See Chapter 4, example (35), or this chapter, example (9), where Maria Dominguez is compared to a hypothetical "you."

systematically embedded in, and partially constitutive of, a sequentially
occasioned justification.

Wider Contexts

The immediate sequential environment of person descriptions often
makes their function very transparent, but not always. In the following
example, a series of person-descriptions, packaged as a distinct entity,
is triggered by a story-telling. To account for the appearance of each
description, we will have to draw on sources other than the present
sequential environment. One source will be later segments of the same
conversation. Evidence regarding "subcultural" orientations of participants will derive from other negotiations.

Maria Dominguez allegedly stole some clothes from "Davidson's,"
a local department store. A portion of the negotiations concerning her
case appears in segment (35) in Chapter 4. The full transcript is in Appendix 3.

(7) [Appendix 3, 001]

1.	PD1:	This is a shoplifting case judge. Um, on the face of it,
2.		it looks pretty bad
3.		(0.8)
4.	PD1:	But
5.	DA1:	Uh-huh
6.	PD1:	Investigating the case uh comes up with some beautiful
7.		defenses that I'm anxious to go to trial on if the Dee Ay is
8.		(1.4)
9.	PD1:	Situation is this (0.2) eghhh. She's a sixty five year old
10.		lady, Mexic- speaks uh (0.2) Castillian Spanish (0.4) she's
11.		from Spain (1.0) Uh eghhh she goes into Davidson's (0.8)
12.		Oh incidently uh- th- by way of background, for twenty years
13.		she's worked in the- in the Catholic Church of- at San Ramon
14.		as the housekeeper for the nuns 'n the fathers 'n all this
15.		stuff (and uh) very religious well known. I've interviewed
16.		half of San Ramon, concerning her background (0.4) wonderful
17.		lady no problems sixty-five years ol' .hhh sh- but on this
18.		particular occasion, she goes into Davidson's eghhh goes
19.		into a (0.2) fitting room (0.4) takes two hundred dollars
20.		worth o' clothes (0.8) pins them up underneath her (0.6)
21.		dress (0.6) and leaves

In this example, the person-descriptions are rather elaborately bracketed off from the story. The descriptions in lines 9–11 are both preceded and followed by small silences and voice clearings that separate them from the story preface ("situation is this," line 9) and the first story entry ("she goes into Davidson's," line 11). This story-entry item is itself followed by an eight-tenths of a second silence, a misplacement marker ("oh incidently," line 12), and a preface to another set of person-descriptions ("by way of background," line 12) which are clearly end-bracketed as well. The last description, "sixty-five years old" (line 17), is a repeat of the very first one in lines 9–10, neatly encapsulating the whole series of descriptions, and is followed by indicators of a change in focus: an inbreath and hesitation (".hhh sh-," line 17).[6] Then PD1 produces another preface ("on this particular occasion," lines 17–18) that contrasts with the prior one ("by way of background," line 12), marked as such with the "but" (line 17), and followed by a repeat of the story entry item "she goes into Davidson's" (line 18) and the rest of the story (lines 18–21).

In sum, through misplacement markers, prefaces, repeats, and other items, a number of person-descriptions are produced next to, but distinct from, a story regarding the referent person. And while in a general sense the descriptions and the story are both "about" the defendant, the exact relation of each of the descriptions to the story and to the overall negotiations requires further investigation.

Subsequent Conversation

In the last three lines of the above fragment, the PD's story tells of the woman taking 200 dollars worth of clothes from the store by pinning them underneath her dress. After this, he asserts that she was under the influence of pain-killing drugs (Appendix 3, lines 036–040) and reports that a consultant pharmacist had said that these drugs could cause a "state of confusion" and "delirium," where a person is "just in a dream world" and does not "know what in the world they're doing"

---

[6]Jefferson (1978: 246, fn. 11) notes,

> It appears that the perturbation occurs at junctures between discrete activity types, and its presence can serve as an index to junctures between discrete activities in otherwise apparently continuous activities like "story preface" and "store entry." Another phenomenon which may indicate activity junctures is the *audible inbreath*.

(044–048). Subsequently, the PD, responding to a question of the judge, tells how much and when the medication was taken (050–054). After the judge remarks on what he has learned (at a judicial conference) on what the drugs might do—pain-killing drugs could produce "some odd effects" (059–060)—the PD provides additional expert opinion on the matter, quoting a doctor who said that with "elderly people" the drugs sometimes have "strange or adverse effects that it wouldn't have normally" (064–068). Then the following occurs:

(8) [071]

1.	PD1:	So we feel that she certainly wasn't acting within her
2.		normal characteristics
3.	J1:	Has she ever had any violations for anything?
4.	PD1:	That's it, she's had nothing, for twenty years she worked up
5.		there in the Church of San Ramon with all these people. She's
6.		a very religious lady. All these uh, these uh Mexican Catholics
7.		up there who just think the world of her they say my god
8.		I couldn't believe it. I spent uh was it Monday this week? . . .
9.		up there talking with 'em and uh they just you know I've got uh
10.		some sisters who're willing to come in and state they've known
11.		her for all this period of time and she's just has a tremendous
12.		reputation for honesty and (very religious)
13.	J1:	What do you want?
14.	PD1:	Want it dismissed

The talk of greatest analytical relevance is that which occurs in response to the judges' query (line 3) and leads up to PD's display of position that he wants the case "dismissed" (line 14).

In lines 1–2, PD1 produces a description of the defendant: "that she certainly wasn't acting within her normal characteristics." This relates to the information the PD had provided regarding the defendant's drug intake and the opinions of the consultants and the judge regarding the effects of the drugs. But it is also heavily dependent on the series of descriptions produced earlier in the conversation, to the extent that the items provided by PD1 in segment (7) document what her "normal characteristics" are. She is an older lady who has worked in church for years, is very religious, and is known by the community.

There is evidence in the present segment that the earlier descriptions in fact do such documenting work. Note that the judge, in line 3, asks if she has "had any violations for anything." The PD, in line 4, answers that "she's had nothing" and proceeds to repeat and reformulate the earlier person-descriptions (two exceptions will be discussed later). Thus, the judge's question is used by PD1 as the *occasion* to reproduce the descriptions of the defendant (lines 4–12) in a topically coherent way.[7] Both judge and public defender, then, exhibit an orientation to the relevance of the woman's past record of behavior. The recitation of activities and assessments in the form of person-descriptions seems to be an effort to document the "real" self, or character, of the defendant by citing evidential characteristics.[8] Then, drawing on cultural assumptions to the effect that facts of a person's biography cannot be contradictory (Goffman, 1961: 63), or that they should be consistent with one another and with the real self of the defendant, the woman's shoplifting behavior, as reported in the PD's story, can be heard as anomalous.

Some conclusions can now be drawn regarding the series of person-descriptions presented in example (7). These descriptions occupy a well-constructed slot at the beginning of a story about the defendant's act. They do not display a sequential link to the PD's eventual proposal in the way demonstrated by earlier examples. Rather, the person-descriptions are integral to a procedure that is developed over a long stretch of conversation, and which provides the reasonableness of the proposed dismissal. Roughly, that procedure consists of (1) producing person-descriptions that work to establish the nature of the defendant's self or character, (2) formulating the defendant's offense so that it appears inconsistent with her character, and (3) explaining the behavior by reference to the "extraordinary circumstances" (drug effects) that could produce it.[9] Thus, the earlier person-descriptions do work to justify the

---

[7]Technically, we can consider the move from "she's had nothing" to "for twenty years she worked . . ." as a topic shift. It depends upon the membership of those descriptions in a class of items we could term "defendant's background" and which would be organized into two subclasses, "things the defendant *has not* done" and "things the defendant *has* done." The topic shift is between subclasses. Cf. Sacks (1968).

[8]Douglas (1967: 281–283) discusses a distinction made in everyday life between "situated" and "substantial" selves, where a substantial self is the reality lying behind situated behaviors. Similarly, Goffman (1974: 293) remarks that a person's acts are regarded as "in part an expression and outcome of his perduring self, and that this self will be present behind the particular roles he plays at any moment."

[9]The contradiction set up between the character of the defendant and the behavior she engaged in is a phenomenon related to the occurrence of "reality disjunctures" in courtroom and other situational discussions of "facts." And the use of "extraordinary circumstances" to explain the phenomenon is one method by which such disjunctures are resolved and the noncontradictory stature of the world is preserved. See Pollner (1974, 1975).

PD's eventual proposal and are a constituent feature of the topical and activity environment, one that occupies broader sections of conversation than we have seen so far.

The Courtroom Subculture

Close scrutiny of the two series of person-descriptions in segments (7) and (8) reveals that two items present in the first series are absent in the second. One is that "she's a sixty-five-year-old lady" (segment 7, line 9), and the other is that she "speaks Castillian Spanish, she's from Spain" (line 10). The rest of the items in the first series are repeated in the second series, indicating their relevance to the procedure by which PD1 argued for dismissing the case. The question arises, then, as to the kind of work, if any, these two person-descriptions perform. A preliminary answer is that some descriptions are produced with an orientation to the courthouse subculture—to "what everybody knows" regarding the relevance and importance of such descriptions.[10] "What everybody knows" should not be viewed as a mysterious content of a person's head, but as a noticeable and describable phenomenon exhibited in conversational practices.

The defendant's age is easiest to account for because it appears as a consequential item in three other segments within the negotiations. First, as noted above, the PD animates talk by a doctor who said, with respect to the medicine the defendant took, "on elderly people it sometimes has strange or adverse effects that it wouldn't have normally" (067–068). The defendant's age is thereby made germane to the question of whether the defendant was behaving intentionally, an issue that was also brought up by DA1 when he argued with the PD's position (see Chapter 4, segment 35).

(9) [096]

DA1: I just can't believe that the drug is- if the drug affects you that badly you gonna do something bizarre. In other words you're gonna walk out swinging around your arm or carrying out (bananas) in your ear or something crazy. Here, she was extremely sophisticated. . .

---

[10]On the importance of the courtroom subculture, see Buckle and Buckle (1977: 119–120, 158), Eisenstein and Jacob (1977: 25–28), Heumann (1978: 120, 152), Mather (1979: 3), and Rosett and Cressey (1976: 81).

Although the judge is somewhat ambivalent about the case (see Appendix 3, especially lines 172–178 and 238–271), he does seem to agree about the effects of age on behavior.

(10) [183]

J1: You know people do do this occasionally and it's like as not, somebody that's older and it- and all of a sudden just does something totally out of character . . .

The defendant's age also becomes a relevant item when the judge appeals to the DA to make some concession (after the DA and PD have disagreed over how the case should be handled):

(11) [212]

J1: What would you be willing to do on it, would you be willing to cut it down, she's an older lady, if you had her on, you know, give her a four eight four if she's got- and if uh therapy and uh checked on

The defendant was charged with violating section 487.1 of the penal code, which is grand theft (the value of property taken was over $200). The judge's suggestion is for a reduced charge, petty theft (section 484); the use of Dominguez's age implicitly proposes certain features about her by virtue of what the description "elderly lady" *typifies* (Schutz, 1973). These features may perhaps include such things as respectability and harmlessness, the latter pertaining to the mention of how her behavior could be monitored in nonpenal ways ("therapy" and "checked on").

Talk regarding the defendant's age occurs at a third point, as discussion focuses on what would happen if the case went to trial:

(12) [280]

PD1: She's such a sweet little old lady uh there's no jury in
     the world's gonna convict her. I just can't believe it.
     Particularly when we have a doctor and a pathologist who
     ⌊say they'll come in and talk⌋
DA2: ⌈It's the sweet little old la⌉dy defense okay

Here, PD1 hypothesizes a jury's sympathetic reaction as following from the defendant's appearance as a "sweet little old lady." DA2 (in overlap with the PD's reminder about expert testimony) utilizes the PD's phrase, but converts it from a description of the defendant to a clichéd characterization of a defense strategy. Thus, both parties exhibit, though in slightly different ways, an orientation to the defendant's age status as relevant to the staging of a trial.

In summary, Maria Dominguez's age was first introduced during negotiations when her defense attorney produced a series of other person-descriptions (segment 7). At different places in the course of talk, and through different means, the public defender, judge, and district attorney all demonstrate its "meaning." For the PD, age was relevant to the effect of drugs on the defendant and to how the jury would react to her. The judge appeared to use her age to invoke the defendant's respectability, harmlessness, or other characteristics associated with the typification "older lady." For the DA, age was an item potentially to be used by the PD in a standard defense strategy. The argument here is not that the descriptive item had the *same meaning* to each one of these actors. Rather, the idea is that a person-description *has meaning* for them and stands as part of the courtroom subculture ("what everybody knows") in the way it is used to do, and is heard as doing, relevant negotiational work.

The second description from segment (7), whose status in the negotiations was not clear, was this:

(13) [010]

PD1:   . . . She . . . speaks uh Castillian Spanish, she's from Spain

The defendant being "from Spain" is a descriptive item occasioned by, and selected with reference to, the first description that she "speaks Castillian Spanish."[11] Thus, taken together, the utterances seem to be characterizing the defendant's language capacity. The reference to her linguistic abilities occurs in one other location in the negotiations, after the DA and judge proposed that the case be continued for a pre-plea report (a "one thirty one point three" report) from the probation department. The PD replies as follows:

---

[11]"Speaking Castillian Spanish" is an activity bound to the category "from Spain." It is in this sense that the second description is occasioned and selected by reference to the first description. It should be noted that these two items together appear to be correcting the prior assertion (cut-off) that the defendant is "Mexican." See example (7), line 9. The correction may be due to the prestige value of being from Spain as opposed to Mexico, or it may be related to the PD's later report that the defendant's case must be settled because she is traveling to Spain.

(14) [231]

PD1: I'll talk with her. Thing of it is she's really upset about
the whole thing, she's just a nervous bundle of- she doesn't
speak any English. Um I'll talk with her and see if she'll
go along with a one thirty one point three but uh . . .

This time there is a negative formulation of the defendant's language
capacity. While it may have been triggered by, and may have made
reference to, the PD's plan to "talk with her," this does not fully explain
its function here or its earlier occurrence.

There is no other talk about this defendant's language, but some
help is provided by parts of another conversation, one concerning a
Chicano defendant, also Spanish-speaking. In the course of discussing
the case, the following utterance is produced:

(15) [Battery]

PD2: He makes a good witness and uh, in his native tongue

The PD's utterance here occasions some joking regarding profanities in
the "native tongue," and then this talk appears:

(16)

1. DA3: Why is there that- that feeling that if they can't
2. speak the language they can harbor no malice or- or
3. criminal intent uh some things are not even challenged
4. PD2: Well I only bring it up to you as a TACtical consideration
5. heh huh
6. DA3: Uh it is that
7. PD2: Uh huh hih. Many a welfare fraud is blocked because she
8. couldn't speak the langua(h)ge er wouldn't cop ta speaking it
9. in court

Here, the DA and PD each draw inferences from the defendant being
a Spanish speaker. The DA heard the PD as proposing that the defendant, by virtue of not speaking "the language," also lacks any evil or
criminal subjectivity (lines 2–3). The PD states, however, that it is a
"tactical consideration" (line 4), and that receives an agreement utterance
from the DA (line 6). The PD then produces an acknowledgment and a
laughter token (line 7) and topically elaborates how it can be a tactical
consideration at trial (lines 7–9).

Both the DA and the PD have thus exhibited an orientation to the "meaning" of the descriptive item concerning the defendant's language capacity. The point, again, is not that the description has the same meaning to each of the actors, except as that meaning is negotiated in discrete episodes of talk. Sequentially speaking, the import of the defendant's language in the last segment was its "tactical" significance in that this, rather than the intentional issue, was implicated in the DA's agreement turn and the PD's topical expansion.

Clearly, then, each of the two items which, at first, appeared to be somewhat anomalous, fit the general pattern of relating to the topical and activity context within which they appear. They display aspects of the courtroom subculture in that they were both produced by a speaker and heard by a recipient as doing relevant negotiational work. What differentiates the age and language items from the other person-descriptions is that they clearly relate to a potential trial scene that would be unfavorable to the DA. They nonetheless provide further support for the proposal that the case be dismissed.

It bears repeating that plea bargaining is not so much an information exchange system nor a mechanism for reaching agreement about facts and character as it is a vehicle for assuming numerous kinds of postures that sustain the viability of a given case action. That the age and language descriptions related to a possible trial for Dominguez should make us appreciate that the other descriptions could well have a dual character. When the PD mentioned that the defendant worked for the nuns and fathers and was well-known in her community, for example, it might have exhibited the "real" self of the defendant *and* given notice to the DA that extensive character testimony would be staged at trial. Indeed, this case was eventually dismissed, and my impression from talking to DA1 after the dismissal was that he still disagreed with the PD's reasoning about the self of the defendant, the anomalous nature of her offense, and the effects of her medicine. While convinced of her guilt (see segment 35, Chapter 4), he was nonetheless wary that a trial would result in acquittal.

Repair

That person-descriptions regularly relate to their topic and activity environment by supporting negotiators' positions is a pattern in negotiational discourse that can be breached. The evidence is that when such a breach occurs, it is noticeable and subject to repair:

(17) [Drunk Driving]

```
 1.  PD2:  Now this is a case which oughta be- which is eminently
 2.        disposable. Uh Lynn Heater is a uh, a young lady,
 3.        beautiful by the way, absolutely beautiful
 4.  J1:   Mm
 5.  PD2:  She looks like Kim Novak right down to the toes. She
 6.        works as a waitress for Bill's¹² new place called- out
 7.        in the shopping center
 9.  J1:   Okay let's get to the case heh =
10.  J1:   ₁h a h  h a h  h a h .hhhhhhh              ₁
11.  PD2:  ʼWell this is all very important becauseʼ this is part
12.        of the defense ₁ya ₁ see, uh as a witness, the jury won't
13.  J1:                ʼHaʼ
14.  PD2:  hear ₁a word₁ she says, they'll be too busy looking at
15.  J1:        ʼHa ha ʼ
16.  PD2:  her. In any event, but . . .
```

The public defender, in line 1, proposes that "this is a case which . . . is eminently disposable" and produces several person-descriptions regarding the defendant's looks (lines 2–5). Those are followed by another description concerning where the defendant works, but the judge produces an utterance ("let's get to the case," line 9) implying that the prior descriptions are not relevant to the discussion and proposing a next turn in which the talk would relate to the case. While the judge's utterance does end in unsolicited laughter (lines 9–10) that suggests a nonserious treatment of the issue, the laughter is overlapped by the PD's "Well this is all very important because . . ." (line 11). This utterance is self-retrieved or made consequential for further talk (Jefferson and Schegloff, n.d.: 14) by PD2 continuing the utterance beyond the simultaneity.¹³ The continuation suggests that descriptions are "part of the defense" (lines 11–12) and it also overlaps additional laughter tokens. As Jefferson (1975: 3) notes, speech that overlaps laughter "undercuts the appropri-

---

¹²"Bill's" is the name of a restaurant.
¹³Two utterances produced in overlap present a problem as to which will be implicated in further talk. A means of achieving implicativeness for one's own utterance is for speaker to continue producing related talk after the other party stops talking or laughing in overlap.

ateness of laughter" and offers "to treat seriously whatever it was the laughter is proposing to treat nonseriously." Here it is not clear that the PD is being entirely serious, except in the narrow and important sense of depicting a trial scenario to support his position—"as a witness the jury won't hear a word she says, they'll be too busy looking at her" (lines 11–16).[14] Juries apparently do make judgments on the basis of the appearance and attractiveness of defendants (Dane and Wrightsman, 1982: 101–103; Kalven and Zeisel, 1966: 202–218; O'Barr, 1982: 41–49). It is not unusual that the PD would be aware of this fact and would use it in an attempt to provide for the relevance of descriptions whose status in the negotiations was at least implicitly questioned.

That district attorneys and public defenders are required to produce relevant person-descriptions is consistent with other studies arguing that in courthouse subcultures attorneys are expected to be "reasonable" in their negotiations (Neubauer, 1974: 217; Eisenstein and Jacob, 1977: 33). Clearly, this requirement is specifically applicable to how defendants are described during bargaining. Not just anything that might be said of a defendant may be deemed relevant or allowable as part of the discourse.

CONCLUSION: PERSON-DESCRIPTIONS AND ACTIVITY CONSTITUTION

In the examples we have examined, a variety of different items were utilized to describe the various defendants. Roughly, these can be divided into two classes. The first includes those descriptions that employ what were referred to earlier as membership categorization devices. For example, "national origin" was a device employed in example (7) to describe the defendant as being "from Spain" and to generate the related (or category-bound) activity-description that she spoke Castillian Spanish. When we consider that persons can be categorized by sex, occu-

---

[14]Note that by discussing the issue of the defendant's looks, the PD abandons the topic of where the defendant works. After this segment, PD2 raises the issue of her eligibility for an alcohol rehabilitation program. See Chapter 5, example (5).

pation, hometown, race, and so on, it is clear that there is a large array of devices available for generating person-descriptions.[15]

A second class of descriptions includes assessment terms, or items that are "opinion" or "subjective" statements about a person's attributes. Thus, in example (5), the public defender described his client as being "strictly honest." Again, there are numerous assessment terms such as good, bad, upstanding, immoral, neat, and so forth, that can be used in person-descriptions.

Categorical descriptions and assessment items[16] can be used singly or together, and the latter possibility yields combinations that increase the number of ways a person can be identified in conversation.

(18) [Drunk Driving]

PD2: Uh mister Larson is a highly educated young economist at
    the college

Here, a person description employs a number of assessment terms ("highly educated," "young") together with a categorical description ("economist at the college") to depict a defendant. One could imagine the use of other categories with the same assessment items or other assessment items with the same category, either of which would radically change the sense of the description.

(19) [Hypothetical]

PD2: Uh mister Larson is a perpetually drunk immature economist
    at the college

In any case, when considered together, the categories, assessments, or combinations of these two classes of descriptions yield numerous pos-

---

[15]It is also the case that categorizing a person in a given way sets up the use of subsidiary membership categorization devices. Maynard and Zimmerman (1983) have shown, for example, that in conversations between persons who mutually categorize one another as students, as a way of "getting acquainted," the use of other devices such as major, year in school, etc., is thereby occasioned.

[16]The distinction between categorical and assessment descriptions here is made on commonsense grounds, but there is some evidence that such a distinction is an achievement of, and made observable in, identifiable conversational practices. See Maynard (1979: Chapter 3).

sibilities for describing persons in conversation. The question was, given all the facts and assessments of a person that might be told about or alleged, how are certain ones chosen?

We have seen that person-descriptions are sensitive to and constitutive of the topic and activity in various episodes of conversation. This means that participants do "topical" and "activity" analyses as they select and produce (or hear) a person-description (cf. Schegloff, 1972: 96). The intimate fit between person-descriptions and their conversational environment is a normative feature of plea bargaining discourse. If it is not evident how a description is relevant to negotiations, the lack of relevance will be noticed and subject to repair or remedy.

With respect to the particular conversations investigated here, this means that description of defendants, and character assessment, are not performed indiscriminately in the way that, for example, jokes are sometimes inserted in conversation (cf. Sacks, 1978: 262). Nor is there an orientation to some sort of "correctness" (Sharrock and Turner, 1980: 20) or "descriptive adequacy" (Atkinson and Drew, 1979: 137). The implication is that there is no abstract set of factors or descriptive variables, the values of which are determined for each defendant when that person's case is discussed. Therefore, as we will see, an assumption about the decision-making process commonly made by researchers investigating the effects of socioeconomic status, race, and other extra-legal characteristics on sentencing outcomes in the criminal justice system is fallacious. The assumption is that such a set of factors does exist. On the contrary, defendants' attributes are systematically made visible in relation to arguments for and against various dispositions, as justifications for the positions taken up by prosecution and defense. Thus, they are highly context-specific rather than abstract.

Defendants' attributes are used to the extent that they can support proposals, position-reports, and their replies in actual negotiations over dispositions. More generally, when persons are talked about in any conversation, descriptions are selected and produced according to what activity is being done: "complaining," "praising," "blaming" (cf. Atkinson and Drew, 1979), "insulting" (Labov, 1972a), "talking objectively," and so forth. Who a person officially is, for others, depends on what activity is being accomplished in their talk.

CHAPTER 7

Modeling Sentencing Decisions

Criminal-justice researchers perennially have tried to determine whether defendants are convicted and punished as much for who they are as for what they have done. Motivating dozens of multivariate statistical analyses of sentencing decisions is a basic concern for justice and "equal treatment before the law" (Hagan, 1975b). The question is whether defendants are treated according to the legal seriousness of their offenses and without regard to age, race, socioeconomic status, sex, or other "extralegal" attributes. Largely, studies addressing this question in the last three decades examined the influence of various *legal* and *extra-legal*[1] factors *on* imposed sentences, rather than investigating the *process* by which various dispositional outcomes are produced.[2]

This has come about in two interrelated ways. First, a fascination with statistical analysis has meant a concomitant lack of commitment to a naturalistic understanding of the negotiation of defendants' official identities, which would mean preserving the integrity of the decision-making process (Matza, 1969: 13–14). Second, it is well known that

---

[1]There is some debate over whether the distinction between *legal* and *extralegal* factors is a proper one (cf. Bernstein, Kelly, and Doyle, 1977a: 750). In the discussion that follows, I will use "offense-related" and "offender-related" as terms to make the distinction, which does not necessarily skirt the issues raised by Bernstein et al. (1977a) and Farrell and Swigert (1978), but is a convenience that is grounded in the way in which such factors are utilized or treated by the legal practitioners in this study. See the discussion of "offense-related factors" below.

[2]Mehan (1979) has made a similar critique of traditional studies of schooling that seek to relate "input" and "output" factors rather than to examine how various outcomes of the educational process are assembled as products of teachers' and students' organized interaction.

upwards of 80 percent of felony and 95 percent of misdemeanor criminal cases are settled by plea bargains (as opposed to trials) in American criminal courts. But the negotiations are seldom, if ever, included in court records; thus, important information is left out of what constitutes a primary source of data for sentencing studies (Neubauer, 1974: 191; Feeley, 1979c: 149). Such considerations lead inexorably to the conclusion that studies of actual discourse are sorely needed.

The tape-recorded data from Garden City Municipal Court provide a unique opportunity for assessing, in a qualitative fashion, how defendant "attributes" are related to dispositions. The proposition is that statistical analyses suffer from methodological problems because interactions among "variables" are extraordinarily complex. Most criminal-justice researchers emphasize the need for more sophisticated models and refined statistical techniques to handle the complexity of relationships among variables. Yet there is a limit to the amount of variance that can be explained—such models and techniques fail to comprehend procedures internal to negotiational discourse and through which sentencing decisions are accomplished. An appreciation of these procedures points to a different "modeling" of the process and to the importance of investigating patterns of commonsense reasoning among legal practitioners.

THEORY AND RESEARCH

Studies of sentencing speak to various sociological traditions, of which four are prominent.

First is labeling theory. Persons using this perspective assume that "factors associated with the values and activities of those responding to a deviant" will account for some or most of the variance in decisions made regarding defendants (Bernstein, Kick, Leung, and Schulz, 1977b: 363).

Second, conflict theory is often the starting point for sentencing investigations, suggesting that race and class are important determinants of case dispositions. The hypotheses generated by conflict and labeling theory often appear indistinguishable, but labeling theory nevertheless simply posits the existence of bias in the criminal-justice process, while conflict theory attributes that bias to power relations inherent in a class society.[3] As Chiricos and Waldo (1975: 754) observe,

> With specific allowances made for such contingencies as the size and degree of threat posed by various groups and interests, this perspective has generally argued that the less powerful a group, the more likely will its behaviors be designated as crime and its members designated as criminals.

A third theory, often counterposed to conflict or labeling approaches, is the functionalist or "legal consensus" perspective, which emphasizes offense-related factors by hypothesizing that items such as prior record and offense charged will be more influential than other factors.

Finally, an organizational perspective focuses on such things as bail, charges, and other decisions as well as sentences. The attempt is to understand the relationship between various subsystems (such as prosecution and probation) in the criminal-justice process (e.g., Hagan et al., 1979).

Prior to the 1970s, much of the research on disposition patterns was methodologically unsophisticated, either not using statistical procedures at all or employing tests of significance in naive ways. A range of offender-related variables—race, age, occupation, income, and sex—were examined, but, as Hagan (1974) pointed out after reviewing the state of the art, statistically significant relationships between these variables and sentences are substantively unimportant when measures of association are computed. For noncapital cases, knowledge of these independent variables increases accuracy in predicting the dependent variable (sentences) by less than one percent. Hagan (1974: 375) concludes that "the central finding of this review of past research is that there is generally a small relationship between extra-legal attributes and sentencing decisions."

In the last decade, research on sentencing and other court decision stages has become methodologically more sophisticated, having utilized multiple regression, path, and log-linear types of analyses. The major

---

[3]A related tradition derives from no explicit theoretical perspective other than a concern with "equality before the law" (see Hagan, 1975a: 536, fn. 4), a focus that fits with that of labeling and conflict theorists. Researchers following this tradition seem to speak primarily to policymakers and others interested in the extent to which the official ideal of equality is being implemented in the courts (e.g., Swigert and Farrell, 1977) rather than to social scientists *per se*.

contribution of this research seems to be an increased appreciation of the complexities of the process by which defendants are routed through the courts. Earlier decision points, such as bail and charge determinations, are now investigated with an eye toward measuring their effects on disposition. Lizotte (1978), for example, shows that race and social class influence sentences by way of bail rulings. Nonwhites and persons in low-prestige occupations fail to make bail more often than others, and "not making bail appears to lead to outright discrimination and longer prison sentences" (Lizotte, 1978: 573; cf. Clarke and Koch, 1976). Other research has investigated the effect on sentencing of recommendations made by probation officers, whose advice is based at least in part on their perception of an offender's demeanor and evaluation of the person's prior record (Hagan, 1975b). One set of studies found, however, that the contributions of the probation officer may be "decoupled" from the disposition by the final agent in the system, the judge (Hagan, 1975b; Hagan et al., 1979).

Besides exploring early stages in the criminalization process, recent research has been sensitive to the influence of previously unmeasured variables. Thus, Myers and Hagan (1979) found that "evidentiary strength," a factor disregarded in much research, increased the probabilities that prosecutors would pursue a case (rather than dismiss it) and take it to trial (rather than allow the guilty plea). Similarly, Bernstein et al. (1977a) and Eisenstein and Jacob (1977: 282) found that, in the courts of several metropolitan areas, evidentiary strength accounted for a small amount of the variance in sentencing. The assessment of offense *victims* has been explored by Myers (1979) and Myers and Hagan (1979), who show that probation officers and prosecutors consider the racial and social status of victims when making recommendations and decisions. Other recently explored factors have included courtroom workgroups (Eisenstein and Jacob, 1977), urbanization (Hagan, 1977), criminal stereotypes (Swigert and Farrell, 1977), changes over time (Thomson and Zingraff, 1981), type of jurisdiction (high or low control of plea bargaining; La Free, 1981), and others.

Offender-related variables, such as race, socioeconomic status, sex, and so on, have differing and even contradictory effects on criminal-justice decision making, depending on both the stage of the process examined and the kinds of other variables that can be controlled. Concerning class, for example, some studies find no substantial effect on sentencing (e.g., Bernstein et al., 1977a; Chiricos and Waldo, 1975, Eisenstein and Jacob, 1977), while others discover varying degrees of effect (e.g., Lizotte, 1978; Swigert and Farrell, 1977).

More consistent findings are generated with reference to offense-related factors. Some investigations turn up significant effects of the "nature of the offense" (e.g., Eisenstein and Jacob, 1977: Chapters 9, 10), others find "prior record" to have an effect (e.g., Feeley, 1979c: 132, 142), and some document the influence of both factors (e.g., Chiricos and Waldo, 1975; Clarke and Koch, 1976; Bernstein et al., 1977a; La Free, 1981). Still, these variables do not explain a large proportion of the variance in sentencing outcomes. "The single finding that *is* consistent throughout this literature," Hagan et al. (1979: 508) note, "is that whether legal-consensus [offense-related] or class conflict [offender-related] factors are the focus of the analysis, the unexplained variance looms large."

The sources of the unexplained variance are usually attributed to a variety of shortcomings in the research design. Frequently cited troubles are the overrepresentation of lower-class defendants (Greenberg, 1977; Hopkins, 1977; Reasons, 1977; Hagan, Nagel, and Albonetti, 1980), lack of longitudinal data (Greenberg, 1977; Hagan, 1974; Thomson and Zingraff, 1981), and absence of control over significant variables such as criminal stereotypes (Swigert and Farrell, 1977) and evidence (Myers and Hagan, 1979). In brief, the problem seems to be lack of adequate data-sets (cf. Hagan et al., 1979), and the implication is that if we had wider variation among independent variables, we would be able to account for more variance in the dependent variables.[4]

This may be true. However, the "subtlety," "complexity," and "intricacy" of the process have also been emphasized (e.g., Chiricos, Jackson, and Waldo, 1972: 564; Myers and Hagan, 1979: 449; Eisenstein and Jacob, 1977: 244, 258; Feeley, 1979c: 153). In view of this, there have been several calls for "new kinds of data on sentencing" (Hagan, 1974: 380), including more intensive observations and descriptions of actual decision making (Feeley, 1979c: 153; Bernstein et al., 1977a: 754; Abel, 1980: 819). As a response to these calls, attention to plea bargaining discourse and actual decision-making processes reveals an endogenous organization, the description of which makes sense of some of the contradictory findings and lack of explanatory power in statistical models

---

[4]The state of research on adult criminal courts is duplicated in the studies of juvenile courts (e.g., see the discussion and review in Horwitz and Wasserman, 1980) and in research on jury decision making (Bennett and Feldman, 1981: Chapter 8).

of sentencing. These models *distort* the process in several ways by exogenously imposing a structure on it.

SENTENCING DECISIONS

Legal practitioners appear to make a distinction between offense-related and offender-related variables. This distinction can be observed in the distinct ways that person-descriptions are used.

Offense-Related Factors: Beginning the Negotiations

When a prosecutor and defense lawyer meet at a settlement conference, Chapter 2 showed, they negotiate a series of cases. Discussion of any particular case is ordinarily started by naming the defendant, specifying the offense charged, and/or reciting the prior conviction record of the defendant. When the charge is mentioned, it is done either by stating its title or by mentioning its penal code section number:

(1) [Petty theft]

PD2:   Okay Jeffrey Walker's a petty theft

(2) [Disturbing the peace]

PD2:   Uh well what about Fridley
DA3:   What about Fridley. That's a four fifteen

(3) [Resisting public officers; Disorderly conduct]

J1:   And now that brings us to Frank Bryan. Is he the poor chap
       sitting out there all by himself?
PD2:   Yeah he's the sweet man with the nice smile. And this is a six
       forty seven "f" and a one forty eight

Previous offenses or "priors," however, are employed as desriptions of the *defendant*, that is, they appear in person-descriptions.

(4a) 8.001 [Drunk driving]

J2:   Uh Rodriquez
PD2:   Now this man has at least two priors that I know of. Is it three
       priors or two priors
J2:   ₁Three priors₁
DA2:   ᵀThree priorsᴵ

Note in the last example that no reference is made to the offense charged, which is drunken driving. Thus, not every discussion begins with the naming of the charge; nor is the defendant's record (if any) repeated for every case. This may be because, unlike other information about the case and defendant, the charge and prior record are listed on the docket sheet for the pretrial conference, and knowledge of them is simply assumed as the negotiation starts.

When the offense *is* named or prior record is cited, then, it is an expressed acknowledgment of what is known about the defendant and the offense, and it sets the context for further discussion. We have seen that, in the Frank Bryan case (segment 3 above), it is precisely over which charge is appropriate that the lawyers subsequently argue (Chapter 5). What will happen to a defendant is also predicated on the number of prior offenses, in accordance with jurisdictional practices that define standard penalties within the limits provided by the penal code. Thus, with respect to the last segment, after answering the PD's question as to whether there were two or three priors the DA continued as follows:

(4b) [Drunk driving]

DA2:   In all cases where there are at least two convictions
PD2:   Okay
DA2:   We would urge that they be referred for a probation and
           sentencing report

In this jurisdiction, then, action on a case is "officially" related not only to stipulated charges, but also to a defendant's prior record, a function that is not accorded other possible (nonrecord, "offender-related") attributes of a defendant.

Offender-Related Factors

The mention of an offender's attributes, Chapter 6 showed, is related to the presentation of positions on what action should be taken in individual cases. An implication of this is that offender-related descriptions are not employed in any mechanical "checklist" fashion when decisions are made but are carefully selected and used contextually to justify negotiators' positions. Furthermore, this raises methodological issues with reference to the statistical modeling of sentencing decisions. An alternative "gestalt" model of decision making permits the investigation of legal practitioners' commonsense patterns of reasoning and conceptions of justice used in negotiations.

Example 1

This is a petty theft case involving a woman who was charged with taking several small items, including needles and thread, from a supermarket. The full transcript is in Appendix 4.

(5a) [006]

1.	PD1:	This lady lives in Sea City, she had her house burned, and
2.		she uh apparently she's staying with relatives. But at
3.		any rate she came up here, she has three small children,
4.		two and a half month old baby, the youngest. Seems to me
5.		that some disposition other than twenty four hours in jail
6.		is-, would be appropriate in this case rather than the
7.		standard

Again, as is evident in lines 5–7, the standard penalty for a person who shoplifts in this juridiction is 24 hours in the county jail. The public defender is arguing, then, that some disposition other than the standard one "would be appropriate in this case" *because of* the biographical items mentioned in lines 1–4. This argument is also apparent in the following segment, which occurred after the PD and DA had discussed the articles the defendant allegedly took from the supermarket: needles, thread, lip medication, a mirror plaque, flashbulbs (019–038).

(5b) [042]

1.	PD1:	The thing of it is, you know, this lady has come- she did
2.		come up here from Sea City, you know, to face the punishment.
3.		She knows that she's facing twenty four hours. No question
4.		about that, she knows that. Um, but it just seems to me
5.		that uh twenty four hours in jail for something like that
6.		is just-
7.	DA3:	Okay, I understand that, I've- I don't see that I can make
8.		an exception on this
9.	PD1:	Okay
10.	DA3:	What do you wanta do
11.	PD1:	Well, I don't wanta continue the case, she'll probably plead and
12.		take the time

Here, PD1 reminds the DA that the defendant did show up in court, possibly attempting to depict her as someone who fulfills her public obligations and who is thus deserving of leniency.[5] The DA, however, while acknowledging the PD's argument, suggests that he cannot make an "exception" and thus rejects the PD's appeal (lines 7–8). Although, in response to the DA's query (line 10), he then appears to concede (lines 11–12), PD1 goes on to make another pitch for his client:

(5c) [055]

1.	PD1:	I don't feel that strongly about it except that I just feel
2.		like that, you know, she was arraigned, she went back to
3.		Sea City, she came up here knowing that she's facing this,
4.		she's got a two and a half month old baby, she's been trying
5.		to support herself and two kids or *three* kids and this- and
6.		uh, I bet you she's probably gone through enough hell as it
7.		is, you know, and I don't think twenty four hours is gonna-
8.	DA3:	I- uh, the judge may be responsive to that

This time, DA3 produces an utterance that is a version of a "pass" (cf. Jefferson and Schenkein, 1977: 89). That is, he simultaneously refuses to make a recommendation of a lesser penalty and yet suggests that PD1 may want to make his appeal in court.

Subsequently, PD1 talked to the defendant and she agreed to plead guilty as charged and accept the standard penalty. Although the judge did not go back on the 24-hour jail term, he did suspend a five-dollar penalty assessment. In summary, the PD here employed a series of "offender-related factors" in the negotiations, including his client's house having burned, her having children to support, and her traveling back and forth to make court appointments. All of these are tailored to the argument, in paraphrase, that she had suffered enough and need not be punished more with the standard penalty of 24 hours in jail. The "suffered enough" theme is recognized to cause juries to be favorably disposed toward defendants in some cases (Kalven and Zeisel, 1966), and the PD may be reminding the DA of that.

---

[5] As Feeley (1979c: 187) has observed, the question for defendants, at least in misdemeanor criminal cases, "is not whether to go to trial, but whether to show up in court at all." Knowing this, courtroom officials may regard a defendant's appearing in court as one factor in his or her favor.

Example 2

This is also a case of petty theft; the defendant, Donald Cleaver, had taken a permit worth $40 that provided parking access to the local college. Negotiations in this case were briefly examined in Chapter 3, and the full transcript is in Appendix 5. As in the last example, there is no argument over the guilt or innocence of the defendant. The negotiations concern the proper disposition, and they show how, as Rosett and Cressey (1976: 102) have argued, criminal-justice personnel often first decide how an offender should be punished, if at all, and then find an offense appropriate to that decision.

The PD began the conversations by telling the DA:

(6a) [003]

PD2:   Jeff, y'know I've scratched my brains trying to think of an
       alternative to theft . . . uh, having to do with failing to
       pay for his parking . . .

In the course of the subsequent conversation, PD2 attempted to establish the propriety of a lesser charge, and, in a manner similar to the last example, person-descriptions are employed as part of that work. Two different descriptions occur in the first line of the following segment.

(6b) [009]

1.   PD2:   He's a young guy, a student out there and the court's file
2.   would have a letter from the dean of students asking for
3.   a, uh any possible courtesy in this case. I think that the
4.   dean of student's position is that uh the guy should not
5.   have a criminal record

The assertion that the defendant is a "young guy" (line 1) is, we shall see, brought up repeatedly. But because the description of him as "a student out there" is intimately related to immediate contexts, it is of focal concern. The two parties knew, from the police report, that the misappropriation of the parking sticker occurred at the college where the defendant was a student. Explicitly identifying Cleaver through his occupation ("student") and specifying that occupation with a locational formulation ("out there") constitutes him as a "course-of-action" type (Schutz, 1973; Zimmerman, 1974) who rightly belongs at the college, and whose offense appears as something done within a round of activities typically motivated and executed by virtue of that identity. That is, as Sacks (1972b) has suggested, police see isolated behaviors of a person on the street and infer that they are not just random activities but are part of a meaningful course of involvements. In a similar sense, the PD here makes the defendant's offense appear related to his college-going activities.

In addition, the phrase "student out there" reflexively links with the formulation of the letter writer (line 2) as "dean of students." That formulation can be heard as discussing not just any dean who has written the letter "asking for a possible courtesy" (lines 2–3), but an administrative official at the locale where the theft occurred and where the defendant is a student. Consistent with the analysis in Chapter 6, the description of the defendant as a "student out there" is intimately related to the topic and activity environment in which it appears.

After the above segment, there is discussion regarding a vehicle code violation that would be an alternative to the theft charge (013–018), and PD2 suggests that "a fine would not be unreasonable" were the defendant to plead to the vehicle code charge (022). The DA, however, asks the PD why "the logic" of the PD's argument would not "apply to every one of the misuse of parking sticker cases" (025–037).

(6c) [038]

1. PD2: My logic is that uhm I don't think that the young man
2.   considered himself a thief and that one of the things we
3.   punish is y- somebody that takes something out of a store
4.   bloody well knows it's stealing, and bloody well knows who
5.   he is and what he's done.

Here, a contrastive device is utilized to support the PD's argument. A hypothetical "somebody" who "takes something out of a store" (line 3) is described as knowing "it's stealing" and knowing "who he is and what he's done" (lines 4–5), whereas the "young man" is characterized as not "considering himself a thief" (lines 1–2).[6] Following this segment, DA3 continued to push for categorizing the offense as a theft (043–066), and the PD again disagrees:

(6d) [069]

PD2: Well I'm suggesting that you could've filed it either way
DA3: Well

---

[6]Compare this to example (35) in Chapter 4 and example (6) in Chapter 6, which also compare defendants to hypothetical persons as a way of justifying a position.

PD2:   This way, you know as a theft charge, it- considering his
        age and his- you know, it's a very serious thing to lay-
        lay a theft charge on somebody like that . . .

The indexical description "somebody like that" retrieves the descriptions of the defendant so far proferred. These include (1) that he's
a young guy, (2) a student at the college where the theft occurred, and
(3) one who did not consider himself a thief. While the DA still exhibited
concern as to whether he would have to "knock down" the charges in
all similar cases (074–080), PD2 argued that this was a "special case"
because of the letter from the dean of students (081–083). Discussion of
how the offense was perpetrated followed (091–114). When DA3 raised
a question about when a theft charge would be "appropriate," PD2
answered in terms that invoke the particular characteristics of the defendant and his incipient career:

(6e) [119]

DA3:   I just want to know, you know in what case it would be uh
        appropriate to stay with the charge of misappropriating
        found property
PD2:   Well, it seems to me, that one of the reasons you have the
        kind of discretion that you have is that you can take a look
        at the person that's being charged and decide what the
        consequences of your action would be you know on any individual
        person
DA3:   Okay
PD1:   Uh you take a young student, I think he's eighteen or
        nineteen years old, he's uh just starting out, trying to get-
        you know, in college, uh and you lay larceny on him. Uh true
        he can come back in a year and get it taken off his record,
        but for many other purposes uh its going to be known, for
        example if he ever tries to get security clearance uh whether
        or not the court seals his records uh they will know about
        the conviction

Subsequently, PD4 joined the discussion and supported PD2's position by suggesting that with these cases "in general," where "students" with no previous record are involved, "this is not something you
want to give them theft on" (150–153). DA3 countered by submitting
that such students "ought to have a heightened sense of responsibility
and appreciation for the consequences of their acts" (166–168). PD4 then
reverted to a generalized form of PD2's earlier argument and stated that
students "don't think of it as theft" (176). Following this, PD2 told a

series of stories regarding how he, as a student, broke rules with impunity (186–218). The DA finally relents but diffuses responsibility by reference to the dean's position (see segment 24, Chapter 3):

(6f) [224]

DA3:   Well uh maybe I can make an exception in this case on the theory that
       if the dean of students doesn't care enough for the enforcement of the
       college's own rules, why should we . . .

After DA3 checked out the section number for the parking violation, the negotiations were concluded through proposal sequences, by which it was decided that the defendant would pay a fifty-dollar fine and a fifteen-dollar penalty assessment (228–238).

The negotiations in the parking sticker case have not been fully analyzed. On the contrary, much of the complexity of these negotiations has been glossed over in order to emphasize and explore the use of person-descriptions. The way in which the PD eventually achieved a desired outcome involved a number of strategems, including the reference to the dean's letter, the telling of stories and so on. Thus, the point is not that descriptions of the defendant unilaterally determine the eventual outcome. Rather, they should be considered as part of a context in which an attempt to obtain a lesser charge for the defendant is enacted. The descriptions of the defendant as a "young man," as a "student" at the college, and as one who did not think of himself as a thief are matters specifically fitted with the disposition requested by the PD (a non-criminal charge).

Discussion

In actual decision making, descriptions of defendants partially constitute the activity of warranting or justifying proposed dispositions.[7] Straightforward as this may seem, it is a neglected feature of the research on the sentencing process. As we have already noted, most models

---

[7]Note that in both examples, the person doing argument was the public defender. This reflects an asymmetry in the negotiation process discussed by Feeley (1979c: 177) and Mather (1979: 70, 94). At least in misdemeanor plea bargainings, prosecutors are "relatively passive." They seem to assume that standard penalties are appropriate for most cases and leave it to defense attorneys to convince them otherwise in particular instances or to make an argument that a given case is not an instance of a "normal crime" (Sudnow, 1965). Thus, it is the public defenders in this study who produce most of the person-descriptions. District attorneys, however, do the same sort of justifying work with person-descriptions when the occasion calls for it. See Chapter 6, example (6).

hypothesize an abstract set of attributes, demographic factors, or pre-established categories as affecting the results of plea bargaining. Presumably, lawyers and judges determine the values of these categories in a checklist fashion; the researcher's task is to find out which categories are regularly used when outcomes (charges, sentences) are decided. The consequences of this presumption are two-fold. Legal practitioners are depicted as "cultural dopes" instead of active agents engaged in judgmental work as they produce decisions (Garfinkel, 1967; Giddens 1979). They also are portrayed as "computerized dopes," as data-processors rather than dramatists who utilize and display specific information about a defendant to enhance the position they advocate.

METHODOLOGICAL PROBLEMS

Where sentencing decisions are an outcome of a plea bargaining system like the one established in Garden City, negotiators may approach a defendant's prior record in a checklist fashion. As we have seen, however, offender-related factors are selectively and contextually employed in arguments for and against specific dispositions. This fact has important methodological implications.

The Problem of Selection

A negotiator may bring out any defendant attribute that would justify some disposition, provided that it is regarded as a relevant and reasonable matter to invoke. But, obviously, not all defendant attributes are thus utilized. Two issues are raised by the selectivity exhibited in the use of person-descriptions in negotiation.

First and most obvious is that while a few theoretically interesting factors have been considered in sentencing research (e.g., age, race, socioeconomic status, sex), other possibly important varibles are neglected. In Example 1, the woman shoplifting defendant was described in terms of her hometown and her status as a mother of children. Although research studies may include parental status as a factor related to sentencing decisions, they rarely examine the effects of a person's hometown. In Example 2, the defendant was categorized as a young guy, a student, and one who did not consider himself a thief. Although researchers regularly consider the effects of age and occupation, it is not the practice to incorporate a variable such as the attributed self-concept of a defendant. The methodological point is not that future studies should include these or other specific categories possibly evoked in negotiations. It is that an almost infinite variety of person-descriptions are potentially useable in any particular negotiated decision. Statistical models cannot capture these, let alone determine their effects on case disposition.

Second, researchers dedicated to statistical analysis may select and study variables that are substantively irrelevant. Clearly, some variables are of theoretical interest but are not pertinent to the dispositions made in specific cases. For instance, in neither Example 1 nor 2 is reference made to the race or socioeconomic status of the defendants, two variables of almost universal interest in multivariate analyses of sentencing decisions.[8]

Therefore, to the extent that disregarded factors may be systematically related to dispositions, and/or to the extent that researchers include variables not considered by practitioners, the models employed in sentencing research are misspecified; they either bias coefficients of significant variables or exaggerate estimator variances (Hanushek and Jackson, 1977: 79–96). It is not enough to respond that henceforth statistical studies will include the proper variables or specify the model more adequately. This solution is precluded because person-descriptions are context related.

The Problem of Context

In negotiations, defendant descriptions do not comprise the categorical, "demographic" identities examined in traditional models of decision-making. In Example 1, for instance, the defendant was described as someone who "had her house burned." She was also depicted as having been arraigned, gone home, and returned to the court. Those

---

[8]It could be argued, of course, that negotiators have other relevant variables "in their minds," even if they do not discuss them, and that their actions are determined by these hidden variables, not what gets exhibited in talk. This argument leads to recommendations for research on negotiatiors' backgrounds and attitudes, perhaps along the lines developed in studies of judicial decision making (Hogarth, 1971; Levin, 1972; Nagel, 1962a,b; Smith and Blumberg, 1967). Two problems arise, however. One is that plea bargaining decisions are mutually determined, thus putting constraints on the degree to which a prosecutor's or defense attorney's private knowledge or beliefs can affect sentencing outcomes. Second, and more important, the use of subjective attitudes and beliefs is a very complex matter. At a minimum, it cannot be presupposed that the subjective processes by which defendant attributes are related to desired outcomes are any less complicated than the public (conversational) display of that relationship. To the contrary, it must be presumed that the subjective reality of such attributes is similar to their intersubjective reality in terms of the selectivity and contextualness of their use.

descriptions combined with traditionally considered attributes (e.g., woman, parent) to provide the warrant for characterizing the defendant as someone who had suffered enough and as a "responsible" person deserving of a lesser penalty. In coding the case for statistical analysis, one would probably pick up the traditional categories but undoubtedly miss the specified details of biography.

It is not just that research schemas overlook and eliminate such details—a problem inherent in any generalizing practice. A deeper trouble is that neither categories nor details stand alone—they are contextually interrelated. In Example 2, one description of Cleaver, the defendant, was that he was a student "out there" (i.e., at the college where the alleged crime occurred). Should the defendant be coded as *employed* or *unemployed* in a dichotomous classification scheme? Perhaps another category, *student*, could be added, and the defendant squeezed into it by the coder. What was crucial, however, was not just that he was a student. The description of the defendant as a student at the college where the crime occurred was involved in constructing the very meaning of his act. It also was related to the report that the dean of the college wrote a letter on the defendant's behalf.

These items constituted Cleaver as a course-of-action type compatible with other character descriptions (young, did not conceive of himself as a thief) that, according to the PD, compelled a lesser charge. In other words, the description "student out there" fit with other aspects of the context of talk and action in which it was employed. Without consideration of contextual details, the meaning of the description is distorted. If the defendant were a student at some other college, for example, his act may have been viewed very differently.

The conclusion must be that temporal, locational, and biographical contexts of categorical descriptions define the relationship between person-descriptions and the dispositions advocated and ultimately administered. As Feeley (1979c: 163) has observed, the "facts" of a defendant's background "can cut two ways."[9] One of the clearest examples of this

---

[9]Feeley cites the example of a defendant with no prior record:

> While a prosecutor might respond with lenience in one case, in another he might decide to follow a harsher strategy, believing that a "firm hand" at an early point might be the most effective deterrent against future misconduct. (Feeley, 1979c: 163)

This raises the possibility that "prior record," in some instances, is used, like offender-related factors, in a selective and contextual way rather than, as argued earlier, a mere "starting point" for further negotiation.

is the research by Gibson (1978), who, in a study of 1,219 felony cases, first showed that race had no effect on sentencing. But he went on to note that, at the individual level, some judges did discriminate against blacks, while others accorded them more leniency than they did whites. Apparently, the antiblack and problack judges balanced each other, giving the impression, at the aggregate level, that race did not influence sentencing practices.

While Gibson (1978) relied on attitudinal data for his analysis, attitudes are just one of many contingent and contextual details determining the way that defendant attributes affect disposition decisions. The net contribution of those attributes is obscured when they are examined independent of the various details. Efforts to code interaction effects and to control for the influence of previously unexamined factors, such as evidentiary strength and criminal stereotypes, reflect a recognition of this problem. When researchers pay attention to such variables, however, they conceive of them as having an external, causal effect *on* decisions rather than as being internal to the negotiation process itself. This is a pivotal distinction that highlights why the introduction of new variables is inadequate to properly specifying a model and why the problem of unexplained variance remains paramount. From the former (external) standpoint, there is a necessity to establish relevant factors and contingencies prior to examining their effects.[10] From the latter (internal) standpoint, all one can predict is that any number of defendant attributes may be used in decision making, and these attributes will be defined as much by their relation to other factors regarding the defendant and his case as by any context-free reference they have. Whether defendant attributes are used at all, which ones are used, and how, cannot be known beforehand. In Feeley's (1979c: 123) terms, factors crucial to the handling of cases were "most visible *during* rather than before the research process."[11] Thus, the negotiation that produces a decision should

---

[10]Chiricos and Waldo (1975: 769), however, observe that "specifying the contingencies" surrounding the relationship of a given factor to sentencing may be a "relatively boundless task." (Their specific concern is with socioeconomic status.)

[11]This issue was also been confronted in an attempt to eliminate plea bargaining in El Paso, Texas (see Daudistel, 1980). There, criminal-justice personnel tried to set up a point system that would help them determine sentences by using certain objective criteria. The system did not work.

> Rather than following the point system literally, the felony court judges rated each case on its own merits. The judges recognized they had not specified all of the variables relevant to sentencing decisions. This is not a criticism of the point system. No matter

not be conceived as an event intervening between cause and effect but as a "formative or creative process in its own right" (Blumer, 1956: 687).

This returns us to the problem of misspecification. Consider the Myers and Hagan (1979) study, which maintains that evidence has been a neglected element in the study of legal decision making.

> Empirically, it means that models of prosecutorial decision making may be misspecified, falsely augmenting *or* suppressing the influence of social attributes (considered in all these studies) by failing to consider and control for the influence of evidence. (Myers and Hagan, 1979: 441; italics in original)

Indeed, race appears unimportant in prosecutorial discretion until the evidence variable is controlled (Myers and Hagan, 1979: 447; cf. Thomson and Zingraff, 1981: 872). But Myers and Hagan's reasoning can be generalized to argue, once more, that evidence is just one example of the contextual way in which offender attributes are related to dispositions; it is just one instance of how failing to consider the influence of various contextual factors may distort our understanding of how given social attributes actually influence case dispositions.

PATTERNS OF COMMONSENSE REASONING

We have shown that research on the relationship between defendant attributes and sentencing has insufficiently recognized the ways those attributes are selectively and contextually employed in negotiations that produce disposition decisions. To the extent that prior research has neglected these methodic features of the bargaining process and used misspecified models, the relative influence of offender-related as opposed to offense-related characteristics on outcomes has not been determined. One problem remains: Traditional studies use a concept of justice only partially applicable to the process in which case dispositions are determined.

The basic concern in assessing whether defendants receive equal

---

how extensive the judges made it, the point system could never be specific enough to be applied in a literal fashion and produce just and equal disposition of cases. (Daudistel, 1980: 71–72)

Practitioners simply do not use "objective" criteria in sentencing decisions in the way that "cultural dopes" might. Disregarding how negotiators do organize the decision process seems to be a tendency, then, not only in social science research but also in programs influenced by such research. See Giddens (1979: 71–72) on this point.

treatment before the law is whether justice is or is not being done. Deciding that, however, depends on how "justice" is defined. A "formally rational" concept of justice (Weber, 1946: 220; Nettler, 1979) dictates that defendants should be considered without regard for such background factors as age, sex, race, and class. This is the common presumption in sentencing research. On the other hand, a "substantive" concept of justice emphasizes treating people as individuals, thus tailoring decisions to fit with known features of each defendant's biography.

It is not sufficiently appreciated that the plea bargaining process is devoted to both kinds of justice. To better understand this fact, a gestalt model of decision making (cf. Nettler, 1979: 40) should guide studies of the sentencing process. This model does not superimpose on the sentencing process a checklist of factors derived from the formally rational concept of justice. Instead, a gestalt model allows researchers to study negotiators' commonsense knowledge. Displays of such knowledge show patterned uses of defendants' attributes and legal practitioners' concrete standards of justice. It is the latter standards that we must understand before attempting to abstractly assess how just the court is.

A Gestalt Model of Decision Making

The following segment of conversation concerns a case of drunken driving, where the defendant had two prior convictions for the same offense. The district attorney has suggested that the defendant should spend 75 days in jail on the present charge (example 43, Chapter 4).

(7) [Drunk Driving]

1. PD2: See here's his problem. The guy lives and works in South
2.   Beach, he's got a good job, well least he's working, he
3.   supports his family, wife and kids, and its his third drunk
4.   driving offense. And uh, if he does seventy five days straight
5.   time he's going to lose his job, his wife's going to be on-
6.   kids, you know, family's going to be on welfare

If we were to use this segment and the person-descriptions within it for itemizing the defendant's demographic characteristics or social attributes, we would obtain the following list. The defendant is (1) employed (lines 1–2), (2) married (lines 2–3), and (3) has children (line 3). (The defendant also is "acknowledged" to have three drunk driving offenses, lines 3–4.)[12] But such a listing fails to capture the way that such items were selected to do the work of soliciting a lesser penalty for the defendant and the way that each description is defined by its relationship to other descriptions and the argument for disposition. Employment is more than just a job; it is how the defendant supports his wife and children. Furthermore, it is not just that he is "married" and has "children," but that his family will be affected if he serves "seventy-five days" in jail. Thus, descriptive attributes are strategically employed, in a selective and contextual manner, to reject the DA's proposed disposition and, later, to argue for weekends in jail.

A gestalt model of decision making encompasses how each of the separate attributes is defined by its relation to other matters in the negotiation, including the other person-descriptions and the activity being accomplished (see Gurwitsch, 1964: 134; Wieder, 1974: 186–190; Maynard and Wilson, 1980: 293). In negotiating individual cases, lawyers do not use a stable set of attributes (e.g., the usual demographic variables) in a checklist fashion. Instead, they assemble a unique set of attributes appropriate to a particular case and argument.

Zimmerman and Pollner (1970) have defined the unitary constellation of such elements as an "occasioned corpus." Although such a corpus is not generalizable from case to case, methods for assembling it are. Thus, the relationship between offender-related factors and sentencing may not be systematic in the way traditional models presuppose, but it is clearly systematic with respect to those practices involved in assembling an occasioned corpus or gestalt of defendant characteristics to justify some particular decision. Recognizing this, we should focus on the structure of legal practitioners' commonsense knowledge, which displays cultural ideas about who defendants are, what they have done, and what justice is (Cicourel, 1964, 1968).[13]

The Structure of Commonsense Knowledge

Investigating commonsense knowledge does not mean inquiring into people's psychologies by assessing their private beliefs or attitudes

---

[12]See the discussion of "prior record" in the section on "offense-related" factors.

[13]For a similar recommendation regarding the study of mental health agencies and psychiatric decision making, see Peyrot (1982), who also emphasizes understanding the organizational context and frame of reference within which professionals operate.

(cf. Gibson, 1978; Thomson and Zingraff, 1981). The task is to describe orderly reasoning practices as they are displayed, and mutually adhered to, in conversation (Coulter, 1979). Examples investigated earlier can be reviewed to illustrate this point.

Recall the case of Frank Bryan, a defendant charged with disorderly conduct and resisting arrest. Of particular interest is how the PD characterized him as a "sweet" man, who got drunk, fought with his family at home, was resistive to the intrusiveness of the police, and who had a prior record simply because he was black and more likely to encounter the police. Also recall Maria Dominguez, who was charged with stealing clothes from a department store. Over the course of the negotiations, the PD developed a reasoning pattern consisting of three parts. First, person-descriptions were used to establish the nature of the defendant's real character. Second, drawing on the cultural assumption that a person's actions must be consistent with an underlying moral character, the theft was described as not "normal." Third, this abnormal behavior was explained by noting that she had ingested a number of drugs. In another case (this chapter, Example 1), a defense attorney attempted to depict his client as a person who had suffered enough by having her house burned, by having to support herself and her children, and by having to travel to and from the court. She was thus deserving of a lenient penalty, even though she had committed petty theft. Finally, consider the case (Example 2) in which the PD characterized his client as a young man, who committed the offense of taking a parking sticker as part of his everyday course of activities as a student, and who did not consider himself as a thief. He was, according to the PD, therefore worthy of a lesser charge than theft.

The reasoning patterns used in these and other cases reveal lay and professional theories about the kinds of persons who commit crimes, why they commit them, and how such persons should be appropriately treated (Cicourel, 1968). Research into gestalt reasoning patterns proceeds of necessity with a relatively small number of cases and does not provide an easy remedy for investigating the "equal-treatment" issue. But clear advantages flow from using the case approach rather than a large-scale statistical design.

First, given that there are differences in history and across regions in sentencing practices (Kleck, 1981; Thomson and Zingraff, 1981), the study of individual cases and reasoning patterns has the potential for revealing in particular times and places discrimination that is not evident in aggregate level data. Race was explicitly invoked in the Frank Bryan case, but as a mitigating factor. The argument was that blacks are victims of police harassment, and this explains Bryan's prior record. Race was similarly used as a mitigating factor in other cases. In different jurisdictions, however, examination of reasoning patterns might reveal that race or other attributes are employed in deprecatory and defamatory ways and thereby affect outcomes.

Second, whether or not typifications influence any given decision, they may still be objectionable if they perpetuate *stereo*typical conceptions of the group to which a defendant belongs. Characterizing the public Bryan as a "sweet man" with a "nice smile" and as a "happy go lucky, good natured guy" (Chapter 2) comes perilously close to the traditional conception of blacks as innately carefree and obsequious. A more blatant exercise in the use of a stereotype was the PD's comment on Lynn Heater, the "beautiful, absolutely beautiful" defendant who "looks like Kim Novak right down to the toes" (Chapter 6). Because of her appearance, said the attorney, the jury would not hear her testimony because they would be "too busy looking at her." Whether the descriptions of the defendant's attractive demeanor affected her courthouse fate might be only one important question. A more crucial issue might be the existence of discourse within which such an argument could even be mustered, *whatever* the effects of the argument. If bias in plea bargaining and other institutional forms of talk were a simple matter of typifications and outcomes, Lipsky (1980: 108) has observed, it "would be more pernicious but easier to root out." If bias operates in subtle and complex ways, if it resides in the way *discourse is organized*, as in the use of negative, stereotypical person-descriptions to justify a given disposition, its remedy is more difficult. Furthermore, its discovery requires an intense, case-by-case analysis.

Finally, a gestalt approach to commonsense reasoning produces knowledge of how judges and lawyers typify persons and offenses for purposes of determining guilt or innocence *in relation to other relevant matters in negotiation*. The examples just reviewed show that various demographic and other attributes of a defendant are salient in negotiations because they are used to construct the person as a good or bad character, thereby providing a way of seeing the alleged offense as a "real" crime or not (cf. Sudnow, 1965). But this is only part of the story. An erroneous implication of this feature of negotiations is that further research regarding the equal-treatment issue should assess the effect of

defendant attributes on the gross typifications employed by legal practitioners. With reference to homicide cases, for example, it has been said
that blacks and individuals with low occupational statuses are more
likely to be designated as "normal primitives" and to thereby receive
harsher penalties than whites or person with higher statuses (Swigert
and Farrell, 1977). Such an approach glosses over the selective and contextual use of defendant attributes in relation to such typifications and
thus suffers from the self-same methodological difficulties outlined earlier.

The main point is that defendant attributes and the typifications
generated from them are used in arguments, and these arguments are
sometimes successful, sometimes not. The PD's appeal to the DA regarding the college student in Example 2 fared well in obtaining a lesser
charge; the PD's statement about the woman with three children in
Example 1 did not influence the DA to relax the standard penalty for
shoplifting. In short, the study of commonsense reasoning reveals the
contingent nature of the negotiation process; typifications are part of a
negotiational environment with many components, including a co-participant's response to one's arguments.

Thus, deciding whether defendants receive "equal treatment" and
justice requires studying how defendant attributes are used in the typification process. It demands a deeper understanding of the full discourse environment in which a corpus of defendant attributes is assembled. A further neglected aspect of that environment is how concepts
of justice are employed by practitioners.

The Concept of Justice

Contrary to sentencing research that uses "formal" rationality as a
standard for measuring the performance of the criminal-justice process,
and much plea-bargaining research that overemphasizes the importance
of "substantive" rationality, both forms are important aspects of actual
decision making.

Maria Dominguez, the defendant charged with shoplifting items
from Davidson's department store (Appendix 3), was "old" (65 years),
a woman, and a member of a minority (Spanish-speaking). These attributes were not abstractly relevant during negotiations in the way that
discrimination would be measured in formally rational terms. Rather,
they were functional parts of an argument for dismissal, selectively and
contextually used to suggest that the defendant was a good person who

would not have stolen had she not been under the influence of drugs. It was precisely on the basis of these background factors, in other words, that a claim for the "fairness" of a particular outcome was made. The same can be said of Examples 1 and 2 in this chapter. To the extent that prosecutors, defense attorneys, and judges make and accept claims like these, we can speak of a courtroom subculture oriented to individual dispositions and substantive justice.

However, Examples 1 and 2 in this chapter also show the district attorney's concern for formal rationality by his emphasis on "standard" dispositions and uniform ways of treating individual cases. And while prosecutors may sometimes yield to a defense attorney's entreatments on behalf of a client (Example 2), there are many times when they refuse to grant "exceptions" because the defendant's circumstances are simply not unique enough (Example 1).[14]

Thus, tendencies toward both substantive and formal rationality appear in plea bargaining, with the defense attorney embodying a substantive orientation and the prosecutor representing a formal one, each party and each principle giving way to the other at various times and in various circumstances. When traditional approaches in sentencing research assess decision making in terms of "equality before the law," they deal with only one approach to the overall problem of justice (Morris, 1981) and methodologically impose that approach upon the decision process instead of coming to grips with the actual practices that compose the process (Horwitz and Wasserman, 1980; Needleman, 1981). The fact that substantive and formal rationality coexist in plea bargaining adds an additional twist to the question of how well the court is administering "equal treatment" and justice.

CONCLUSION

To date, researchers have taken the contradictory and inconclusive findings of statistical studies as having ambiguous or negative import for theory. With respect to the labeling perspective, Bernstein et. al. (1977a: 754) have argued that "the emphasis that interactionists place on the role of the deviants' social attributes in explaining variation in societal reaction seems very much overstated." Similarly, Chiricos and

---

[14]See the discussion of examples (9) and (10) in Chapter 3.

Waldo (1975: 769) have remarked, with reference to conflict and legal consensus (i.e., "traditional") theories:

> the capacity of conflict criminology to account for variations in criminal process must be seriously questioned at this point and it is certain that conflict does no better than traditional perspectives in criminology when it comes to explaining—in empirically sustained terms—the class and racial characteristics of convicted and sentenced criminals.

From an organizational perspective, Bernstein et al. (1977b) have argued that less attention be paid to offender characteristics and more to bureaucratic stages, constraints, and priorities.

But our case materials suggest that the lack of explanatory power in all these theoretical views stems from the following problems. First is the necessity to model defendants' attributes as elements selectively and contextually assembled in a specific gestalt for each case. Second is the requirement to not only study commonsense reasoning and the use of attributes to typify offenders and acts for deciding guilt or innocence, but to examine the typification process in relation to other aspects of the negotiational environment. Third, the complexity of the question of justice should be acknowledged and approached from an understanding of how discourse is organized within the criminal-justice process.

CHAPTER 8

A Discourse System for Negotiation

The concern for discovering whether equal treatment exists in sentencing decisions is only one aspect of a general preoccupation among social scientists with the issue of justice. For those who study plea bargaining, this preoccupation is expressed in two major and implicitly connected questions about the process. First, to what extent are nontrial means of case disposition fair and accurate in terms of separating the guilty and the innocent (e.g., see Newman, 1966: 4)? Second, in view of the fact that trials offer formal safeguards for ensuring fair and accurate decisions, why is plea bargaining so prevalent? That is, what accounts for the high proportion of guilty pleas?

Neither of these questions has prompted inquiry into the structure of bargaining as a discourse phenomenon, perhaps because this would seemingly direct attention away from the justice issue. Thus, we know very little about basic patterns of negotiation as constructed through participant's actual talk. It is true that examining talk does make it difficult to answer the first question about the fairness and accuracy of plea bargaining. In fact, studying the organization of discourse necessitates suspending *a priori* standards of accuracy and fairness.[1] If we want to discover the intrinsic order of negotiation, we must examine it on its own terms only. Nevertheless, a focus on discourse can shed light on the second question about plea bargaining: why so many criminal cases are resolved by guilty pleas rather than trials.

[1]This point was made in Chapter 1. I follow Lynch (1979: 304) in not claiming to present a "value free" approach, but one which is indifferent to the *particular evaluative stance* taken in most sociological and legal studies of plea bargaining. The organization of plea bargaining as an achieved, interactional orderliness is not capable of being apprehended without such a policy of indifference.

THEORIES OF PLEA BARGAINING

This should not imply that a discourse study can supply a theory
that completely explains the prevalence of negotiated decisions. However, current theories suggesting that high rates of guilty pleas are due
to court overload, a concern with substantive justice, or the exchange
made between prosecution and defense plainly fail to accommodate
some facts about plea bargaining, and even to recognize others. It may
be that each theory lacks an account of human agency (Giddens, 1979)
to provide for how legal practitioners settle cases as an everyday practice
in direct interaction. Analyzing discourse can make sense of some of
the known facts about plea bargaining. It also reveals a diversity to
outcomes that has not previously been appreciated. Finally, investigation of plea bargaining discourse shows a structure to negotiation, consisting of a set of practices that systematically induce nontrial decisions.
The agency of criminal-justice personnel, in terms of their practical and
instrumental activities, is thereby reintroduced as a phenomenon fundamental to understanding the bargaining process.

Overloaded Courts

It is commonly believed that plea bargaining is an administrative
response to overcrowded urban courts. In Blumberg's (1967: 21) terms,
for example, plea negotiation "consists of secret bargaining sessions,
employing subtle, bureaucratically ordained modes of coercion and influence to dispose of large case loads in an efficacious and rational manner." More recently, Littrell (1979) has also stressed the importance of
"pressures of administration" and the "bureaucratic imperative of efficient dispositions" in accounting for the large number of guilty pleas.
In brief, it is frequently said that without plea bargaining courts would
not run smoothly and efficiently.

However, as previously discussed, much empirical evidence dis-
credits this notion. First, confidence in the belief that plea bargaining
can be explained by overcrowded court dockets is undermined by research showing the practice to be an intrinsic part of both high-volume
and low-volume courts in contemporary America (Feeley, 1979c: Chapter
8; Buckle and Buckle, 1977: 63; Miller et al., 1978: 18). Second, investigations into the history of plea bargaining (e.g., Alschuler, 1979; Friedman, 1979; Heumann, 1978) have shown that guilty pleas became an

important mode of case disposition in the late nineteenth and early twentieth century in this country, so arranging such pleas appears not to be a recent response to higher crime rates and increased caseloads. Plea bargaining has *accommodated* pressures put on the courts by increased caseloads (Alschuler, 1979: 236) and thus contributed to increased *rates* of guilty pleas (Friedman, 1979). These increased rates must also be seen, however, in relation to a number of fortuitous historical events, including the availability of the guilty plea, the resistance to the use of bench trials, the rise of public prosecution as a profession (Langbein, 1979), the creation of modern police departments and the consequent decline of court authority (Haller, 1979), the emergence of a "new penology" emphasizing the individualization of punishment (Mather, 1979: 282; Rosett and Cressey, 1976: 53–54), and the growth of criminal law (Mather, 1979; Alschuler, 1979).

Plea Bargaining as Substantive Justice

Plea bargaining, then, is not caused by increased workloads in the courts. In recent years, researchers have devised other explanations of the phenomenon. One theory is that plea bargaining represents the attempt to individualize justice, a matter Newman (1966: Chapters 8–9) explores at length in his American Bar Foundation study. The argument is that abstract and general laws must somehow be made to fit specific acts, persons, and circumstances. Grave injustices are done when prescribed penalties are uniformly administered to similarly situated persons; real justice involves adapting penalties to individual characteristics of the offender and the offense. Over a decade ago, the Supreme Court (Brady v. United States, 397 U.S. 742,751) articulated this point by noting that negotiations between prosecution and defense mediate the law and the actualities of the world. The drive toward individualized justice is the critical explanatory principle used in recent studies of plea bargaining by Feeley (1979c: 272–274), Rosett and Cressey (1976: 37–40), and Utz (1978: 141–142).

While this explanation accounts for some of the negotiated cases, it fails to make sense of others. A number of researchers, following Schelling (1963), make a distinction between "explicit" and "implicit" plea bargaining. In explicit bargaining, adversarial stances are taken on the "facts" of the case and the appropriate disposition, and a compromise is reached. Implicit bargaining refers to established court practices

for providing leniency without haggling between lawyers (e.g., see Newman, 1966: 60–61; Miller et al., 1978: 6–7; Buckle and Buckle, 1977: 129;
Friedman, 1979: 253–358; Mather, 1979: 66–68).[2] Using this distinction,
Friedman (1979) finds that, between 1950 and 1970, 36 percent of guilty
pleas in Alameda County, California, were due to implicit bargaining
and 40 percent were due to explicit bargaining.

In summary, while the notion that plea bargaining is a way of
individualizing justice may be applicable to cases that are explictly bargained, it is inappropriate to the explanation of why a nearly equal
percentage of guilty pleas are obtained without extensive consideration
of the particular circumstances of the offender and the offense. Implicit
plea bargaining seems to reflect a desire of court personnel to mitigate
the harsh penalties provided in the law (Newman, 1966: 112; Rosett and
Cressey, 1976: 158; Utz, 1978: 139). But when this is done as a routine
matter, the negotiation process more closely resembles procedural or
rational justice where decisions are made "without regard for persons"
(Weber, 1946: 215). Put differently, instead of imposing legislatively man-
dated penalties, court personnel in particular jurisdictions establish a
"going rate" for "normal crimes" (Feeley, 1979c: 67–68; Mather, 1979:
66; Neubauer, 1974: 238; Sudnow, 1965), and this rate is utilized as a
matter of course. Thus, to repeat a point demonstrated in Chapter 7, it
seems that routine, rational justice *and* substantive decision-making processes coexist within the scope of courtroom discretion.[3]

Plea Bargaining as Exchange

Another explanation for the high rate of guilty pleas posits a system
of exchange from which both prosecution and defense obtain benefits.
On the one hand, prosecuting and defense attorneys, convinced that 90
percent of defendants are factually guilty (Heumann, 1978: 156), regard

---

[2]The difference between explicit and implicit bargaining is similar to that between "adversary" and "routine" justice, discussed in Chapter 5.

[3]We can here take a cue from Weber (1946: 217), who recognized that "nonbureaucratic
forms of domination display a peculiar coexistence: on the one hand, there is sphere of
strict traditionalism, and, on the other, a sphere of free arbitrariness and lordly grace."
He concluded that "combinations and transitional forms between these two principles
are very frequent" (Weber, 1946: 217). With respect to bureaucratic administration, however, Weber (1946: 20) overemphasized the degree to which rational and substantive
justice "collide" with each other instead of similarly existing in what he called "combinations" and "transitional forms."

plea bargaining as the most effective way of reducing their caseloads while at the same time doing justice. The orientation they adopt has been described as "the attitudes of bureaucracy, emphasizing the maximization of production and the minimization of work" (Alschuler, 1979: 236) and is said to reflect the personal and professional "interests" of court personnel (Buckle and Buckle, 1977: 150–154; Nardulli, 1978: 53; Heumann, 1978: 156). Defendants, on the other hand, desire to minimize the time the adjudication process takes (Feeley, 1979c), to "return to the streets" as fast as possible (Buckle and Buckle, 1977: 153), and to obtain some perceived sentencing concessions. It is easy to conclude, then, "that disputes settled through negotiation and/or pleas of guilty provide mutual benefits for *all* involved parties" (Feeley, 1979c: 272, original emphasis).

One trouble with using the exchange perspective to explain plea bargaining is that it ultimately converges with the very definition of the practice, which, as we noted in Chapter 4, is regularly referred to as a courtroom transaction in which the prosecution and defense trade benefits. When defendants plead guilty, they receive some dispositional "consideration," in the form of reduced charges or sentences, from the state. The latter, in turn, gets the convictions that it desires (Alschuler, 1968: 50; Baldwin and McConville, 1977: 23; Bottoms and McClean, 1976: 123; Feeley, 1979c: 185; Grosman, 1969: Chapter 7; Klein, 1976: Chapter 1; Miller et al., 1978: xii). The problem arises when this visible exchange process is used to explain itself. From the exchange process, researchers infer a "system of rewards and sanctions" whereby participants "accomplish personal and professional objectives in the court" (Buckle and Buckle, 1977: 159). However, it is clearly circular to then explain the willingness to settle cases informally and the high number of such cases on the basis of these rewards and sanctions.

Exchange perspectives on the plea bargaining process also suffer from a close kinship with what Ekeh (1974: 9–19) has characterized as the "individualistic orientations" in American versions of social-exchange theory (Homans, 1958, 1961; Blau, 1964), that is, the tendency to reduce social activity to the behavior and expectations of individuals while neglecting processes structured at the level of the collectivity. Plea bargaining experts, for example, hint at a mechanical and stylized process into which participants are socialized (Alschuler, 1975; Eisenstein and Jacob, 1977; Heumann, 1978). This suggests a subculturally maintained methodicity to negotiation that has not received serious attention.

Put differently, exchange theory is overrationalistic and therefore un-
derstates the importance of routine in everyday interaction (Collins,
1981).[4] Applied to plea bargaining, the perspective emphasizes how
participants cognitively weigh benefits and costs with respect to guilty
pleas and trials.[5] As a result, we have little understanding of plea bargaining as a collective *way of life* within the court, a mode of discourse
consisting of socially organized practices. While accommodating personal and professional interest, the discourse and its "outcomes" can
neither be reduced to those interests nor to participants' rational analyses
of costs and benefits. More importantly, the organization of the discourse
produces a disproportion of informally arranged dispositions.

Summary

Common to the three perspectives on plea bargaining is lack of
attention to human agency. That is, the theories ignore the question of
how negotiators actively produce decisions in criminal cases by depicting
legal practitioners as reacting to pressures exerted on the court by exogenous factors (large caseloads, general laws, harsh penalties) or as
acting in accord with cognitive assessments, rather than as enacting
practices that make plea bargaining a coherent and locally organized
behavioral phenomenon. Studying such practices, and thereby incor-
porating an account of human agency, we can link the large number of
nontrial dispositions to a discourse *system* through which negotiators
decide what must be done in particular cases.

The theoretical review calls attention to some facts that our analysis
must fit. First, while caseload pressure does not explain the high proportion of guilty pleas, plea bargaining lends itself to handling high
caseloads when they arise. Second, insofar as individual characteristics
and circumstances are considered as some cases are "explicitly" bar-

---

[4]On the general importance of routine in "street-level bureaucracies," see Lipsky (1980:
81–86).
[5]Objections to the rationality inherent in exchange theory are summarized by Heath (1976:
75), who also defeats at least the more simplistic criticisms (Heath, 1976: 75–89). My
objection, note, is not that the exchange perspective rests on a rationalistic foundation.
In many ways, the decision to plea bargain a given case is a rational choice for the involved
parties. The problem is in *overrationalizing* the process in a cognitive sense when it can
be investigated as a system of routines. These, then, are not nonrational nor irrational,
but rational in a mundane, practical sense.

gained, and a standard penalty for "normal crimes" is utilized in cases where "implicit" bargaining occurs, both substantive *and* rational justice are accomplished through plea bargaining. Finally, while plea bargaining is not explained by exchange theory, that perspective does describe what happens at an abstract level. Now we need to investigate specific mechanisms by which prosecution and defense reciprocation is made to happen in actual interaction.

DECISION-MAKING PATTERNS IN PLEA BARGAINING

When Garden City defense attorneys and prosecutors meet at pretrial conferences, a list of cases has been scheduled for official action. The meetings occur in a designated courtroom, and a judge is periodically present to help settle intractable cases, ratify negotiated decisions, and hear pleas. For each case, defense and prosecution must decide on some disposition (which may be anything from a dismissal to a jail sentence), must agree to a trial date, or must continue the case for reconsideration at a later time. These are the only options for a given case at the settlement conference, which is to say that "no action" on a case is precluded. The instrumental task faced by the lawyers in each case, then, is to assign or obtain one of these outcomes. Whichever is the result, an entry will be made on the defendant's file and on a summary sheet for the pretrial conference.

The question is, how are these decisions made? We have seen that in general participants employ a basic unit termed a "bargaining sequence." Each such sequence consists of two turns: one in which a party makes a position visible by means of a *report* of a preference or by means of a *proposal*, and a second in which the other party *replies* by exhibiting alignment or nonalignment with the presented position. A decision is achieved for a case when each of the parties aligns with the same position, whether that be for dismissal, guilty plea, trial, or continuance.

This achievement is not as simple as it seems. It can be realized through three different paths or patterns. Each pattern involves (A) the presentation of an attempt or attempts to resolve how the case should be handled. Every attempt can be considered an "opportunity" for prosecution and defense to arrive at a mutually acceptable disposition. When any opportunity is not taken, the system allows (B) the option of delaying determination of a disposition by continuing the case or setting it for trial. Both (A) and (B) are accomplished through one or more bargaining sequences being systematically employed within single episodes of negotiation on a particular case (see Figure 2 on page 190).

The three kinds of opportunities for determining a disposition embody logical possibilities, given the two parties and the "sides" they represent: (1) one party exhibits a position and the second aligns with it; (2) both parties exhibit positions and one relinquishes an initial stance to align with the other; and (3) the parties compromise.[6] But two major points need to be stressed here. First, knowing that there are three logical possibilities does not tell us *if* they will be realized, *how* they are realized, nor how cases will be distributed among them. We will see that, empirically, they all do occur. Each kind of opportunity is presented in order and may or may not be successful depending on what else happens in the talk regarding any given case. Furthermore, a distinctive patterning appears in the way cases are distributed among the possibilities. A second point is that, in the bargaining literature, each of the three possibilities is usually considered as a separate bargaining "game." Schelling argues that Possibility 1 involves "implicit" bargaining, which is akin to what Stevens (1963: 18) calls a "take it or leave it" or an "unnatural purposive game." Possibility 2 is discussed as a "move-symmetrical" bargaining game (Schelling, 1963: 268–270). And 3 is treated as the real negotiation game (Stevens, 1963: 27–37); or, in the experimental literature, the sequential presentation of demands and subsequent concessions is viewed as a *necessary* feature of negotiation (Rubin and Brown, 1975: 14).[7] The evidence here is that the three possibilities are not sep-

---

[6]The three opportunities here are not to be confused with what Ikle (1964) refers to as the "continual three-fold choice" that faces a negotiator:

1. to accept agreement at the terms he expects the opponent would settle for (the "available" terms),
2. to discontinue negotiations without agreement and with no intention of resuming them, and
3. to try to improve the "available" terms through further bargaining. (Ikle, 1964: 59–60)

Clearly, these choices are different from the opportunities I discuss, but a more important point is that Ikle's (1964) unit of analysis is the individual and his perspective is psychological, in that the three choices exist for each party and one is taken by the party according to the calculation of probable gains and losses associated with each choice. In contrast, the approach here is empirical and sociological. The three opportunities are derived from observable patterns in actual discourse as it is interactively constructed.

[7]Pruitt (1981) discusses a "strategic choice model" of negotiation containing three elements roughly related to the patterns I discuss: (1) conceding unilaterally, (2) standing firm and

arate games, and that the last one is not an invariant happening in bargaining. Rather, all three patterns occur within a single discourse system for negotiation. That is, they are outcomes contingently produced in an organized fashion as negotiation proceeds in each case.

While it has been recognized that continuances and trial dates are delay options often used strategically to win concessions on charges or sentences (Feeley, 1979c: 175; Mather, 1974: 299–211; Rosett and Cressey, 1976: 21), the related point that these outcomes do not, then, represent the "failure" of negotiation (Utz, 1978: 35) has been given insufficient attention. Delays of this sort should be viewed in relation to the methodic ways in which they are decided upon. As sequential phenomena, proposals for continuances and trials occur after opportunities for immediate disposition have been presented, and for the purpose of achieving specific bargaining ends. This fact has important implications to be spelled out later.

The negotiations in each of our 52 cases fit one of the three patterns, but not all of the cases can be analyzed and discussed. (They are summarized in Table 1.) A sample of the 52 cases—negotiations that exemplify each pattern—will be considered. Additionally, because some negotiations include the judge, segments illustrating his participation as a type of "third-party" intervention will be investigated. Space limitations dictate that the examples be selected partly on the basis of brevity. Nevertheless, one case is extensively analyzed in order to make clear how the relation of the decision-making patterns to one another constitutes a *system* of negotiation.

Pattern 1A. Unilateral Opportunity: One Party Takes up a Position with Which the Other Aligns

The most straightforward way in which a decision is made is for an "offer" to be put forward by one party and accepted by the other. In example (1), the defendant (Delaney) was charged with malicious mischief ("mal mish") because, according to the police report, he "tore up a bar" after being refused more drinks than he already had.

---

acting competitively, and (3) collaborating or using coordinative behavior. Although Pruitt suggests these strategies can be combined and specifically discusses competiveness and coordination as sequential stages of negotiation (Pruitt, 1981: 131–135), the emphasis is on the separateness of the strategies, because the choice of one lessens the possibility of selecting another (Pruitt, 1981: 15–16).

Table 1. Cases Settled by Each Decision-Making Pattern

1A.	Unilateral opportunity: One party takes up a position with which the other aligns		15
	Proposal by PD	9	
	Proposal by DA	6	
1B.	Delay post–unilateral opportunity		12
	Continuances	6	
	Trials	6	
2A.	Bilateral opportunity: Each party advances a position; one relinquishes and aligns with the other's		13
	Position advanced first	6	
	Position advanced second	7	
2B.	Delay post–bilateral opportunity		8
	Continuances	4	
	Trials	4	
3A.	Compromise		3
3B.	Delay post–compromise opportunity (continuance)		1
	Total		52

(1) [Malicious mischief]

1. PD2: Okay uh is there an offer in Delaney
2. DA3: Yeah, plea to mal mish and uh, uhm modest fine and uh
3.   restitution
4. PD2: Okay, fifty dollars
5. DA3: Yes

Here, DA3 indicates the charge to which the defendant should plead guilty, and suggests, in general terms, the sentence. PD2 aligns with this position while proposing the amount of the fine (line 4). DA3 agrees to that (line 5), and the bargain is consummated.

When a recipient accepts a counterpart's initial offer, it may reflect a "concerting of expectations" achieved implicitly before the offer is made (Schelling, 1963). The concerting of expectations is no mystical process, as Schelling (1963: 93) argues. It lies in the empirically demonstrated ability of participants to read situations in a like manner and infer what resolution will be mutually acceptable. In plea bargaining, such a process is surely aided by participants' participation in the court-room subculture.[8]

When the defense attorney and prosecutor do not achieve conver-gence on their own, the judge may participate in the discussion and display an attitude toward a proposal just after it has been made. This point was made in Chapter 4, with reference to the following segment:

(2) [Speed contest]

```
1.   J1:   Next is Jerry Romney, which is a two three one oh nine bee
2.   PD2:  Ya we haven't discussed that yet but if you'll take a speeding
3.         and a thirty five dollars
4.                              (0.6)
5.   J1:   Oh I'm sure the people'll do that, right
6.                              (0.4)
7.   J1:   Looks like ⌊it's just⌋ breaking traction
8.   DA3:              ⌊Sure  ⌋
9.   DA3:  Sure
```

We might speculate about why the judge's intervention should lead the prosecutor to accept a proposal he might otherwise hesitate to accept. For example, the prosecutor might be sensitive to the judge's power or status, the judge might have validated a position the DA was already inclined to accept, or DA3, as a member of the courtroom workgroup (Eisenstein and Jacob, 1977), may have been unwilling to disrupt rela-tions for the modest return of a higher sentence in a minor case. What-ever the reasons for the prosecutor's alignment with the PD's proposal, the judge's participation did not necessitate a compromise or some other form of resolution. Rather it enabled the initially stated position of the PD to be accepted. Thus, third-party intervention may facilitate a par-ticular outcome in negotiation. It need not change the structure of align-ments through which the outcome is achieved. In this case, opportunity for agreement on disposition was presented unilaterally; the basic de-cision-making pattern consisted of one party making an offer and the other agreeing to it.

[8]See the discussion of "going rates" for normal crimes in the section on Plea Bargaining as Substantive Justice above. For a review of experimental literature on how the concerting of expectations is related to the emergence of "mutually prominent alternatives," see Pruitt (1981: 57–70).

Pattern 1B. Delay Post–Unilateral Opportunity

If some factor prevents the recipient of an offer from aligning with it, then a continuance or trial may be suggested.

Continuances. Posed after one party has taken a position, continuances occur because the defense or prosecution needs additional time to obtain information relevant to make a reply to the other's offer. For example, in a drunk driving case the DA suggested reducing the charge to reckless driving, but with a regular drunk-driving penalty. Because an initial test of the defendant's blood alcohol level was ambiguous, the PD requested time to have the blood alcohol level remeasured, a regular procedure in some drunk driving cases.

(3)

DA2:   Ya wanna continue it for two uh two weeks to re-do the blood?
PD2:   Sure

Here, the DA grants PD2's request by formally suggesting a continuance. After the blood test, presumably PD2 would be in a better position to decide whether the offer of reckless driving should be accepted or whether a further reduction or even dismissal of the case should be pursued. Indeed, when the blood was retested, the alcohol level was above the statutory limit, and PD2 accepted the DA's original offer. The defendant pleaded guilty to reckless driving and received the regular drunk-driving sentence.

In the last example, it was the PD who, at least implicitly, asked for a continuance. In the next case, the DA proposed a continuance after the PD, arguing that his client had not really committed an offense, suggested dismissing the case.

(4) [Misdemeanor exhibition of speed] (judge's chambers)

DA1:   What I recommend is a continuance so I can get a, you know,
       narration from the officer as to what happened.

Subsequent statements from the officer upheld the charge, and the defendant pleaded guilty.

Not all proposals for continuance exhibit a concern with getting necessary "facts" that would bear on a party's negotiational stance. We will see that continuances may be requested for other reasons, such as the sheer benefit of delay. Such postponements are not proposed after a unilateral opportunity for resolution has been presented, but at a later point in the negotiations.

Trials. Trial proposals occurring after an initially suggested disposition indicate intransigence of a particular kind. On the one hand, the district attorney may propose a guilty plea and sentence in the face of a claim of innocence by the defense. On the other hand, the defense attorney may suggest dismissing a case that the DA thinks is worth pursuing. Either way, the guilt of the defendant is a salient issue and the case is often characterized as a "dismiss or go." In the following example, discussion begins with the PD telling a version of the incident:

(5a) [Petty theft]

J1:   Let me come back to Kathy Nelson
PD3: Um this is a very unusual petty theft your honor. Uh Nelson's employed in Sands, and there's been some theft of employee purses and-
J1:   She herself is an employee?
PD3: She's employed and uh there's been some theft of employee purses, employee money from a little room that they have in the department that she works in. And uh she goes back into the room to make some phone calls and she sees a strange purse, and she's lookin' in it, and the store detective comes in and uh she gets busted. And she says no, I wasn't going through that purse to steal, I had no intention of stealing anything. I didn't recognize the purse. I knew there'd been the thefts, I lost some money, and uh I wasn't trying to steal anything. Um the store detective says she was trying to hide some money. She says that's not true.

After further discussion, the judge solicits an offer from the DA.

(5b)

J1:   Well what can you do on it, maybe the DA isn't as tough as the judges'd be on this one . . .
DA1: Well I'd want her on probation for a good suspended time and probably uh in the neighborhood of fifteen days in jail

Subsequently, the DA proposed a more specific amount of time suspended (60 days), while still holding to the 15 day jail sentence. In the next segment, the judge assesses the proposal (line 4) and the PD reports his client's "rigid" position (lines 5–7).

(5c)

1. J1: If she's the hysterical type she's not gonna wanna go to
2.   jail at all, on the other hand
3. PD3: Yeah
4. J1: For what this is, uh fifteen days ain't bad
5. PD3: Well in one sense it's reasonable except that she doesn't
6.   budge. She is emPHAtic that she was NOT going through those
7.   purses to steal anything. She is just absolutely rigid
8. J1: Well so it's gotta go, that's it arright
9. PD3: That's what I think

After the PD's report of his defendant's position, the judge proposes a trial (line 8), to which both PD3 and DA1 agree (DA1's assent is nonverbal). In this case, the lawyers were able to settle at a later date, and the trial did not actually take place.

In summary, (4), (5), and (6) ended with delay of the disposition decision, by continuance, or by setting the case for trial. Both these options, however, were exercised after concrete proposals for presently settling the case had been made by one party and disavowed by the other.

Pattern 2A. Bilateral Opportunity: Each Party Advances a Position; One Relinquishes and Aligns with the Other's

A negotiator may reject a proposal but continue discussion by suggesting an alternative disposition. Then, the party who first made an offer may agree to the counter proposal. Alternately, the initial offerer may stand firm while the person making the counter offer eventually backs down. The following case, discussed briefly in Chapter 4, illustrates the situation where the counter offer is accepted. The PD starts negotiations by telling what happened.

(6a) [Drunk driving]

PD3: Um his girlfriend was in the car up to about five or ten minutes
      before the detention. He'd had something to drink seven, seven
      thirty at night, he had three beers, and uh he had a little whiskey
      earlier in the day, went to sleep, woke up to take her to work,
      drops her off at work. He's got his kid with 'em and he's driving
      home. And um, he says I was not doing anything wrong, said I
      didn't feel the alcohol, I wasn't under the influence. And she
      says well I was in the car with him, he was driving perfectly,

> and I wouldn't have went with him, I would've taken the car myself
> if I thought he couldn't drive

After this, the DA provides his own characterization of the offense (lines 1–6 below), plus a display of position regarding how the case should be handled (lines 6–7).

(6b)

1. DA2:   What we've got here is a- for driving is, we got a couple
2.   of unsafe lane changes. He's weaving at least three times
3.   within a single lane, he's outside of the lane, he's on
4.   ((highway)) one fifteen, least a couple times. He's speeding
5.   along you know at sixty. He really doesn't do very well on the
6.   field sobriety. It's a triable drunk driving. We're
7.   obviously offering a reckless

Thus, the state's offer is for a charge (reckless driving) downgraded from the original drunk driving offense.[9] However, in subsequent talk, the PD suggests an even lesser charge. "Movers," in the following segment (line 1), refer to traffic violations that are infractions rather than misdemeanor crimes like drunk or reckless driving.

(6c)

1. PD3:   Well what about some movers
2. DA2:   It's really a question of whether're not- We'd have a
3.   pretty good shot at convicting him of driving under the
4.   influence

When the DA did not accede (lines 2–3) to his suggestion, PD2 went on to discuss conflicts in the stories told by arresting officers, the dis-

---

[9]Note here that since "reckless driving" is a lesser charge than "drunk driving," the DA's offer might be considered as a concession. However, once again it should be pointed out that there are "going rates" for such offenses as drunk driving and it was standard practice in the jurisdiction studied to reduce drunk driving to reckless driving on first offenses where the blood alcohol level was borderline. Persons were legally considered to be driving under the influence of alcohol if their blood showed an alcohol content of one-tenth of one percent. Because the defendant's in this case was just at that level, the offer of reckless reflects a well-known negotiational starting point for typically borderline cases. However, there still may be the *appearance* of a concession being made by the state when the defendant is presented with the offer of reckless driving. See the discussion in Alschuler (1975: 1194) and Neubauer (1974: 238–244).

putable blood alcohol level of the defendant, and other items that he thought weakened the state's case.

After this, the judge indicates the "borderline" status of the case (line 1, below), assesses the DA's offer as "good" (line 4), and finally displays a favorable attitude toward the PD's proposal for moving violations (lines 6–7).

(6d)

1. J2: Yeah it's one of those that's on the borderline. If the guy
2.   says well I don't want to take the sure thing, I wanna take the
3.   chance, that's pretty much up to him. I'd like to, you know,
4.   dispose of the case, I think it's a good offer, but on the
5.   other hand um the jury might choose to believe that his
6.   driving ability was not impaired . . . it could be best to give it
7.   to him, and that's just give him you know, the speeding and
8.   the illegal lane change uh

Following this DA2 changes his position:

(6e)

DA2: I've reconsidered my position and I'll offer a 22348a and a 22107
      and would recommend a hundred and twenty five dollar fine.

The 22348a charge is speeding, and the 22107 is an unsafe lane change, the "movers" specifically suggested by the judge. This was clearly an alignment with the course of action *originally* proposed by the public defender as an alternative to the DA's initial preference for reckless driving. The DA therefore relinquished that position although he proposed the penalty (6e) to which the PD agreed. We also saw this alternation in who produces bargaining openers in example (1). It appears that having two kinds of currency in plea negotiations (i.e., charge and sentence) allows a general practice whereby the party who relinquishes on one is allowed to decide the other.[10] This preserves an appearance of autonomous participation for both parties.

---

[10]This is not to lose sight of the fact that the core issue in plea bargaining is the question of punishment (Rosett and Cressey, 1976: 80–81). Negotiations on both charge and sentence are ultimately related to that issue. By giving in on the charge, in example (6), the DA was considerably restricted in the parameters of the sentence he could propose.

It is not always an initially exhibited position that is yielded in favor of a second proposal. In some cases, a second position is given up, as the following shows.

(7a) [Drunk Driving]

1. DA2: We haven't talked about McCall
2. PD2: No, we haven't, is there an offer in the case
3. DA2: Yeah a reckless with a drunk driving dispo

The DA's proposal (line 3) is to have the defendant plead guilty to a reduced charge, but with the penalty regularly assigned to drunk-driving cases. This was a $315 fine, plus a 15-day jail sentence that would be suspended for two years of probation (if the defendant violates probation, he must serve the 15 days). The PD, however, makes a counter offer.

(7b)

1. PD2: I'll offer you a reckless with a straight fine . . .
2. DA2: I think he oughta be on probation
3. PD2: Ah hah well then ya gotta convict him
4. DA2: Okay
5. PD2: I mean I'll ask him if he wants the reckless but I'll have to tell
6. him what I think of it

By "straight fine" (line 1), PD2 indicates that he does not want the suspended sentence and probation. DA2 rejects that suggestion (line 2), which occasions PD2's challenging the DA to a trial (line 3). When DA2 takes up the challenge (line 4), PD2 performs a "backdown," indicating that he would reluctantly pass the DA's offer to his client.[11] Subsequently, the defendant accepted the offer, pleaded guilty to reckless driving, and received the full sentence originally proposed by the DA. Again, a decision was reached on disposition after one party gave up a position to align with the other's. In this case, the one producing a

---

[11]In Chapter 3, we discussed the PD's capacity for framing a client's position in such a way as to exhibit a relatively independent assessment of it while talking to bargaining co-participants. Here, a related capacity of the PD appears to be framing a DA's offer, while talking to the defendant, so as to make defense "advocacy" a visible part of the interaction.

second offer (the PD) relinquished it in favor of the first proposal (made by the DA).

Note the following facts about the bilateral pattern. First, from the existence of unilateral opportunities, we know that it is not an essential feature of plea negotiation that contrasting positions be taken up before a decision is reached. Second, the order of presentation does not determine which position will "win." At times, the first party making an offer will relinquish and agree to a suggested alternative. At other times, the party proposing the alternative will yield and assent to the action initially presented.

Thus, bilateral opportunities are neither required nor do they reflect any preestablished decision-making procedure. Whether a decision will fall into the pattern depends upon methodical developments achieved within the course of negotiations. Given one party's displayed position, a second party may make an alternative proposal that helps articulate arguments regarding weaknesses in the other's case (segment 6c), induces a third party (the judge) to display a view of the case (segment 6d), tests the firmness of an opponent's position, being a posture from which oneself is willing to retreat (example 7), or accomplishes other strategic ends. Then, depending on the outcome of these moves, one party may yield and align with the opponent's position.

Pattern 2B. Delay Post–Bilateral Opportunity

As when only one party has made a concrete offer that the other consistently refuses, both parties may propose dispositions with neither willing to align with the other's. Again, there is the option of delaying the determination of disposition by agreeing to a continuance or trial. The use of this option after opposite sides have each proposed a disposition (pattern 2A) is much different from its invocation after only one position (pattern 1A) has been presented.

Continuances. Suggestions for continuance at the earlier stage of negotiation—following a unilateral opportunity—are made to appear necessary for obtaining information relevant to providing a reply. Later in negotiations—following a bilateral opportunity—continuances are employed as pure bargaining tactics that might weaken an opponent's resolve. Consider the following, which is from a case in which the defendant allegedly took a package of "Mini-wash" soap from a store. (A portion of this segment was analyzed as example 6 in Chapter 6):

(8a) [Petty theft]

1.	DA3:	What ya wanna do
2.	PD4:	Why don't you let me plead her for a fine . . .
3.	DA3:	Why
4.	PD4:	Well she has no previous record, it's a very small item, uh
5.		she says she was going to pay, she says when they stopped her,
6.		she offered to pay, uh
7.	DA3:	I have difficulty making this other than the standard
8.		disposition
9.	PD4:	For a dollar 'n some odd cents worth of Mini-Wash?
10.	DA3:	Yeah, I mean I can buy the logic, within the limits of the, you
11.		know, the items of necessity by somebody very poor, but a
12.	PD4:	Yeah
13.	DA3:	cosmetic item by a young um lady who's just uh in too much of
14.		a hurry to go pay for it, uh I can't buy that

Clearly, the PD and DA have different views of the case, and these match contrasting positions regarding disposition. While PD4 is willing to have the defendant plead guilty to the petty theft charge, he proposes that the penalty be a fine (line 2). The DA, however, wants the "standard disposition" (lines 7–8), 24 hours in jail.

Following this segment, the PD repeated that the defendant planned to come back and pay for the soap and noted that this would have been aided by her living "very close to the store." Still, the DA asserted, "I can't see making the exception here." Then:

(8b)

1.	PD4:	Well, on this particular case, let's continue it for a couple
2.		of weeks, let me talk to her and see what she says about it
3.	DA3:	Uhhhhh
4.	PD4:	Uhm I don't mind twenty four hours. Thing is there's
5.		something to the case

PD4's proposal for a continuance is dealt with by DA3's minimal utterance (line 3). Although PD4 then seems to align with the DA's position (line 4), he immediately adds an utterance that prefaces further arguments for his own position. First, PD4 stated that "in the past, we've had exceptions." To this, DA3 replied that this is an "ordinary, average, mickey mouse petty theft" and that exceptions cannot be made for these. Second, PD4 reiterated the "insignificance" of the stolen object, arguing that there was nothing in the defendant's record which indicated she was regularly involved in shoplifting. He further remarked that 24 hours in jail, therefore, did not "make any sense." When DA3 disagreed, a third tactic of PD4 was to revert to the contention that this case was exceptional and did not warrant the standard disposition. This followed:

(8c)

DA3:   We can disagree as to the wisdom of it but I think it applies in
       this case
PD4:   Okay
DA3:   Wanna continue it two weeks?
PD4:   Uh why don't we continue this one three weeks. I want to look
       into it a little better. And it's a first continuance. Okay?
DA3:   Sure
PD4:   Arright. And I wanna see if I can find out something more about
       it that'll make a difference to you

Thus, a continuance was agreed to in this case following extended discussion in which neither the prosecution nor defense was willing to yield from his original position. And while PD4 wanted the continuance to "find out something more,"[12] it was apparent during the negotiation that both parties had the relevant "facts" at hand and the real issue was their different views of those facts and of whether this was a routine or exceptional case. This is much different from the continuances suggested after a unilateral opportunity, which are proposed so that the recipient of an offer can obtain information necessary to taking an initial stance on disposition.

   Trials.   As with continuances, suggestions for trial after both parties have advanced particular dispositions are unlike trial overtures made after a single proposal. In the unilateral (1B) situation, the issue of the

---

[12]While it was PD4 who originally proposed the continuance in (8b), in (8c) DA3 makes the offer and PD4 is in the position of accepting it. Thus, while PD4 may believe "finding out something more" may "make a difference" to the DA, the latter may also be oriented to the way the delay may bring about a weakening of the PD's position. Rosett and Cressey (1976: 22) have observed, "time is a major weapon used by both sides to bring about the settlement of cases without trial."

defendant's guilt figures prominently in the decision. In the bilateral (2B) case, the defendant's guilt is less of a problem. Instead, 2B trials are suggested because defense and prosecution, assuming the party's guilt, disagree over what charge or sentence is appropriate for the defendant (cf. Mather, 1979: 140; Rosett and Cressey, 1976: 101–102).

Example (7) might have resulted in an agreement to try the case if the PD had not retreated from the challenge he put to the DA. In that case, there was no discussion over whether the PD's client had committed an offense. It was assumed he was guilty, and the question was whether the sentence should be the regular drunk-driving penalty or a "straight fine." The following is a similar example (from Chapter 3), but in this case, the trial challenge (line 7), once accepted (line 8), was not retracted.

(9) [Drunk driving]

1.	DA3:	What are you proposing we do with this
2.	PD2:	If you want a reckless and a hundred and eighty dollar fine,
3.		he'll do it
4.		(6.0) ((DA3 looks through file))
5.	DA3:	Should do at least one weekend nothing less, it's what it
6.		says here
7.	PD3:	Well. In that case you get to try it
8.	DA3:	Okay
9.	PD2:	You refuse his offer
10.	DA3:	Yes
11.	PD2:	Okay

Thus, a trial decision was made because PD2 did not relinquish his position for a reckless charge and fine (lines 2–3), and the DA remained firm on the recommended "at least one weekend" (line 5) in the county jail. The defendant's guilt was not a question, and the risk each *appeared* to take was not who would win or lose the trial but who would win or lose the sentencing after the defendant would probably be found guilty at trial.

In fact, a week later, just before a trial would begin, the prosecutor agreed to accept the defendant's offer. Clearly, setting a trial date is functionally similar to deciding on a continuance; both delay determining a disposition. The difference between continuances and trial appears to be in the posture a party takes. Trial decisions contain an element of challenge or bluff not present in continuances.

Pattern 3A. Compromise: Each Party Takes a Position and Relinquishes It for an Intermediate One

We have examined two basic ways in which a decision can be reached if parties take opposing sides on disposition. The first solution is for one party to relinquish; the other is to delay by agreeing to a continuance or a trial. Another way is for the parties to compromise, that is, to give up their former stands and take up a position somewhere between them. This pattern was visible in the determination of sentence in the Frank Bryan case. The PD proposed a $25 fine, the DA suggested $75, and the PD responded, "Why don't we compromise and make it fifty." When the DA accepted the compromise offer, negotiations were brought to a close.

Of course, there can be further rounds of counterproposing, or other negotiating work, involved in obtaining a compromise. Recall the following example (from Chapter 5), which shows how concessions can be traded on both charge and sentence as a compromise is methodically accomplished. The PD started the bargaining by proposing that the defendant be charged with driving 45 miles an hour in a 25-miles-an-hour speed zone.

(10) [Speed contest]

```
 1.   PD2:   Forty five in a twenty five, I mean you know what are
 2.          we doin' here
 3.   DA3:   I'll be happy uh- would you give me forty five in a
 4.          twenty five on that?
 5.   PD2:   Twenty five dollar fine
 6.   DA3:   How 'bout a fifty dollar fine
 7.   PD2:   How 'bout a twenty five dollar heh fine heh real misdemeanors
 8.          go for fifty dollars
 9.   DA3:   How 'bout thirty five including p.a.
10.   PD2:   Eh yeah, I think that's not a bad deal
```

This is a classic example of what many students consider to be "real" bargaining. Still, compromise is not a necessary or automatic component of negotiation. It is, instead, a phenomenon tenuously achieved as one party's stance is contingently tied to that of the other. The analysis in Chapter 5 showed how, on a turn-by-turn basis, participants employ various procedures for testing the other's position and signaling their own willingness to engage in a compromise before actually consummating it.

The judge may sometimes steer a middle course after neither defense nor prosecution have relinquished initial positions. The following is from a case in which a male defendant, Robert Abbey, was charged with battery against a police officer who attempted to break up a barroom brawl involving the defendant. The PD and DA had discussed the case before stepping into the judge's chambers for further negotiation. After PD2 provided some characterizations of the defendant and the case, this ensued:

(11a) [Battery against a police officer]

1.	J2:	What's the offer in the thing, c'mon
2.	PD2:	Well the offer's ninety days, he's already done fifty four days.
3.		he'd plead for fifty four days time served
4.		(1.0)
5.	DA1:	The offer's ninety days with six months suspended for a period of
6.		two years
7.	J2:	What's with this guy Abbey, we know he's a con, he's been in
8.		for awhile
9.	PD2:	Yeah. It was not an unfair fight judge, one against four . . .

Two competing positions are exhibited regarding how the case should be disposed (lines 2–3, 5–6), and there is a substantial discrepancy between them. The judge, after passing up an opportunity to comment on the PD's offer (line 4),[13] occasions further discussion of the defendant (lines 7–8). This is followed by talk regarding the incident in the bar (line 9) and (not shown here) about the defendant's record and living circumstances. The judge argued that the defendant was basically a rough character who lived in an environment where violence was not unusual.

(11b)

J2: I feel like you're not gonna TEACH him anything, you're not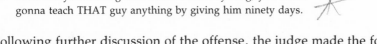
     gonna teach THAT guy anything by giving him ninety days.

Following further discussion of the offense, the judge made the following proposal:

---

[13]Note that PD2, in lines 2–3, first reports the state's offer, and then his own position. This may reflect the order in which the two positions were originally presented, but the effect also is to make the "fifty four days time served" *sequentially implicative* (Schegloff and Sacks, 1974: 231). That is, it projects the relevance of a response directed to it and not the "ninety days" quoted in line 2. That move does not succeed in getting such a response (silence, line 4). Instead, DA1 corrects PD2's report of the prosecution's offer by specifying further aspects of it.

(11c)

1.	J2:	What I was gonna suggest is that we do exactly the same thing
2.		but instead of ninety I hit 'em with sixty days, he serves the
3.		next six days out and he's finished
4.	PD2:	I think he'll go for it.

The judge's suggestion could be heard as a compromise position because it was for something less than the DA wanted and something more than the PD desired. When PD2 produced a candidate acceptance (line 4), this occasioned the settling of details and a closure of the negotiation. The case thus demonstrates that compromise can be achieved without the principal parties testing and signaling each other. What is needed is a third party (the judge) who exhibits a view of the case and proposes a median position with which the two negotiators can align. Again, this is not a required means of settling what should be done, but a methodic achievement.

Pattern 3B. Delay Post–Compromise Opportunity; A Discourse System for Negotiation

Just as other decision modes can falter, attempts at compromise are not always successful. A possibility then is postponement of a disposition decision.

The data provide only one case in this category, and it results in a continuance. Generalizing from this one instance, it appears that postponements that occur after a compromise attempt are similar to those proposed following a bilateral opportunity. Thus, the obstacle to resolution is not a debate over the guilt or innocence of the defendant, but irreconcilable defense and prosecution views on what charge or sentence is appropriate.

Review and analysis of the case will not be redundant, however, but can be used to document how the individual decision-making patterns (1A through 3B) actually comprise a discourse *system* for negotiation. That is, the case usefully highlights how the patterns are related to one another in an ordered fashion.

A consideration of two notions, *opportunity* and *option*, is crucial here. Each of the patterns 1A, 2A, and 3A, describes an opportunity for a disposition decision, defined by (1) a proposal or other bargaining opener, and (2) the relation of that proposal to what has occurred before. Thus, if the opener of a prosecutor or a defender is the first one in the discussion, a unilateral opportunity for agreement—by pattern 1A—is present. If the offer occurs after one party has already exhibited a position, a bilateral opportunity—pattern 2A—is available. If neither party aligns with the other, one can move to an intermediate position and thereby open an opportunity for compromise, which is pattern 3A. Each opportunity may be followed by the *option* of postponing determination of disposition (patterns 1B, 2B, 3B). Refer to Figure 2. In each case the possibility that a given pattern will be the outcome depends on decisions to take or pass over successively realized opportunities or to exercise various options according to contingencies that develop within the course of negotiations.

The case to be examined is that of Cliff Johnson, a 61-year-old man who was found rummaging through a car and was arrested by the police (see Appendix 6). The defendant was on probation at the time of his arrest and already had a 35-day suspended sentence hanging over his head. Because the new arrest was a violation of probation, it necessitated serving the suspended sentence. Thus, Johnson was in jail when the DA and PD met to discuss the case. The PD remarked that the "defendant is very frank about what he does" and that he admitted to getting caught in the act of stealing (040–041), although he was discovered before he actually removed anything from the car. After the DA told a story regarding a similar defendant (043–054), the negotiators briefly discussed the defendant's probation violation hearing (065–070). Then:

(12a) [094] [Breaking or removing vehicle parts]

1. DA3: I want some time on this
2. PD1: Oh well don't be too hard on him
3. DA3: How about three months
4. PD1: Nah that's too much
5.   (4.0)
6. PD1: That's too much
7. DA3: How about four months with credit for time served
8. PD1: How about uh, how about wiping it out with forty five days
9. DA3: With credit for the time served? That he's done already?
10. PD1: Yeah credit for the time he's been in

In line 3, DA3 makes a proposal for a three-month jail sentence. If PD1 had accepted the proposal, a decision would have been reached and, as in examples (1) and (2), the discussion could have been brought to a close. Instead, PD1 rejects the suggested sentence and assesses it as "too much" (line 4). That occasions a substantial silence (line 5), an indication

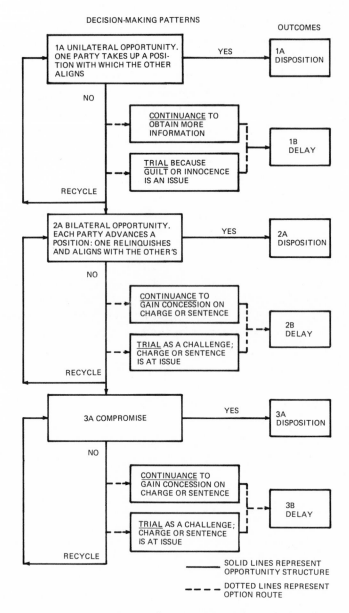

DECISION-MAKING PATTERNS

OUTCOMES

Figure 2.   A discourse system for negotiation at the pretrial conference.

that both parties are waiting to see who will make the next move. PD1 again characterizes the proposal as too much (line 6), and then DA3 proposes slightly less than three months of jail time (line 7)—"four months with credit for time served" would be four months minus the 35 days being served for the probation violation. Although the proposing party has "come down" from the initial offer, such a strategy is a *recycling* of a unilateral opportunity because the second party has not yet suggested an alternative course of action.

However, PD1 does subsequently take a concrete stand of his own, proposing "forty five days" (line 8). Following this, DA3 questions PD1's position (line 9, which may also display "incredulity"), and obtains a reply establishing that the 45 days would include "credit for the time served" (lines 9–10). With these utterances (lines 8–10), then, the unilateral opportunity for determining a disposition (1A) is passed by. Furthermore, the option of a postponement (1B) is not invoked. Rather, each party takes a position, *seriatim*, and it is clear that there is a substantial discrepancy between them.

One way the discrepancy can be eliminated is for one party to give up his own position and accept the other's, thus taking up a bilateral opportunity (pattern 2A; see examples 6 and 7). In this case, however, the discrepancy in positions regarding how to handle the case is preserved in contrasting prosecution and defense views of the defendant's character and his offense. The following occurred immediately after line 10 of (12a):

(12b) [104]

1. PD1: He's just an old codger that
2. DA3: Steals a lot
3. PD1: Yeah but you're not gonna be able to-
4. DA3: Yeah well the old codgers that steal a lot are just as big of
5.   thieves as-
6. PD1: Uh he didn't steal anything in this one though
7. DA3: Oh god knows he was trying

While neither party aligned with the other's position on sentence, they also did not use the delay option (pattern 2B, see examples 8 and 9). Next, the DA presents opportunity for compromise (3A):

(12c) [111]

1. DA3: Uh I'll give you ninety days with credit for time served
2. PD1: Nah that's no good

DA3's proposal is for one month less than his last suggestion. This is a substantial reduction, since the sentence would be about one-third shorter. Still, PD1 rejects the offer. Following this, DA3 argued he could "get more" jail time, PD1 disagreed with this by arguing that it was "too much time" (114), and the two negotiators discussed the defendant's record. The DA concluded that the record was not "terribly significant" (128). Then:

(12d) [130]

1. DA3:   What did I say? Three months for that, ninety days
2. PD1:   Give him forty five
3. DA3:   Give him sixty
4. DA3:   ₁C- c'mon sixty   ₁   ₁last offer₁
5. PD1:   ⌈Oh come on Jeffrey⌉ come ⌈o::::n J- ⌉ .hhh listen forty five, give
6.   him forty five and credit for time served, that ₁'s plenty₁ good
7. DA3:   ⌈Na:::::h ⌉
8. PD1:   Uh listen he didn't steal anything it isn't tampering it's
9.   not a theft
10. DA3:   It's a good burg is what it is, it's a good auto burg

In line 1, DA3 reasserts his suggestion of "three months," which first proffered the possibility of compromise. PD1, however, counters that suggestion by reiterating his own prior position for "forty five" days (line 2). Next, DA3 produces a proposal for "sixty" days (line 3), which is another intermediate position relative to their last ones, and is a recycling of the opportunity for compromise.

In their subsequent overlapping turns, however, DA3 and PD1 both make an appeal on behalf of their own positions: DA3, in line 4, indicates his "sixty" is a "last offer," while PD1, in line 5, issues pleadings ("come on Jeffrey, come on J-") that preface a repeat of the PD's proposed disposition (line 6).[14] An assessment "that's plenty good" (line 6) is overlapped by DA3's rejection (line 7), and then PD1 claims that the

---

[14]Note that there is considerable competition for turn space here. PD1's first "come on Jeffrey" is overlapped by DA3's appeal "c-c'mon sixty," and is repeated. This is an instance of a "segmental adjustment," a way of signaling to the other party that speaker is not dropping and the other party should (Jefferson and Schegloff, n.d.). The repeated appeal ("C'mon J-") is cut off just when DA3's next utterance, "last offer" (line 4), is completed. PD1 then starts up a next utterance with an inbreath and a "listen," items that push PD1's repeated proposal for 45 days (lines 5 and 6) until later in the turn. This may allow PD1 to hear whether DA3 is starting another utterance. When it is apparent that DA3 is not, PD1 produces his proposal "in the clear," that is, outside of overlap.

defendant "didn't steal anything," and that the act "isn't tampering, it's not a theft" (lines 8–9). But DA3 responds with a contrasting characterization of the case, "it's a good burg is what it is, it's a good auto burg" (line 10). Thus, while the difference in sentence proposals diminishes to 15 days, that discrepancy is maintained through successive reassertions of each party's position and opposing assessments of the case.

To summarize, three segments of the negotiations regarding Johnson display concrete prosecution and/or defense positions. The prosecution proposed four different dispositions (three months, four months with credit for 35 days, 90 days with credit, and 60 days with credit), each successive one being a downgraded version of the prior. The defense, on the other hand, suggested one course of action (45 days) and held this position across the series of segments. Through this, three types of opportunities for settlement—unilateral (1A), bilateral (2A), compromise (3A)—were presented, sometimes recycled, and ultimately passed by. Postponement options (trial, continuance) were neither posed nor exercised after opportunities 1A and 2A. However, a proposal for postponement did occur after the above attempts at a compromise (3A) were made:

(12e) [144]

1. PD1: Well why don't we do this. Let's put it over til after the
2. probation violation hearing . . . just put the thing over for
3. a week . . .
4. DA3: I think it was coming up this Friday
5. PD1: Coming up this Friday
6. DA3: Uh any reason not to dispose of it then
7. PD1: No okay put it on for Friday
8. DA3: Arright
9. PD1: Okay

In open court, the case was "continued" until Friday, the day of the probation violation hearing.

DISCUSSION

There are two main implications of the empirical analysis. The first concerns the outcomes of plea bargaining in relation to the means by which they are achieved. The second concerns the way negotiators' use of the discourse system provides large numbers of negotiated dispositions.

Outcomes

Often, plea bargaining and trial are viewed as the two major outcome variables in the justice process.[15] However, even with those cases where lawyers do agree upon a dismissal, charge, or sentence, there are three clearly defined patterns that render these outcomes heterogeneous rather than homogeneous. In other words, not all negotiated dispositions are bargained in the same way. Examining the different decision patterns yields important information and suggests directions for future research.

Table 1 (p. 174) shows that, for these data, the largest number of cases is settled simply by one party taking a position and the other agreeing to it without taking any oppositional stance on disposition.[16] Furthermore, in only a small number of cases is there a visible compromise. Thus, it is clear that settling cases by agreement is not the same as "compromise"; the overwhelming majority is resolved by the defense or prosecution aligning with the other's initial position by way of taking up a unilateral or bilateral opportunity. In the literature on negotiation, this is considered to be a different bargaining game altogether, or at least a rare phenomenon (Ross, 1970: 149). A special name, "Boulware," is assigned to the practice of taking up a single position and adhering to it.[17] The presumption seems to be that one's first proposal should be an extreme position that will help define the boundaries of the dispute,

---

[15]See, for example, La Free (1981). The title of Mather's (1979) ethnographic treatment of plea bargaining in Los Angeles felony courts, *Plea Bargaining or Trial? The Process of Criminal Case Disposition*, depicts the dichotomy, although the author's argument is that it is a false dichotomy.

[16]Also note the following information in Table 1. For pattern 1A, more proposals are made by the PD than the DA, although it is difficult to say whether the difference is important. For pattern 2A, the numbers of first-advanced and second-advanced positions which ultimately "won" are nearly even. Finally, the numbers of continuances and trials (1B, 2B, 3B) are almost equal.

[17]The "Boulware" approach was named after an officer of the General Electric Company. Stevens (1963: 34–37) discusses the technique as used in labor negotiations.

but that one should eventually move toward some middle ground.[18] In their investigation of felony plea bargaining, Eisenstein and Jacob (1977: 32) suggest that "in the course of negotiations, both parties are likely to move from their original positions toward a mutually acceptable outcome." If the evidence here is representative, this is rarely the situation in misdemeanor plea bargaining. Future research should explicitly investigate if indeed there are differences between felony and misdemeanor plea bargaining patterns.[19]

A summary point is that when the ends of negotiational interaction are viewed in relation to the *means* by which they are achieved, the dichotomy between plea bargaining and trial outcomes is clearly too simple. The question is not only why are some cases settled and some cases tried, but why are some cases settled in one way and some in others? The variety of negotiated decisions has yet to be considered, for example, in the literature on discrimination in sentencing. For researchers and policymakers interested in the factors affecting disposition, an issue is whether systematic variation exists in the types of cases or defendants associated with given decision-making patterns.[20]

Finally, consider those decisions made at the pretrial and settlement conference that delayed determination of disposition by continuance and trial. These outcomes also have different meanings and different paths. With continuances occurring after unilateral opportunities, the requesting party displays a need for information relevant to reply to a proposal for disposition. With similarly situated (1B) trial decisions, the issue of

[18]In their review of experimental research, Rubin and Brown (1975: 267) report, "Bargainers achieved higher outcomes when they make extreme initial demands, coupled with gradual concessions, than when they made a large initial concession and remained at that level." Similarly, Gulliver (1979: 164) suggests that the "predominant" form of bargaining is what he calls "convergent concession-making," which can involve a "gradual inching toward agreement" or "substantial concessions" to achieve a decision. But see Gulliver's (1979: 164–165) subsequent discussion of the variety of ways that concessions are expected and made.

[19]Mather's (1974: 198) evidence suggests that felony plea bargaining may be similar to misdemeanor negotiations, in that most cases in the Los Angeles Superior Court were "light" and "dead bang"—that is, not serious and settled with little haggling.

[20]In my data, such variation does not seem to exist, at least by type of case. Petty theft, drunk driving, and battery cases (the ones for which I have multiple entries) are all distributed evenly across the decision-making patterns. In felony plea bargaining, Mather (1979) suggests that seriousness of offense and offender characteristics lead to more extended bargaining and, by imputation, to bilaterally patterned decisions or compromises.

guilt and innocence is a salient factor. Delays occurring after bilateral or compromise opportunities are less concerned with either information-getting or the defendant's guilt. Rather, 2B and 3B continuances and trials are set because defense and prosecution, assuming the defendant's guilt, refuse to yield from their last-stated positions regarding what charge and/or sentence is appropriate in the case. Thus, these continuances and trials are not ends in themselves, but are used as bargaining strategies in their own right, whose desired effect is on the penalty the defendant will receive.

Arranged Dispositions

Proposals for trials and continuances are employed not just anywhere in negotiational discourse. They occur when neither party aligns with the other's position—that is, after unilateral, bilateral, or compromise opportunities have been refused. Put differently, rather than reflecting initial negotiating positions, postponements are arranged after specific dispositions have been proposed. An implication of this is that even if a negotiator "wants" a trial or continuance, the request for delay must be presented as "no other choice"; that is, one must make or hear a proposal for immediate settlement before such an action is broached.

In our 52 case corpus, dismissals or guilty pleas were ultimately obtained in 46 and trials were set in six, an 88 percent plea-bargaining "rate." My argument is that this phenomenon is achieved organizationally in terms of the structure of negotiational discourse. A *systemic* preference for negotiated dispositions is evidenced in the way that decision opportunities and options are regularly provided.[21] Proposals for trials and continuances always follow attempts at agreement on disposition. Moreover, achieving later decision patterns requires that earlier oppor-

---

[21]The argument here draws on the discussion of "preference" in the organization of repair in conversation, as discussed in Schegloff, Jefferson, and Sacks (1977). In observing a preponderance of self-, as opposed to other-correction of errors in conversation, they find this preponderance is produced by the sequential ordering of repair positions, and the way opportunities are organized for locating and remedying of troubles (or repairable items) so as to favor self-correction. The "opportunity structure" is participant managed and the quantity of self-corrections is therefore explained by practices intrinsic to conversation. The "preference" for self-correction refers not to beliefs or attitudes of participants, but to their interactionally organized achievement.

tunities be presented. That is, the occurrence of a bilateral opportunity necessitates that a unilateral one has been passed up, and compromise can only be attempted after unilateral and bilateral chances have been serially given. Delays, however, are optionally proposed. In short, continuance and trial possibilities may be ignored as the full range of opportunities is explored (see example 12).[22] The reverse does not happen—delay options are never offered in the absence of suggestions for disposition.[23] Finally, even when delay is the decision, it is a certainty that the case will be negotiated again, either when the continuance expires or on the eve of the trial. Opportunities for disposition will once more be presented immediately and delays proposed later, if at all. Thus, *rounds* of negotiation often occur, and each round exerts a systemic "pressure," by the way that opportunities and options are ordered, for an arranged guilty plea.

Proposals for continuances and trials represent more than just strategic delay. They also indicate a reliance on "formal" mechanisms for achieving an ultimate disposition. Continuances, for instance, keep the cases in the court system and also allow the filing of pretrial motions. Trials may have to be postponed until the court can make room for them and represent the ultimate in official court ceremony. At the level of discourse, trials and continuances occur less often than dispositions because the structure of negotiation puts a priority on the here-and-now, informal resolution of cases, and deters delay and formal modes of decision making in the patterned ways that proposals for these outcomes are presented.

[22]Delays, then, may be accountably "last resort" decisions, (Emerson, 1981), whose rational, necessary character (Garfinkel, 1967) is exhibited in the prior employment of those disposition attempts. Furthermore, plea bargaining has a kinship with the means by which negotiations are conducted in a wide variety of settings where disputes or conflicts have arisen. In business, MacCauley (1963) has discussed the hesitancy among manufacturing corporations to invoke the legal process in their exchanges and disputes. The use (or threatened use) of legal sanctions is a last resort invoked when other dispute settlement attempts fail. Similarly, Ross (1970) has documented the reluctance of involved parties to use trials as a means of settling insurance claims.

[23]In the one case in which a DA asserts that he is going to trial and is initially unwilling to entertain any other proposals, it was disruptive and resulted in the PD suggesting that their talk was not plea bargaining. See Chapter 5, example (5) and discussion.

CONCLUSION

The existence of a discourse system for negotiation has implications for the standard theories of plea bargaining and the methodological issues attached to them.

First, with respect to the exchange perspective, it may be true that district attorneys and public defenders wish to attain certain personal and professional goals and want to "maximize production and reduce work." But the exchange that is implemented for these reasons happens through a system of negotiation in which routine practices and not rational calculation are the central phenomenon (cf. Collins, 1981). Moreover, the system actuates and induces guilty pleas independent of whatever reasons the participants may have for agreeing to the exchange. We have seen, for example, that either of the parties may wish to delay the disposition or may, in fact, want a trial. Regardless of these wishes or wants, the delay option is presented or sought only after opportunities for immediate disposition are made available.

Second, although one theory explains plea bargaining as being a means for administering substantive justice, we have seen that formally rational justice is also involved. The described negotiational system can accommodate both forms, just as it accommodates both "explicit" and "implicit" negotiation. The most expeditious way of handling a case is through pattern 1A, where one party exhibits a position and the other aligns with it. If the agreement represents a standard penalty for the offense, negotiation is "implicit" and the decision is a formally rational one, made "without regard for persons."[24] On the other hand, as disagreement with an initially presented position occurs and more positions are exhibited, negotiation is "explicit" and involves justifications, descriptions of the defendant's character, arguments over the facts of the case, and so forth, all of which are made to fit the positions taken up. Thus, the negotiation can become visibly adversarial, and the decision may display a substantively rational character. Consider the economy of a system that allows for the accomplishment of both kinds of justice; rational and substantive justice do not require disparate forms of negotiation; both are contingent upon how a basic discourse organization

---

[24]Implicit negotiation here only refers to the use of standard charge reductions and sentences. Bargaining sequences, in simple or elaborated form, are still utilized to reach decisions. See Chapters 4 and 5.

is related to other methodic bargaining practices. In other words, "implicit" and "explicit" bargaining are not separate games; they are both realized within one negotiational system.

This raises the third theoretical implication. As discussed, there is evidence that the ratio of guilty pleas to trials has risen over the past century and that explicit, as opposed to implicit, bargaining has also increased, at least since World War II (Friedman, 1979). Neither of these proportions need imply more *use* of plea bargaining. Instead, it can be seen that the discourse system of negotiation allows for variation in the number of trials and explicitly or implicitly bargained guilty pleas. That is, whatever the external organizational logic of the society, it is in and through a robust local social organization, which itself has an independent contribution to gross outcomes, that the effects of distant organizational processes will be implemented.[25] The mechanism lies in the way in which different settlement opportunities are presented, seized, or passed up. For example, as caseload pressures build, more opportunities for immediate settlement can be taken. As such pressures diminish, those opportunities may be taken less often and more continuances and trials can be agreed to. Nonetheless, the system will remain weighted toward informal here-and-now resolution so that even as nontrial and trial proportions vary, nontrial dispositions will remain predominant.

My general recommendation is consistent with a critique of social theory mustered by Giddens (1976, 1979). Phenomenal aspects of a society should be comprehended not simply as reflections of large-scale institutional and historical forces but as contingent outcomes of members' (or, in this case, professionals') practical activity, including sequences of talk socially organized in and through everyday discourse in real settings. Similarly, the courtroom "subculture" needs to be discussed not only in terms of beliefs, attitudes, interests, and other cognitive concepts, but also as a set of activities or skills involved in its ongoing production and reproduction. Clearly, the close inspection and rigorous analysis of negotiations is a means for fulfilling this recommendation in the study of the criminal-justice process. Such inspection and analysis reveal exactly how nontrial dispositions are produced in direct interaction. They also disclose distinct patterns of negotiation and

---

[25]See the discussion by Lipsky (1980: 182–183) on how political and economic structures of the larger society affect street level bureaucracies.

heterogeneous bargaining outcomes that any comprehensive theory of case processing must address. Finally, because clear benefits derive from the microanalysis of plea bargaining, and because the criminal court is but one aspect of the society's wider dispute-processing networks (Sarat, 1979), other dispute-processing forums may well benefit from similar microanalyses.

CHAPTER 9

Inside Plea Bargaining

The empirical materials presented in preceding chapters can be tied together by treating a theme sketched at the outset—plea bargaining as an "inside" activity. Such treatment also flags other issues to be explored.

PLEA BARGAINING AND BUREAUCRACY

Plea bargaining is an inside activity because it is a discourse carried on by professionals in a bureaucratic manner. Even in the Garden City jurisdiction, where plea bargaining is a calendarized event occurring in a public courtroom, it is routinely protected from scrutiny and participation by others. Moreover, it is carried on while a variety of related and unrelated activities are pursued in simultaneity or in sequence with it. Some of these—such as the judge hearing pleas from defendants— prevail over plea bargaining. But others are clearly subordinated to it as negotiations are ritually and ecologically protected from intrusion.

The temptation is to condemn the court and plea bargaining for such an exhibition of bureaucratization. The sociological need, however, is to understand the structure of face-to-face interaction that infuses the term "bureaucratic" with specific meaning in this jurisdiction and this court. My general strategy, in fact, has been to examine the organization that lies behind the phenomena presented to us as "bureaucracy," "bargaining," "character assessment," and so on. This strategy reveals, for example, that defendants contribute to courtroom social order partly as a way of shaping a biography that could justify a minimum sanction from the court. The argument is consistent with prior studies establishing the importance of "character assessment" in various phases of the criminal-justice process. Rather than being a "finding," however, this feature was taken as a starting point for a deeper investigation into the organization of discourse as it is used to accomplish "character assessment" and related activities as visible features of plea bargaining.

PLEA BARGAINING AS A PRODUCED SET OF DISCOURSE PRACTICES

Characters are assessed as people are described. Person-descriptions are sensitive to, and constitutive of, the topical and activity environment of the conversations in which they appear. In plea bargaining, obviously enough, a central topic is "what should be done" with defendants, and a core activity is taking positions on that issue. Person-descriptions support those positions, as demonstrated by their use in places where justifications of positions have been sequentially occasioned, their part in arguments regarding what should be done with a defendant—which are pursued over long segments of talk—and their fit with other aspects of the courtroom subculture.

The concern in all of this is to identify and describe procedures of talk that are not dependent on probability sampling for their generality. The assumption is that it is possible to study a corpus of data and discover formal structures of talk that are indifferent to the parties speaking, the kinds of cases discussed, the various strategies employed, and so forth (cf. Sacks et al., 1974: 700). It is by way of these structures, however, that particular identities of participants, specific features of cases, and other distinctive characteristics of plea bargaining discourse are accomplished.

While this approach has its own shortcomings—such as analytically deemphasizing the complete context within which plea bargaining occurs—it has clear advantages. For example, we were able to put order in some of the perceived diversity in plea bargaining. When used strictly, *plea bargaining* refers at most to charge and sentence bargaining. But the personnel I observed, and those studied by other investigators, use plea bargaining to refer to obtaining dismissals, continuances, and even trials. Even more diversity is apparent in the fact that lawyers can either rapidly decide an action for a case or pursue, at some length, different versions of what the case is really about. In addition, some cases are resolved with little or no visible "compromise," while in others both parties make clear moves from their original positions to an intermediate one.

Rather than assigning different names to these surface variations or faulting the use of plea bargaining as a generic term, the task has been to locate procedures that provide for plea bargaining as a reasonable "account," in Garfinkel's (1967) terms, of the complete range of lawyers' negotiational discourse over criminal cases. Close examination of their discourse reveals a bargaining sequence at the basis of charge bargaining, sentence bargaining, arranging continuances, setting trials, compromise, routine handling, and adversariness. Each of these characteristic kinds of discussions and outcomes is an achievement, contingently accomplished by the systematic deployment and elaboration of the bargaining sequence. The bargaining sequence is occasioned or made relevant during negotiations by procedures indicating that its timing is a delicate issue. That is, announcements and solicits of a bargaining opener allow collaborative arrival at delivery of the first part of a bargaining sequence, a matter that appears particulary important when no "discussion" has taken place. Bargaining sequences are not only occasioned in specific ways; depending on whether a bargaining opener receives a positive or negative reply, the sequence elicits specific forms of subsequent talk. In both ways—by being locally occasioned and sequentially implicative—bargaining sequences articulate externally with other aspects of negotiational discourse. The sequence is elaborated internally by various direct and indirect responses that relate it to gaining information, disagreement, and additional bargaining strategies.

Bargaining openers include *proposals,* by which a negotiator presents a possible course of action to be accepted or rejected by his co-participant. Some openers are discussed as *position-reports* that seem to provide variable reply options. A person hearing a report can focus on issues of perspective regarding a displayed position or can directly accept or reject the position. But these different ways of producing the bargaining sequence are not just options to be casually employed. Rather, they are involved in specific kinds of negotiational work, including the topicalizing and detopicalizing of issues regarding "what really happened," "who" the defendant is, how strong or serious the case is, and how these matters are viewed by the defense and prosecution.

That the bargaining sequence is the basic component of negotiation can be discerned from the fact that it appears in all but one of the 52 cases recorded. Its absence in the one was complained about and rem-edied in a way that highlighted the importance of mutuality as ordinarily sustained in and through the sequence. In some negotiations, of course, a number of bargaining sequences may be serially occupied with arriving at an acceptable decision about a given defendant's fate. Examining the serial use of bargaining sequences reveals three patterns whereby agree-ment is reached. These patterns include unilateral, bilateral, and com-promise opportunities. When any opportunity is not taken, participants may move on to the next or may exercise the option of delaying dis-position by continuing the case or setting it for trial.

It is easy to view these patterns as logical ways in which a two-party dispute can be settled. But beyond the logic of these patterns, they are concretely ordered relative to one another, and that ordering is an achievement of methodic ways of presenting, taking, and declining op-portunities and options for specific outcomes. Moreover, each oppor-tunity and option is responsive to contingencies that develop within the course of negotiation. Thus, the system of negotiation is not a mechanical means by which decisions are reached. Rather, it is a structure that is dynamically produced by participants in conjunction with their practical concerns and as part of their ongoing interaction.

In various ways, therefore, plea bargaining can be viewed as an inside activity in a sense more profound than is conveyed by merely noting that it seems to be bureaucratic. It is an inside activity because it consists of participants' methods for constituting its objective-appear-ing, noticeable features. Assessing character, arguing, compromising, making an exchange, and coming to agreement are "glosses" (Garfinkel and Sacks, 1970) for organized discourse practices that lie behind these phenomena and accomplish them as visible, reportable, negotiational entities. It is not enough to suggest that "assessing character," for in-stance, is a prominent feature of plea bargaining. We should investigate how that activity is done, and how it is related to other elements of the discourse. "Compromise," for another example, should not be taken as an invariant and inevitable feature of negotiation. Instead, it must be understood as an outcome constituted by manipulation of a generalized structure of talk—the bargaining sequence—whose properties and or-ganization are themselves worthy of detailed attention. Furthermore, compromise is the infrequent result of participants systematically pre-senting and passing up other decision-making opportunities and op-tions. For participants and others, phenomena such as character assessment and compromise often are either performed or observed as simple and obvious matters. It is possible, however, to go inside these otherwise uninteresting and taken-for-granted practical actions to discover, describe, and analyze real social order (Garfinkel, 1967: 7–8). Concrete gains are made in terms of fully understanding what happens in direct interaction and how such interaction is put together.

INSIDE ACTIVITY AND OUTSIDE CONCERNS

Because plea bargaining discourse is socially organized by participants as part of their real-time interaction, an appreciation of its fundamental structure necessitates starting with problems posed by participants within their natural interaction. The focus, as in this study, must be on how the structure of discourse is an ongoing, moment-by-moment production. After all, participants themselves describe and analyze what they are doing in and through their talk. Stated differently, the observer must be concerned with *subjects'* orientations in talk and not problems posed by this or that academic discipline. This point bears repeating, because many investigations of plea bargaining seem to have been motivated by questions of justice as articulated by jurists and social scientists concerned, for example, with whether plea bargaining accurately separates the guilty from the innocent and whether it does so fairly, according to law and without undue coercion.

Nowhere are such outside concerns more evident than in the research on sentencing. In attempting to discern the extent of bias in the criminal-justice process, researchers have tested propositions deriving from a variety of theoretical perspectives, but the fundamental issue remains that of discrimination, as is clear in the following typical passage.

> Our primary objective in this paper has been to describe and in some instances to demonstrate common pitfalls in the detection of sentencing discrimination. We are sure that some readers will claim that we are engaged in a futile effort, since studies have yet to show convincingly the existence of disparity in the criminal justice system. We maintain, however, that in a *society based on equality*, such research should be encouraged and its techniques continually subjected to careful scrutiny. (Thomson and Zingraff, 1981: 878–879, emphasis added)

The "society based on equality" phrase seems to be a somewhat careless and unreflective use of, in Gidden's (1979: 187) terms, an ideological aspect of American society's symbol system. The point here is not that the society is based on *inequality,* though that could be assumed as easily as its converse. Rather, it is to suggest that using, as a beginning point for research, problems posed by a society's characterization of itself, or those set up by theories that display, as a prominent feature, a similar and abstract preoccupation with fairness and equality, risks neglecting aspects of social organization lying at the center of a society's everyday activities.

Thus, an implicit feature of prior social-scientific, statistical modeling of sentence decisions is the positing of decisionmakers as "judgmental" or "computerized" dopes. If practitioners performed according to the presuppositions inherent in that modeling process, they would determine case outcomes in a routine and mechanical fashion, scanning a checklist of items similar to ones salient in the researcher's schema. But investigation of actual negotiation practices reveals that defendant attributes are selected to support an argument for a specific disposition and that they are defined more by their relatedness to other factors regarding the defendant and the defendant's case than by any context-free reference they may have. Thus, a proper model of how defendant characteristics play a part in lawyers' decision making would incorporate how these practitioners assemble a set of elements in a gestalt contexture.

The argument is not meant to imply that the large-scale and quantitative study of sentencing decisions cannot or should not be done. Rather, such a study should take into account the vagaries of the social process whereby such decisions are produced (cf. Eisenstein and Jacob, 1977: 244). Those vagaries attest to the richness and artfulness of that process, but this does not mean that, in all its complexity, the decision-making process is not patterned or structured. To locate systematic features of the social process, however, we must look at participants' actual practices—at their methods—and not let the dominant methods of empirical social science presuppose the nature of the social world for us. Specifically, to understand the actual organization of plea bargaining and to adequately confront questions of justice we need to examine endemic patterns of commonsense reasoning and concepts of justice as displayed in plea bargaining discourse.

Attention to the methodic production of plea-bargaining discourse reveals that a *discourse system of negotiation* makes a contribution to the disproportionate number of guilty pleas in the court, independent of such exogenous factors as "overcrowded courts," the desire for substantive justice, and the exchange relations between defendants or defense attorneys and prosecuting attorneys. Ever since plea bargaining was "discovered" in the early part of this century (Alschuler, 1979), lawyers and social scientists have gone to great lengths to explain why it is so prevalent, and why it results in so many guilty pleas instead of trials. However, their theories and assumptions push researchers in one of two directions away from examining the face-to-face interaction wherein plea bargaining occurs. They depict courtroom officials as reacting to outside pressures, including overcrowded courts or abstract laws and harsh penalties established by legislative bodies, or they attribute the occurrence of a large number of arranged guilty pleas to the personal and professional interests or benefits of involved parties. Either way, the result is a de-emphasis of acting subjects and their inside production and reproduction of structures that constitute various phenomenal aspects of the court process. Practitioners *construct* and *execute* a system of negotiation that works to bring about a preponderance of arranged dispositions rather than trials.

PLEA BARGAINING AS AN INSIDE INSTITUTIONAL ACTIVITY

Throughout, I have stressed how participants use *practices* and *methods* to *achieve* and *accomplish* prominent features of plea bargaining. They do this as members of lay and professional subcultures who have mastered the natural languages of those subcultures (Garfinkel and Sacks, 1970: 342). This emphasis on accomplished and achieved matters maximizes attention to the "produced" character of social interaction in terms of discourse structures invariant to particular settings. The bargaining sequence, for example, hypothetically occurs in a variety of social contexts. Proposals and replies can be used in places as diverse as flea markets, car lots, legislatures, boardrooms, and so on. By examining the structure of the sequence in one setting (the court), we can hope to learn about negotiation as a generic phenomenon. That is, procedures for building the sequence and methods for occasioning, elaborating, and relating it to subsequent talk are assumed to be exhibited in these other settings as well.

Nevertheless, the attention to transsituational structures can minimize the importance of reproduced and institutional aspects of plea bargaining discourse. Contextual elements of plea bargaining talk reside

in more than just the immediate sequential environments of given utterances. As negotiators frame the different positions they animate, for
instance, they thereby exhibit the importance of a variety of organizational forms in which they are embedded. These include their associations with defendants and witnesses, involvements in their own offices
and professions, connections with other agencies (e.g., police and schools),
and relationships with the court and its own activities (e.g., trial). We
can thus speak of negotiating procedures as being sensitive to an array
of social networks within and surrounding bargaining encounters. Framing practices draw on and make visible these networks to render current
talk reasonable and sensible, and they simultaneously reproduce the
very structure that constitutes those networks (Wilson, 1982).

We have only begun to probe the complete context of plea bargaining discourse. For example, we need to investigate how various negotiational activities, including character assessment, the discussion of
"facts," and the assumption of bargaining positions, are related to socially organized means of gathering information that produce a "documentary reality" (Smith, 1974), such as police reports, the defendant's
record, and other items used in negotiation. Because the results of plea
bargaining become a further element in the record-keeping system of
the criminal-justice process, that system may exert an influence on how
negotiations are conducted (Frankel, 1981). Clearly, further understanding is required about the relation of plea bargaining to activities organized both before and after its occurrence, on which it depends and to
which it is reflexively related (Maynard and Wilson, 1980). Plea bargaining, that is, is an inside activity whose relationship to outside concerns can be more fully analyzed now that the ground has been prepared.
Our investigation has revealed what actually happens in plea bargaining
in terms of the structure of direct interaction. As with other types of
institutional discourse, the next step should be to recover, in the discourse, more distantly organized social and historical processes.

Adapted Transcribing Conventions

1. A: Oh you do? R[eally]
   B: [Um hmm]

   A left hand bracket marks the point of overlap, while a right hand bracket indicates where overlapping talk ends.

2. B: That's how I felt=
   A: =Really

   Equal signs indicate "latching"; i.e., no interval between the end of a prior utterance and the start of a next.

3. A: And I'm not use ta that
             (1.4)
   B: Yeah me neither

   Numbers in parentheses indicate elapsed time in tenths of seconds

4. A: Are they?
   B: Uh huh they are because. . . .

   Ellipses indicate where part of an utterance is left out of the transcript

5. A: It was unbelievable. I had a three point six? I think.
   B: You did.

   Punctuation markers are not used as grammatical symbols but for intonation. Thus a question may be constructed with "comma" or "period" intonation and "question intonation" may occur in association with objects which are not syntactically constructed questions.

6. B: I did oka::y

   Colon(s) indicate the prior syllable is prolonged. The more colons, the longer the prolongation.

7. A: That's where I REALLY want to go

   Capital letters indicate various forms of stressing, and may involve pitch and/or volume.

These conventions are adapted from the work of Gail Jefferson.

8. A: I told them that there was-   The dash indicates a "cut off" of the
        well there IS a job opening   prior word or sound.

9. B: Tha(h)t was really neat   The "h" within a word or sound in-
                                            dicates explosive aspirations, e.g.,
                                            laughter, breathlessness, etc.

10. B: You didn't have to worry   The "h" indicates audible breathing.
        about having the .hh hhh   The more "h's," the longer the breath.
        curtains closed   A period placed before it indicates in-
                                            breath; no period indicates outbreath.

11. A: Well ((cough)) I don't know   Materials in double parentheses are
                                            explanatory or indicate features of
                                            audio materials other than actual
                                            verbalization.

12. B: (Is that right)   Materials in single parentheses indi-
                                            cate transcribers are not sure about
                                            words contained therein. If no ma-
                                            terial is within the parentheses, none
                                            of the talk was decipherable.

The Frank Bryan Case

001	J1:	And now that brings us to Frank Bryan. Is he the poor chap
002		sitting out there all by himself
003	PD2:	Yeah he's the sweet man with the nice smile and this is a six forty
004		seven "f" and a one forty eight . . . See he's drunk and he comes
005		home to his own house where he had a fight with his family, and he's
006		out in his own front yard apparently having such a fight or at least-
007	DA3:	His mother having called the police
008	PD2:	Mother having ca(h)ll(h)ed the (h) co(h)ps. Its a family thing,
009		he's screaming and saying fuck and all that kind of stuff . . . And
010		this is, I mean, the same very happy go lucky good natured
011		guy, as you can tell he's sitting out in the courtroom and when
012		the police come into his own home, his castle, he decides he
013		ain't going without making some trouble. He does take a menacing
014		stance, but on the other hand he doesn't attempt to strike an
015		officer. I assume that the officer's high degree of professionalism
016		prevents my client from getting himself into further trouble
017	DA3:	Yeah the (pushing foul) ( ) apparently which caused that uh
018		laceration above his uh ( )
019	PD2:	He's terribly sorry he did this, I believe they took him to jail,
020		did they not?
021	DA3:	They did and it was somewhere in the process of being uh, he
022		did resist being handcuffed and resist walking from the residence,
023		in the process of that resistance he quote collapsed and struck
024		his head on the floor unquote
025	J1:	heh
026	PD2:	Yeah well he might of had a certain amount of justice all
027		ri(h)ght heh hih I don't heh thi(h)nk the police were putting
028		up with him
029	DA3:	One senses that uh uh other than that it was a lotta talk
030		of uh assuming fighting stances and then running away
031	PD2:	Yeah it's a verbal uh one forty eight and a real six forty
032		seven ef. Now I would like to settle this case

033	DA3:	Well I'd like to settle it
034	J1:	You(h)u al(h)ways sa(h)y tha(hah)t . . .
035	DA3:	Uh- I think it's a case that oughta be uh settled, it's uh-
036	PD2:	Okay
037	DA3:	strikes me as a dandy one forty eight uh b- probably a better
038		one forty eight than a six forty seven ef if you want to
039		be very strict about it
040	PD2:	Well I see it as a six forty seven ef, uh he didn't lay hands
041		on any officers, if he hadn't been so drunk I assume nothing-
042		none o' this would of happened. Well I don't think it's
043		worth any jail time no matter what it is
044	DA3:	I was being academic when I said that uh
045	PD2:	Oh
046	DA3:	I think technically it's a better one forty eight than it is a
047		six forty seven, he put the officers through their uh mettle.
048		In- in uh collaring 'im they hadta pursue 'im through the house
049		and all that sorta stuff
050	PD2:	And they did a very fine job of it, I have to- I wanted
051		to add the officer's uh conduct was highly commendable, and
052		if my client accidentally tripped and conk(h)ed his head, heh I
053		am su(h)re tha(h)t-
054	DA3:	On the other ha⌊nd⌋
055	PD2:	⌈jus⌉tice was done
056	DA3:	I don't know that the substantial interests of justice require
057		any more than a plea to six forty seven ef
058	J1:	He's been here uh now for uh, six hours
059	DA3:	So've I your honor
060	PD2:	I- I belie(h)ve heh heh
061	J1:	We'll give you credit for time served
062	DA3:	Yes heh heh heh
063	PD2:	Okay uh, twenty five dollar fine does that sound justice- uh
064		justiciable
065	DA3:	Well um um uh
066		(0.8)
067	PD2:	I made it up, I'm sorry I didn't look at the (dictionary), I
068		(made it up)
069	J1:	He's gonna dismiss the one four eight
070	PD2:	Okay
071	J1:	'n you plead to the six four seven ef
072	PD2:	Yeah
073	J1:	And what would you realistically-
074	PD2:	Well what are you asking for, lemme- I mean I always usually go
075		along with whatever Jeffrey ((DA3)) says
076	J1:	How long was he in jail
077	DA3:	He bailed out uh, I can't tell from my note here, other than
078		the fact that uh, does your honor indicate the time that ( )

079   J1:   We never know, how long they were down there
080   PD2:   Well let me ask him, I assume his momma bailed him out after
081   she called the co(h)ps on him heh fin(h)d out wha(h)t was all
082   about, finally
                      ((PD2 leaves room and returns 45 seconds later))
083   PD2:   It sounds to me like between ten to twelve hours in jail
084   DA3:   He has uh one prior conviction in this jurisdiction with
085   the um sheriff's office of, interestingly enough, uh striking
086   a public officer and uh disturbing the peace
087   PD2:   Will you knock it off, you wanna make a federal case out
088   of this
089   DA3:   No, I- I just think that it's not uh this uh happy go lucky
090   chap's uh first encounter with uh (the law)
091   PD2:   Statistically if you got black skin you are highly likely
092   to contact the police, uh substantially more likely than
093   if you're white, now c'mon, what do you want from him. He's
094   got a prior
095   J1:   Well we know he spent ten hours and uh maybe (   )
096   some more. And what do you think would be reasonable, Jeffrey
097   (6.0)   ((DA3 looks through files))
098   DA3:   Seventy five dollar fine
099   PD2:   Why don't we compromise and make it fifty
100   DA3:   It's done
101   PD2:   Arright

The Maria Dominguez Case

```
001  PD1:  This is a shoplifting case, judge. Um on the face of it, it
002        looks pretty bad
003                              (0.8)
004  PD1:  But
005  DA1:  Uh huh
006  PD1:  Investigating the case uh comes up with some beautiful
007        defenses that I'm anxious to go to trial on if the Dee Ay is
008                              (1.4)
009  PD1:  Situation is this (0.2) eghhh. She's a sixty five year old
010        lady, Mexic- speaks uh (0.2) Castillian Spanish (0.4) she's
011        from Spain (1.0) Uh eghh she goes into Davidson's (0.8)
012        Oh incidently uh- th- by way of background, for twenty years
013        she's worked in the- in the Catholic Church of- at San Ramon
014        as the housekeeper for the nuns 'n the fathers 'n all this
015        stuff (and uh) very religious well known. I've interviewed
016        half of San Ramon, concerning her background (0.4) wonderful
017        lady no problems sixty five years ol' .hhh sh- but on this
018        particular occasion, she goes into Davidson's eghh goes
019        into a (0.2) fitting room (0.4) takes two hundred dollars
020        worth o' clothes (0.8) pins them up underneath her (0.6)
021        dress (0.6) and leaves
022                              (1.2)
023  PD1:  And they pick her up outside. She's with a companion. They
024        pick her up outside, and they uh cite her for petty theft, later
025        discover how much was involved and hit her with four eighty
026        seven point one
027                              (1.6)
028  PD1:  She had no explanation except to say that she was sorry, her
029        companion with whom she lives is here in court today, says that
030        night she, the companion was crying, saying look what've you
031        done, why are you doing this and all the lady could say is what've
```

032		I done? It wasn't 'til the next day that she realized, when
033		she found the ticket in her purse that the police had given
034		her, what she had done. And
035	J1:	Yeah
036	PD1:	Then in subsequent investigation uh it was discovered that she
037		had taken two different drugs, one for her arthritic condition,
038		she'd taken more than what she should've, and another drug.
039		Combined them which was improper. And was obviously under
040		the influence of drugs
041	J1:	What're the drugs, ya got any idea
042	PD1:	Darvoset
043	J1:	Yeah
044	PD1:	And seconal. Now I've checked with the county pathologist and
045		he's researched the thing out. He says that if those drugs are
046		mixed it will cause a state of confusion, delirium, and put the
047		person in a situation where they're just in a dream world, don't
048		know what in the world they're doing. I've also talked with a
049		pharmacist at Middleton Medical who says the exact same thing
050	J1:	Uh well, let's see, ya don't know how much she had
051	PD1:	Well we got that too. She's taken uh- she took uh ((looking at
052		file)) she took ONE uh seconal and three darvoset at approximately-
053	J1:	One seconal an' THREE darvosets?
054	PD1:	That was it. At approximately an hour and a half before this
055		occurred. And uh the doctors say it- that could easily (cause
056		it)
057	J1:	Well it could, in fact I was just- at this judicial conference
058		I was at the last few days, one of the things they went over
059		was the various sedatives and saying about seconal, some odd
060		effects this way and it tends to peak out a little later than
061		other drugs so it would probably be about maximum potentiality
062		around that time anyway. Wouldn't do that with most people but
063		it could do that
064	PD1:	She's the- they say that it uh- that I talked with her doctor
065		who- well, she has two different doctors, ONE prescribed one
066		drug and one prescribed the other, and the doctor said he didn't
067		know the effect except that on elderly people it sometimes has
068		strange or adverse effects that it wouldn't have normally. And
069		he suggested that I talk with the county pathologist which I
070		did, and also with a pharmacist who's out at Middleton Medical.
071		So we feel like that she certainly wasn't acting within her
072		normal characteristics
073	J1:	Has she ever had any violations for anything?
074	PD1:	That's it, she's had nothing, for twenty years she worked up
075		there in the Church of San Ramon with all these people. She's
076		a very religious lady. All these uh, these uh Mexican Catholics

077		up there who just think the world of her they say my god I
078		couldn't believe it. I spent uh was it Monday this week? yeah
079		Monday this week up there uh, no Friday of this week up there
080		uh er last week, talking with them, and uh they just y'know I've
081		got uh some sisters who're willing to come in and state they've
082		known her for all this period of time and she's just has a
083		tremendous reputation for honesty and (very religious)
084	J1:	What do you want?
085	PD1:	Want it dismissed
086		(2.2)
087	PD1:	Wasn'- she was obviously not acting on 'er own free will
088		(1.0)
089	J1:	Well
090		(3.0)
091	PD1:	They'll never- you'll- they'll never get a conviction
092		(0.8)
093	DA2:	₁Do you understand how much manual dexterity it takes to₁
094	DA1:	₁M a y b e w e w o n ' t b u t u h : : : : : : : ₁
095	DA2:	₁operate a booster operation ₁
096	DA1:	₁I just can't believe that the drug₁ is- (1.4) if the drug affects
097		you that badly you gonna do something bizarre
098	PD1:	Well that's w₁hy don't you- ₁
099	DA1:	₁In other words₁ you're gonna walk out swinging
100		around your arm or carrying out (bananas) in your ear or something
101		crazy. Here she was extremely sophisticated. Go into the dressing
102		room, pin it up underneath her coat, um her uh dress like that.
103		Extremely sophisticated. Uh I just can't buy it
104		(1.0)
105	DA1:	The whole defense is gonna rest really on, do you believe
106		she actually took those drugs. 'Cause nothing else during
107		that day indicates that she did
108	PD1:	Well-
109	DA1:	She didn't walk funny, she didn't garble
110	PD1:	Well now look
111	DA1:	She signed her name correctly, and very neatly on the ticket
112		The- all the physical functions were not the ones that say
113		hey something's wrong with this gal
114	PD1:	Okay except for the fact that the lady she lives with and
115		who was there says that when she got home that night she,
116		the lady, was VERy upset the- not the defendant but the other
117		lady, and she was trying to talk with her to say what, you
118		know, what made you DO this and the other lady kept saying
119		you know what did I do? And when she told her what she had
120		done, uh the defendant just didn't- just let it go in one
121		ear and out the other as though it didn't really make any

122		difference. She said that the uh witness said that the
123		defendant ate a good meal, went to bed and went to sleep,
124		and she, the witness, uh spent most the night worrying and
125		crying and being very concerned. The NEXT day, when Mrs.
126		Dominguez found the ticket in her purse, and asked what it
127		was, and then she was told that again what had happened.
128		Then SHE breaks down and starts crying, and then she's been
129		upset and to this day she claims that she doesn't remember
130		what in the world happened there
131		(3.0)
132	J1:	She got anything else going on in her life, you know no
133		divorce, no-
134	PD1:	Oh no no
135	J1:	cancer, no-
136	PD1:	No she's uh- there is a possibility that she'll be going
137		back to Spain, uh she's been living down here for a couple
138		years and there's talk about her going back to Spain
139	J1:	Why did she have seconals?
140	PD1:	Uh it was, I don't know it was uh prescribed by-
141	J1:	Is she having some sleep difficulties now?
142	PD1:	Apparently, I don't know. There's a Doctor Carlson who
143		prescribed the seconals. Doctor Avalon prescribed the
144		darvoset
145	J1:	Avalon's a GP, Carlson I think is a skin doctor, there may
146		be another Carlson
147	DA2:	What time of day was this
148	PD1:	This happened at like four thirty in the afternoon on Monday
149	J1:	Were they kinds of clothes that would fit her or
150	PD1:	NO and that's another thing. None of the clothes would fit.
151		There were two different sizes, one was large and the other
152		one was small. Those were the two sizes, and she takes uh-
153	J1:	She just took stuff in other words
154	PD1:	Yeah
155	J1:	Not necessarily stuff for her
156	PD1:	YEAH now like th- like fancy nightgowns and uh, let's see
157		I've got a whole list of the stuff here
158		(2.0)
159	PD1:	Eh yeah just, you know, it doesn't make much sense there
160		was a- there were two blouses, a large and small, there
161		were two nightgowns, a large and a small, there were-
162	J1:	A large and a small?
163	PD1:	Yeah, there were camisoles whatever those are.
164	J1:	Kind of a slip
165	PD1:	Yeah is that what they are, and they have the size of thirty
166		four, thirty six or peTITE thirty-four peTITE, a thirty six

167		and two beige teddies, whatever teddies are, uh size thirty
168		four B, and-
169	J1:	Larry are you an expert on such things?
170	PD1:	And uh, you know it just didn't make any sense, the stuff
171		that she was taking
172	J1:	Well sometimes people have strange dissociative reactions
173		like this and just uh do these kinds of things. I suppose
174		from what you've said I'm inclined to think something like
175		that was in the picture. I'd think she'd probably legally
176		knew what was going on, would be just guess from what you're
177		saying but uh but I bet you're not gonna sell the Dee Ay
178		either
179	PD1:	I can't-
180	DA1:	heh heh no I don't think so
181	PD1:	I can't see a jury ever convicting her, I just can't believe
182		a jury would convict her
183	J1:	You know people do do this occasionally and it's like as not,
184		somebody that's older and it- and all of a sudden just does
185		something totally out of character and the uh fact that these
186		are not for her is really very significant. I mean she's
187		got a large and a small, they're not for somebody else either,
188		they're just taken
189	DA1:	Well I don't, I'm not saying we haven't got problems with
190		the case judge. But it's just some kind of case that I just
191		don't- I think she knew what was going on, when she starts
192		pinning, you know, if she'd just carried them out the door
193		or something like that or tried something very unsophisticated
194		I may be (on a little different) posture. But going in a
195		store and pinning up underneath the clothes, that's a pro.
196		somebody who thought about it
197	J1:	What'd she use for pins
198	PD1:	She had-
199	DA1:	She brought 'em in
200	PD1:	She had pins so apparently uh, I don't know where she got
201		the pins
202	J1:	Uh how was she caught
203	PD1:	Well uh-
204	J1:	Mirrors or was she very very bulgy
205	PD1:	No uh ay store detective, um female was going through there
206		and she saw that a shawl that was hanging in was put in one
207		of the louvres, and that made her suspicious so she looked,
208		went down and looked underneath the thing and-
209	DA1:	Another sophistication
210	J1:	Yeah
211		(2.8)

212	J1:	What would you be willing to do on it, would you be willing
213		to cut it down, she's an older lady if you had her on, you
214		know, give her a four eight four if she's got- and if uh
215		therapy and uh checked on
216	DA1:	I'd give her a four eight four
217	J1:	Maybe that's just as well for her, she's running a risk if
218		she gets a grand theft
219	DA1:	How about a four eight four and a referral to probation
220	PD1:	No
221	DA1:	How about a one thirty one point three report
222	J1:	Hey what about a one thirty one point three
223	PD1:	Well I wouldn't mind, the only- my problem is if we're going
224		to try it I wanna try it you know when it's set now because
225		I'm gonna be gone for about two weeks on vacation, that's
226		my last time to try it unless you continue it
227	J1:	That's why you smiled so all day today. Couldn't figure it
228		out
229	PD1:	Yeah I could hardly wait
230		(1.2)
231	PD1:	So if you- I'll talk with her. Thing of it is SHE's really
232		upset about this whole thing, she's just a nervous bundle
233		of- she doesn't speak any English, um I'll talk and see
234		if she'll go along with a one thirty one point three but uh
235		(3.0)
236	PD1:	It- the thing of it is, it's so totally out of character
237		for her
238	J1:	Something seems odd. Well we'd be also be interested to
239		know what she had the seconals for because there may be
240		something else going on that the seconal may give us clue
241		to . . . you might then have something to go to probation
242		on and probation might then uh say okay. 'Cause I'm sure
243		if it's demonstrated that she's got some odd effect, you
244		guys'd go along and say well that's all we need to know and
245		and that's all HE needs to know too. On the other hand
246		these kinds of things more are likely to occur, it seems
247		to me in uh later life simply because of people uh having
248		as I said what's called dissociative reactions, just sort
249		of acting strangely for some hours and not even remembering
250		it. WELL there's uh a couple of Carlsons, and so I don't
251		know which it is so, that might help ya, might not help ya
252	PD1:	Well I've talked with uh Avalon
253	J1:	Bill Avalon?
254	PD1:	Bill Avalon is the one I talked with. Uh I didn't talk with
255		the- he just prescribed the darvoset, and that's for
256		arthritic condition
257	J1:	Yeah. Well that's a pain killer and-

258	PD1:	Reacts the same, you know
259		(2.6)
260	DA1:	Well how about a one thirty one point three report
261	J1:	Ya wanna do that
262	PD1:	What is that going to prove, what is it going to show
263	J1:	Well it just might be, if you're able to set it up so that
264		you can show the probation officer look this is what happened
265		or get the probation officer to talk to Anderson or have
266		a controlled experiment or something so the probation officer
267		says WE think that this what likely occurred they might then
268		say well although we recommend such and such a sentence we
269		also think as they sometimes put in there, there's a real
270		question of whether the person knew what was going on. My-
271		I would guess against it. I would think the odds are that
272		probation, even with what might be going on, is not gonna
273		pick it up would be my guess
274	PD1:	Well then we just- then we'll just wind up right back in
275		trial
276	J1:	Yeah then you'd be in trial three weeks from now
277	PD1:	Be after my vacation anyway
278	J1:	Well she'd be a little older she might be a little uh, if
279		they are unconvinced by this story, she might-
280	PD1:	She's such a sweet little old lady uh there's no jury in
281		the world's gonna convict her. I just can't believe it.
282		Particularly when we have a doctor and a pathologist who
283		⌊say they'll come in and talk⌋
284	DA2:	⌈It's the sweet little old la⌉dy defense okay
285	J1:	Who's the pathologist you talked to
286	PD1:	Uh Paxon
287	DA1:	'Kay what do you want in here you wanna go to trial or you
288		wanna one thirty one point three. A one thirty one point
289		three report would help us lean towards dismissal if that's
290		a recommendation
291	PD1:	Well let me go talk with her
292	DA1:	What I got here in this, I think we can try it
293	J1:	Okay
294	PD1:	Let me go try

((PD1 leaves room and talks to his client. The following occurs
when he returns:))

295	PD1:	. . . I told her that there was a possibility that if we went
296		to a one thirty one point three, and the dee ay uh then
297		views the case, they may dismiss. If they didn't dismiss
298		we could still go to trial. She said that's fine, whatever
299		will be most convenient with everybody else, so
300	DA1:	I don't care

301   PD1:   Ya wanna put it over ta one thirty one point three I'm not
302   opposed to it
303   J1:   Uh wanta do that
304   DA1:   It'd be over into next month, he doesn't get back in time
305   PD1:   I won't be back until after the fourth

((Dominguez case is continued to obtain "131.3" report. Pretrial
and trial dates are set for four weeks and five weeks later,
respectively.))

The Lucinda Smith Case

```
001  PD1:  I have um, Lucinda Smith is a petty theft
002  DA3:  Mm hmm
003  PD1:  case
004  DA3:  Goes in and takes a- some needles, and I think some thread
005  PD1:  Um my argument would be the same thing as John's. It doesn't
006        seem to me that twenty four hours in jail- This lady lives
007        in Sea City, she had her house burned, and she uh apparently
008        she's staying with relatives. But at any rate she came up
009        here, she has three small children, two and a half month
010        old baby, the youngest. Seems to me that some disposition
011        other than twenty four hours in jail is- would be appropriate
012        in this case rather than the standard
013  DA3:  Who was caring for the child when she was-
014  PD1:  She had it with 'im
015  DA3:  Oh did she?
016  PD1:  She came up here on the bus to visit a lady and the lady's
017        out there now with her
018                            (1.0)
019  PD1:  Uh, and on the way, she stopped by the market, she got uh
020        needle and thread and then something else
021                            (11.0)
022  DA3:  Needles. Lip quencher
023  PD1:  That was- she says she had that, she had uh lip quencher
024        with her. And she had some, the FLASHbulbs she said she
025        had with her
026  DA3:  Yeah they show lip quencher, uh thread, dial a needle
027  PD1:  That's the needles
028  DA3:  Yeah. Um, a mirror plaque
029  DA3:  And um
030  PD1:  She took the threh- what she says she took from the store
031        was the thread-
032  DA3:  a few flashbulbs
```

033   PD1:   needles, mirror
034   DA3:   And not the flashbulbs huh?
035   PD1:   Pardon? Not the flashbulbs, not the-
036   DA3:   They must of had uh their label on 'em for them to conclude
037   that that was the case
038   PD1:   I don't know. This is what she tells me
039   DA3:   Okay
040   (7.0)
041   DA3:   Well, there's uh- there's some dispute about that
042   PD1:   The thing of it is, you know, this lady has come- she did
043   come up here from Sea City, you know, to face the punishment.
044   She knows that she's facing twenty four hours. No question
045   about that, she knows that. Um, but it just seems to me
046   that uh twenty four hours in jail for something like that
047   is just-
048   DA3:   Okay, I understand that, I've- I don't see that I can make
049   an exception on this
050   PD1:   Okay
051   DA3:   What do ya wanta do
052   PD1:   Well, I don't wanta continue the case, she'll probably plead
053   and take the time
054   DA3:   Okay, you make a pitch and might get a low key-
055   PD1:   Well, I don't know. I don't feel that strongly about it except
056   that I just feel like that, you know, she was arraigned, she
057   went back to Sea City, she came up here knowing that she's
058   facing this, she's got a two and a half month old baby, she's
059   been trying to support herself and two kids or three kids
060   and this- and uh, I bet you she's probably gone through enough
061   hell as it is, you know, and I don't think twenty four hours
062   is gonna-
063   DA3:   I- uh, the judge may be responsive to that

The Donald Cleaver Case

```
001  PD2:   Um where were we
002  DA3:   Oh, I think we're gonna talk about
003  PD2:   Cleaver. Yeah um Jeff, y'know I've scratched my brains
004          trying to think of an alternative to theft . . . uh, having
005          to do with failing to pay for his parking . . . he did not
006          deprive anybody of their property in that he was very careful
007          to look for somebody that had two stickers, and only take
008          one of them so that they would still be able to h(h)ave
009          free parking . . . he's a young guy, a student out there and
010          the court's file would have a letter from the dean of students
011          asking for a, uh any possible courtesy in this case. I think
012          that the dean of student's position is that uh the guy should
013          not have a criminal record. And uh, Joe ((PD4)) what was
014          that parking uh, you had a parking sticker problem
015  PD4:   Twenty one one one three ay
016  PD2:   Of the vehicle code? What does it say?
017  PD4:   It covers uh various parking violations including illegal
018          parking on state property
019  PD2:   Arright. Well if you'd be willing to stipulate it's a
020          factually related offense-
021  DA3:   Yeah I tell you what um-
022  PD2:   I think a fine would not be unreasonable
023  DA3:   Well-
024  PD2:   I'm trying to remove it from the theft category
025  DA3:   Tell me this, why in any one of these parking permit cases,
026          would not the same argument be made
027  PD2:   Well I think it's a good argument if we're not- because I'm
028          trying to separate it from theft ya see
029  DA3:   Oh arright I understand that, I appreciate what your endeavor
030          uh to do is, but in every one of these um uh appropriating
031          found property to one's own use, um which you and I as lawyers
```

032		know is um a variation on a theme of theft, failure to return
033		lost property or make diligent effort to find the owner
034	PD2:	Mm hmm
035	DA3:	Why would that, your effort, or the logic of your effort not
036		apply to every one of the rather, well to several misuse of
037		parking sticker cases, uh
038	PD2:	Well, my logic is that uhm I don't think that the young man
039		considered himself a thief and that one of the things we
040		punish is y- somebody that takes something out of a store
041		bloody well knows it's stealing, and bloody well knows who
042		he is and what he's done
043	DA3:	I- that would apply with equal force to every case in which
044		an individual allegedly loses or finds uh uhm a parking
045		sticker on the ground, they're always somehow wind up on the
046		ground and somebody always finds it on the ground and says
047		neato! I can, uh you know, use this without having to pay
048		a parking fee. Now I don't think that- that it occurred
049		to him, uh
050	PD2:	Well how's it different from crashing the gate, let's say
051		he drove his car through there and crashed the gate without
052		destroying anybody's property
053	DA3:	Fair question, snuck in and parked
054	PD2:	That's what we're pleading him to, ya see
055	DA3:	Arright, but, I appreciate that, but-
056	PD2:	Yeah that's what I'm suggesting
057	DA3:	But in terms of sort of the moral turpitude of the matter
058	PD2:	Mm hmm
059	DA3:	Uh one who uh does an end around run on the parking kiosk,
060		or in this case appropriates a
061	PD2:	Yeah
062	DA3:	quote found unquote parking sticker, but it's the same purpose,
063		parking uh all day without uh having to pay out the moneys.
064		One must appreciate that one is getting away with uh not
065		having to spend the amount of money one would- one would
066		otherwise have to spend to accomplish the same thing
067	PD2:	Oh it's true
068	DA3:	Arright so I don't think that- that it- I mean
069	PD2:	Well I'm suggesting that you could've filed it either way
070	DA3:	Well
071	PD2:	This way, you know as a theft charge, it- considering his
072		age and his- you know, it's a very serious thing to lay-
073		lay a theft charge on somebody like that . . .
074	DA3:	Yeah I know and granting among lawyers that it's a variation
075		on theft, still appropriating lost property is rather fair
076		statement what it is. Uh- and that's what he did, and he
077		used it as one would use uh appropriated property to his own

078		use, in this case to beat a fee, um if we knock this down
079		to that, whatever it is vehicle code section, we knock 'em
080		all down and I-
081	PD2:	Well maybe ya don't have to do that, this is a special case
082		in that the dean of students has written a letter to the
083		court. Have you seen it?
084	DA3:	No I haven't
085	PD2:	Okay well-
086	DA3:	Maybe it would be useful for me to see that . . . uh my
087		inclination is ta say that it is uh fairly stated as a theft
088		charge, not- I mean viewed in the abstract, but also the
089		fact that this apparently happens fairly often. I haven't
090		seen any case yet in which the individual was observed
091		unhooking the parking ticket from the bumper or the rear
092		view mirror, uh they ALways wind up on the ground somehow
093		and uh, that's always the explanation given, a fair inference
094		in at least some of them is that uh, somebody stole it
095	PD2:	These parking stickers you see are made so that they have to
096		be stuck on bumpers
097	DA3:	Well not all of them. A lot of these cases involve uh, ya
098		see, if you own more than one car you get a motor pool sticker
099		which is hung on a piece of cardboard, and ya hang that in
100		your rear view mirror
101	PD2:	Is this one of those
102	DA3:	Uh this happens to have been hung from the bumper
103	PD2:	Well what I mean is, apparently the person who HAD it, was
104		also playing some game with the parking people, because they
105		are suppose to be stuck to the bumper and uh-
106	DA3:	Well I-
107	PD2:	Course they get, you know if you have more than one, it's not
108		convenient, so apparently the owner of the sticker did something
109		that they weren't supposed to be doing with the sticker anyway
110		which was instead of attaching it to the bumper so it could
111		not be moved, they had it attached to some plate
112	DA3:	But that- let's assume that the owner was not permitted to
113		do that and the owner was trying to steal a ( ) on the
114		college. That hardly inures to the benefit of the defendant
115	PD2:	Well I'm- we're not accusing the defendant of stealing it
116	DA3:	Yeah WE have. Not of stealing it, but of a variation on the
117		theme of theft
118	PD2:	Well
119	DA3:	I just want to know, you know in what case it would be uh
120		appropriate to stay with the charge of misappropriating uh
121		found property
122	PD2:	Well, it seems to me, that one of the reasons you have the
123		kind of discretion that you have is that you can take a look

124		at the person that's being charged and decide what the
125		consequences of your action would be you know on any
126		individual person
127	DA3:	Okay
128	PD2:	Uh you take a young student, I think he's eighteen or
129		nineteen years old, he's uh just starting out, trying to get-
130		you know, in college, uh and you lay larceny on him. Uh true
131		he can come back in a year and get it taken off his record,
132		but for many other purposes uh it's going to be known, for
133		example if he ever tries to get security clearance uh whether
134		or not the court seals his records uh they will know about
135		the conviction
136	DA3:	Well
137	PD2:	They apparently go beyond what our um- Joe ((PD4)), let me
138		ask you something. The uh- you made one of these arrangements
139		what was it, last week or week before
140	PD4:	On what
141	PD2:	Uh having to do with this parking sticker business and uh
142		crashing the gate
143	PD4:	Yeah
144	PD2:	You know and Jeffrey is asking me, well why not every case
145	PD4:	Yeah, well I think really uh-
146	PD2:	This is a case where the dean of students has written into
147		court a letter on the student's behalf
148	PD4:	Actually, I think uh, where you have- I think I had a pretty
149		good case in which to make a number of points. Okay maybe
150		you do too, I don't know, but as far as the cases in general
151		seems to me that when you have these people who're students
152		with no previous record, this is not something you wanna give
153		them theft on
154	DA3:	Yeah um
155	PD4:	Seems to me they oughta be filed to begin with as something else
156	DA3:	Don said something that uh, you know, that one can- one
157		of the things that the dee ay can do in looking- in deciding
158		what to file or what to dispose of is, you know look to the
159		individual. Well we're dealing with a self-admitted clientele
160		out there, who don't have the range of people that you have
161		if you took a cross section of you know life on the streets
162		and deciding whether a given individual merits uh
163	PD4:	Mm hmm
164	DA3:	You know special dispensation. You know they're all students,
165		they all have futures before them. Which of course implies
166		they also have or ought to have a heightened sense of
167		responsibility and appreciation for the consequences of their
168		acts, uh particularly with, you know a future beckoning before

169		them and I-
170	PD4:	Uh I don't think that's true, in fact I think maybe if you're
171		oh about eighteen, nineteen, twenty, you're just not experienced
172		enough. Many of them have never been in court before. They
173		don't think about the consequences because they don't SEE
174		this as a theft. They see it as uh, you know, getting some
175		free parking. Okay maybe if you analyze it, it's theft, but
176		they don't think of it as theft
177	DA3:	They can make a distinction between that and the guy who
178		boosts the bandana at the drug store
179	PD4:	Well there is a distinction
180	PD2:	It's stealing, it's something that his parents have told
181		him about
182	PD4:	Yeah everybody thinks of that in terms of stealing, but
183		these kids don't think of parking sticker in terms of
184		stealing
185		(2.0)
186	PD2:	Just kind of ARE eff. You remember that phrase
187	DA3:	I do indeed
188	PD2:	You know the acid test is this . . . I was out there before
189		they build those goddam kiosks
190	PD4:	Ye(h)s heh heh heh
191	PD2:	And I recall that if you had any class at all you had a
192		faculty sticker. Now in order to get a faculty sticker, you
193		had to do it to a member of the faculty you know. Seems to
194		me I knew a certain teacher of languages and uh I had a
195		dynamite sticker, I had all kinds of little things going.
196		I recall that getting a faculty sticker and then arranging
197		to live in married student housing back in the days when
198		you really had to be married to live in married student
199		housing. Now I suppose you could, you know, you could have
200		filed one of these charges in ALL those cases. If anybody
201		had asked me in those days if I felt like a thief, I mean,
202		or you know or brought up this issue, you know I would have-
203	DA3:	Your head lay easy on the pillow did it
204	PD2:	Oh god yes, heh I didn't- uh I also crumbled up my ROTC
205		uniform and stuck it in a locker ya know, just-
206	PD4:	Heh!
207	PD2:	just to heh heh heh heh heh I heh heh I mean it was kind
208		of a sign, I had to wear that uniform, but on the other hand
209		I didn't have to press it, we(h)e hee and it was quite a
210		thing to behold, an ROTC uniform tha(h)t had been
211		deli(h)berately put under a pi(h)le of books heh heh for
212		a week
213	PD4:	heh heh heh heh

214	PD2:	I mea(h)n heh, it achieved a certain- you know it made it's
215		own subtle statement about-
216	DA3:	heh heh heh hah hah hah
217	PD2:	Course they got even with me, I got drafted while I was in
218		co(h)lle(h)ge, the justice was done eventually
219	DA3:	You just don't appreciate the breaks that-
220	PD2:	I suppose not
221	DA3:	God and gov'ner Reagan gave ya
222	PD2:	Yeah
223		(2.4)
224	DA3:	Well uh maybe I can make an exception in this case on the
225		theory that if the dean of students doesn't care enough for
226		the enforcement of the college's own rules, why should we
227		feel all that uh- what was the section found uh
228	PD4:	Twenty one, uh two one one one three ay
229	DA3:	Hm
230	PD4:	I'm almost sure it is, I can show you
231	DA3:	What do you want in a fine
232	PD2:	Mm what's reasonable. Fifty dollars
233	DA3:	Fifty's fine
234	PD2:	Fifteen dollar penalty assessment
235	DA3:	Mm hmm
236	PD2:	Total sixty five dollars
237	DA3:	Mm hmm
238	PD2:	Arright

The Cliff Washington Case

001	PD1:	Cliff Burton Washington . . . he uh was just released from
002		jail
003	DA3:	Mm hmm
004	PD1:	And uh was rummaging through a couple of cars
005	DA3:	Mm hmm. He's going to do some time isn't he
006	PD1:	And he's doing time
007	DA3:	Is he? on another violation?
008	PD1:	Well I- they put him in jail on this and he hasn't been-
009	DA3:	Hasn't been out?
010	PD1:	He hasn't been out
011	DA3:	Oh. When did he go ta jail on this thing, uh the twenty ninth
012	PD1:	Yeah that's when they picked him up, he's been- hasn't been
013		out since. In addition to that he's got a probation matter
014		that's uh pending, he's- and I've talked with Paxton about it,
015		we're going to- uh he's going to be found in violation
016	DA3:	Is that on that petty theft he was in jail on
017	PD1:	You know, I don't have- I don't know what it is right now,
018		but it's a- he was on probation and he has, uh and I don't
019		know the nature of the charge. He had uh forty eight days
020		with credit for thirteen days so he has thirty five days
021	DA3:	Yeah, Bill Severt's note indicates that this guy on the twenty
022		ninth pre-trial date was placed on probation uh with thirty
023		five days suspended for petty theft charge that dealt with
024		taking items out of cars at the Suburban News parking lot
025	PD1:	Well see I didn't handle that case, but I do have the probation
026		matter now
027	DA3:	Well I wonder. Let's see, oh yeah okay here we are, let's see
028		here's this, let's see if this is it
029		(3.2)
030	DA3:	Yeah this is the one, this is the old one
031	PD1:	So he's going to wind up doing the thirty five days

032   (4.0)
033   PD1:   He's an elderly guy who just doesn't seem to comprehend a great
034   deal
035   DA3:   He just doesn't seem to pick up real quick does he
036   PD1:   No. He just uh doesn't seem to grasp things at all
037   DA3:   Hm. I mean is it uh
038   (3.8)
039   PD1:   He's just not smart I guess, I don't know, you talk with him
040   and he's very frank about what he does, you know I mean he
041   doesn't try to- he says yeah, he says I got caught. Uh, but
042   I don't know
043   DA3:   I don't either. God I remember, I may have told you this
044   anecdote. Uh out in Basintown, dealing with, what was it, it
045   was either prelim petty with a prior or it was a petty theft
046   case, anyway the guy was charged with boosting a carton of
047   cigarettes out of a liquor store and I'd been hearing all these
048   stories about how it just happened that this item or that found
049   it's way into the pocket of the poor defendant and all these
050   sad stories, and I asked this old gentleman uh you know what
051   his story was and he said uh I stole the cigarettes and I said
052   what? and he said, and he gave me this sort of contemptuous look
053   for a (young-) I stole the cigarettes. I'm a thief, I've been
054   a thief for a long time
055   PD1:   Heh heh
056   DA3:   Now here's how we're gonna- here's how we're gonna defend
057   the case and th(h)ere's
058   PD1:   heh HAH HAH hah
059   DA3:   kind of elaborate and rather incorrect search and seizure notion
060   but he was ve(h)ry up front kind of gu(h)y heh heh
061   PD1:   Well this guy doesn't- he's just like that except he doesn't
062   have any defenses
063   DA3:   heh heh heh
064   PD1:   heh heh heh heh .hh .hh
065   DA3:   Well um he's been in since twenty ninth and is gonna have done
066   his thirty five days by the time he get's around to a hearing
067   PD1:   Well the hearing is I think on the sixteenth
068   DA3:   Fifteenth actually
069   PD1:   Is it?
070   DA3:   Yeah according to the note uh made yesterday . . .
071   DA3:   I kinda want some time on this uh, although I don't think it
072   has to be a great deal more, in this case. He didn't break
073   anything, he didn't take anything
074   PD1:   He didn't take anything, in this case
075   DA3:   Yeah
076   PD1:   All he did is he got in the car and he, the owner of the car

```
077            says that some things were displaced
078   DA3:     Mmhmm
079   PD1:     But he did not take anything. So there was no theft
080                                    (12.4)
081   DA3:     He's lucky he's not (lookin' at a bird)
082                                    (5.6)
083   PD1:     He's a guy who's just- hasn't got any matza. He's just a dumb
084            dimwit
085                                    (4.2)
086   PD1:     Let's see how old of a guy he is, he's (9.0) nineteen sixteen
087   DA3:     Mm hmm
088   PD1:     Sixty one
089                       (39.0)     ((shuffling paper, reading file))
090   DA3:     He's not employed is he
091   PD1:     No I think he just sort of bums around lookin' for a home
092   DA3:     Well
093                                    (0.4)
094   DA3:     I want some time on this
095   PD1:     Oh well don't be too hard on him
096   DA3:     How about three months
097   PD1:     Nah that's too much
098                                    (4.0)
099   PD1:     That's too much
100   DA3:     How about four months with credit for time served
101   PD1:     How about uh, how about wiping it out with forty five days
102   DA3:     With credit for the time served? That he's done already?
103   PD1:     Yeah credit for the time he's been in
104   PD1:     He's just an old codger that
105   DA3:     Steals a lot
106   PD1:     Yeah, but you're not gonna be able to-
107   DA3:     Yeah well the old codgers that steal a lot are just as big of
108            thieves as-
109   PD1:     Uh he didn't steal anything in this one though
110   DA3:     Oh god knows he was trying

                    ((interruption by PD2 occurs here
                    regarding when DA3 will be available))

111   DA3:     Uh I'll give you ninety days with credit for time served
112   PD1:     Nah that's no good
113   DA3:     I could get more
114   PD1:     No:: shoot. That's just too much time for that guy
115   DA3:     Well he hasn't got anything else to do with it does he. Besides
116            break into cars
117                                    (4.6)
118   DA3:     Where's that uh- we have all this (          ) on this guy
```

119		and I don't have a rap sheet. Do you have a rap sheet
120	PD1:	No
121	DA3:	How could we not have a rap sheet on a guy like this
122		(6.4)
123	DA3:	What? Oh here it is. I was looking at it before.
124		(7.4)
125	PD1:	Do ya think he's a petty thiever
126	DA3:	There's no convictions on a couple of those . . . he escapes
127		on most of these things. Well I can't say that it's uh
128		terribly significant, here from the looks of it
129		(3.4)
130	DA3:	What did I say? Three months for that, ninety days
131	PD1:	Give him forty five
132	DA3:	Give him sixty
133	DA3:	₁C- c'mon sixty ₁ ₁last offer₁
134	PD1:	⌐Oh come on Jeffrey⌐ come ⌐o::::n J- ⌐ .hhh listen forty five, give
135		him forty five and credit for time served, that₁'s plenty₁ good
136	DA3:	⌐Na::::::h ⌐
137	PD1:	Uh listen he didn't steal anything it isn't tampering it's
138		not a theft
139	DA3:	It's a good burg is what it is, it's a good auto burg
140	PD1:	Oh I don't know, he coulda been mistaken about his car heh
141		heh heh
142	DA3:	Uh huh righ(h)t, about which of his cars was parked in the
143		jailhouse lot. Uh huh . . .
144	PD1:	Well why don't we do this. Let's put it over until after the
145		probation violation hearing . . . just put the thing over for
146		a week . . .
147	DA3:	I think it was coming up this Friday
148	PD1:	Coming up this Friday
149	DA3:	Uh any reason not to dispose of it then
150	PD1:	No okay put it on for Friday
151	DA3:	Arright
152	PD1:	Okay

References

Abel, R.L.
1980 Redirecting Social Studies of Law. *Law and Society Review,* 14:805–829.
Alfini, James J. (ed.)
1981 *Misdemeanor Courts: Policy Concerns and Research Perspectives.* Washington, D.C.: National Institute of Justice.
Alfini, James J., and Rachel N. Doan
1977 A New Perspective on Misdemeanor Justice. *Judicature,* 60:425–34.
Alpert, Geoffrey P., and Donald A. Hicks
1977 Prisoners' Attitudes Toward Components of the Legal System. *Criminology,* 14:481–482.
Alschuler, Albert
1968 The Prosecutor's Role in Plea Bargaining. *University of Chicago Law Review,* 36:50–112.
1975 The Defense Attorney's Role in Plea Bargaining. *The Yale Law Journal,* 84:1179–1314.
1976 The Trial Judge's Role in Plea Bargaining. *Columbia Law Review,* 76:1059–1154.
1979 Plea Bargaining and Its History. *Law and Society Review,* 13:211–245.
Antonio, Robert J.
1972 The Processual Dimension of Degradation Ceremonies: The Chicago Conspiracy Trial: Success or Failure? *British Journal of Sociology,* 23:287–297.
Arcuri, Alan F.
1976 Lawyers, Judges, and Plea Bargaining: Some New Data on Inmates' Views. *International Journal of Criminology and Penology,* 4:177–191.
Atkinson, J. Maxwell
1979 Sequencing and Shared Attentiveness to Court Proceedings. Pp. 257–286 in George Psathas (ed.), *Everyday Language: Studies in Ethnomethodology.* New York: Irvington.
1982 Understanding Formality: The Categorization and Production of 'Formal' Interaction. *The British Journal of Sociology,* 33:86–117.
Atkinson, J. Maxwell, and Paul Drew
1979 *Order in Court.* London: MacMillan.

Austin, J.L.
   1965   *How to Do Things with Words.* New York: Oxford University Press.
Baldwin, John, and Michael McConville
   1977   *Negotiated Justice: Pressures to Plead Guilty.* London: Martin Robertson.
Barkan, Steven E.
   1977   Political Trials and the *Pro Se* Defendant. *Social Problems,* 24:324–336.
Becker, Howard S.
   1958   Problems of Inference and Proof in Participant Observation. *American Sociological Review,* 23:652–660.
Bennett, Lance
   1978   Storytelling in Criminal Trials: A Model of Social Judgment. *The Quarterly Journal of Speech,* 64:1–22.
   1979   Rhetorical Transformation of Evidence in Criminal Trials: Creating Grounds for Legal Judgment. *The Quarterly Journal of Speech,* 65:311–323.
Bennett, W. Lance, and Martha S. Feldman
   1981   *Reconstructing Reality in the Courtroom.* New Brunswick, N.J.: Rutgers University Press.
Bernstein, Ilene Nagel, William R. Kelley, and Patricia Doyle
   1977a Societal Reaction to Deviants: The Case of Criminal Defendants. *American Sociological Review,* 42:743–755.
Bernstein, Ilene N., Edward Kick, Jan T. Leung, and Barbara B. Schulz
   1977b Charge Reduction: An Intermediary Stage in the Process of Labelling Criminal Defendants. *Social Forces,* 56:362–384.
Bittner, Egon
   1974   The Concept of Organization. Pp. 69–82 in Roy Turner (ed.), *Ethnomethodology.* England: Penguin.
Blau, Peter
   1964   *Exchange and Power in Social Life.* New York: John Wiley.
Blum, Alan F., and Peter McHugh
   1971   The Social Ascription of Motives. *American Sociological Review,* 36:98–190.
Blumberg, Abraham
   1967   *Criminal Justice.* Chicago: Quadrangle.
Blumer, Herbert
   1956   Sociological Analysis and the Variable. *American Sociological Review,* 21:683–690.
Boden, Deirdre
   1981   *Talk International.* Unpublished masters thesis. Santa Barbara: University of California.
Bogdan, Robert, and Steven J. Taylor
   1975   *Introduction to Qualitative Research Methods.* New York: John Wiley.
Bottoms, Anthony E., and John D. McClean
   1976   *Defendants in the Criminal Process.* London: Routledge and Kegan Paul.
Brickey, Stephen L., and Dan E. Miller
   1975   An Ethnography of a Traffic Court. *Social Problems,* 22:688–697.
Buckle, Suzann R. Thomas, and Leonard G. Buckle
   1977   *Bargaining for Justice: Case Disposition and Reform in the Criminal Courts.* New York: Praeger.

Burger, Thomas
1976 *Max Weber's Theory of Concept Formation.* Durham, N.C.: Duke University Press.
Burstein, Carolyn
1980 Criminal Case Processing from an Organizational Perspective. *The Justice System Journal,* 5:258–273.
Carlen, Pat
1976 *Magistrate's Justice.* London: Martin Robertson.
Carlin, Jerome E.
1966 *Lawyers' Ethics: A Survey of the New York City Bar.* New York: Russell Sage.
Casper, Jonathan D.
1972 *American Criminal Justice: The Defendant's Perspective.* Englewood Cliffs, N.J.: Prentice Hall.
Chiricos, Theodore G., and Gordon P. Waldo
1975 Socioeconomic Status and Criminal Sentencing: An Empirical Assessment of a Conflict Proposition. *American Sociological Review,* 40:753–772.
Chiricos, Theodore G., Phillip D. Jackson, and Gordon P. Waldo
1972 Inequality in the Imposition of a Criminal Label. *Social Problems,* 19:553–572.
Churchill, Lindsay
1978 *Questioning Strategies in Sociolinguistics.* Rowley, Mass.: Newbury House.
Cicourel, Aaron
1964 *Method and Measurement in Sociology.* New York: Free Press.
1968 *The Social Organization of Juvenile Justice.* New York: John Wiley.
Clarke, Stevens H., and Gary G. Koch
1976 The Influence of Income and Other Factors on Whether Criminal Defendants Go to Prison. *Law and Society Review,* 11:57–92.
Clynch, Edward J., and David W. Neubauer
1981 Trial Courts as Organizations. *Law and Policy Quarterly,* 3:69–94.
Cohen, Michael D., James G. March, and Johan P. Olsen
1972 A Garbage Can Model of Organizational Choice. *Administrative Science Quarterly,* 17:1–25.
Collins, Randall
1981 On the Micro Foundations of Macrosociology. *American Journal of Sociology,* 86:984–1014.
Conley, John M., and William M. O'Barr
1977 *Behavioral Analysis of the American Criminal Courtroom.* Durham, N.C.: Duke University Law and Language Project (Research Report No. 4).
Conley, John, William M. O'Barr, and E. Allen Lind
1978 The Power of Language: Presentational Style in the Courtroom. *Duke Law Journal,* 1978:1375–1399.
Coulter, Jeff
1979 *The Social Construction of Mind: Studies in Ethnomethodology and Linguistic Philosophy.* Totowa, N.J.: Rowman and Littlefield.
Cressey, Donald R.
1953 *Other People's Money: A Study in the Social Psychology of Embezzlement.* Glencoe, Ill.: Free Press.

Cyert, Richard M., and James G. March
  1963 *A Behavioral Theory of the Firm.* Englewood Cliffs, N.J.: Prentice Hall.
Dalton, Melville
  1959 *Men Who Manage.* New York: John Wiley.
Dane, Francis C., and Lawrence S. Wrightsman
  1982 Effects of Defendants' and Victims' Characteristics on Jurors' Verdicts. Pp. 83–115 in Norbert L. Kerr and Robert M. Bray (eds.), *The Psychology of the Courtroom.* New York: Academic Press.
Danet, Brenda
  1980a 'Baby' or 'Fetus'? Language and the Construction of Reality in a Manslaughter Trial. *Semiotica,* 32:187–219.
  1980b Language in the Legal Process. *Law and Society Review,* 14:445–564.
Danet, Brenda, and Nicole C. Kermish
  1978 Courtroom Questioning: A Sociolinguistic Perspective. Pp. 412–441 in Louis N. Massey, II (ed.), *Psychology and Persuasion in Advocacy.* Washington D.C.: Association of Trial Lawyers of America, National College of Advocacy.
Darley, J. M., and B. Latane
  1973 Bystander Interaction in Emergencies: Diffusion of Responsibility. *Journal of Personality and Social Psychology,* 27:100–108.
Daudistel, Howard
  1980 On the Elimination of Plea Bargaining: The El Paso Experiment. Pp. 57–75 in William F. McDonald and James A. Cramer (eds.), *Plea Bargaining.* Lexington, Mass.: D. C. Heath.
Davis, Anthony
  1970 Sentences for Sale: A New Look at Plea Bargaining in England and America. *Criminal Law Review* (March and April):150–162, 218–229.
Douglas, Jack D.
  1967 *The Social Meanings of Suicide.* Princeton: Princeton University Press.
Dunstan, Robert
  1980 Context for Coercion: Analyzing Properties of Courtroom 'Questions'. *British Journal of Law and Society,* 7:61–77.
Edelman, Murray
  1964 *The Symbolic Uses of Politics.* Urbana: University of Illinois Press.
Eisenstein, James, and Herbert Jacob
  1977 *Felony Justice.* Boston: Little, Brown and Co.
Ekeh, Peter
  1974 *Social Exchange Theory: The Two Traditions.* Cambridge: Harvard University Press.
Emerson, Robert
  1969 *Judging Delinquents: Context and Process in Juvenile Court.* Chicago: Aldine.
  1981 On Last Resorts. *American Journal of Sociology,* 87:1–33.
Ervin-Tripp, Susan
  1972 On Sociolinguistic Rules: Alternations and Co-occurrence. Pp. 213–251 in John J. Gumperz and Dell Hymes (eds.), *Directions in Sociolinguistics.* New York: Holt, Rinehart, and Winston.

Etzioni, Amitai
1961   *A Comparative Analysis of Complex Organizations.* New York: Free Press.
Farrell, Ronald A., and Victoria L. Swigert
1978   Prior Offense Record as Self-Fulfilling Prophecy. *Law and Society Review,* 12:437–458.
Feeley, Malcolm
1973   Two Models of the Criminal Justice System: An Organizational Perspective. *Law and Society Review,* 7:407–425.
1979a Perspectives on Plea Bargaining. *Law and Society Review,* 13:199–209.
1979b Pleading Guilty in Lower Courts. *Law and Society Review,* 13:461–466.
1979c *The Process is the Punishment.* New York: Russell Sage Foundation.
Flacks, Richard
1975   Making History vs. Making Life: Dilemmas of an American Left. *Sociological Inquiry,* 46:263–280.
Frankel, Richard M.
1981   *I Wz Wondering—Uhm Could Raid Uhm Affect the Brain Permanently D'Y Know? Record Keeping in the Context of Communicative Interaction.* Paper presented at the annual meetings of the American Sociological Association. Toronto: August.
1983   The Laying on of Hands: Aspects of the Organization of Gaze, Touch, and Talk in a Medical Encounter. Pp. 19–54 in Sue Fisher and Alexandra Todd (eds.), *The Social Organization of Doctor–Patient Communication.* Washington D.C.: Center for Applied Linguistics.
Friedman, Lawrence M.
1979   Plea Bargaining in Historical Perspective. *Law and Society Review,* 13:247–259.
Garfinkel, Harold
1967   *Studies in Ethnomethodology.* Englewood Cliffs, N.J.: Prentice Hall.
Garfinkel, Harold, and Harvey Sacks.
1970   The Formal Structures of Practical Actions. Pp. 338–365 in John C. McKinney and Edward Tiryakian (eds.), *Theoretical Sociology: Perspectives and Developments.* New York: Appleton-Century Crofts.
Gibson, James L.
1978   Race as a Determinant of Criminal Sentences: A Methodological Critique and a Case Study. *Law and Society Review,* 12:455–477.
1980   A Role Theoretic Model of Criminal Court Decision-Making. Pp. 83–99 in Peter F. Nardulli (ed.), *The Study of Criminal Courts: Political Perspectives.* Cambridge, Mass.: Ballinger.
Giddens, Anthony
1976   *New Rules of Sociological Method: A Positive Critique of Interpretive Sociologies.* New York: Basic Books.
1979   *Central Problems in Social Theory: Action, Structure, and Contradiction in Social Analysis.* Berkeley: University of California Press.
Glaser, Barney, G., and Anselm L. Strauss
1965   The Discovery of Substantive Theory: A Basic Strategy Underlying Qualitative Research. *The American Behavioral Scientist,* 8:5–12.

1967   *The Discovery of Grounded Theory: Strategies for Qualitative Research.* New York: Aldine.

Goffman, Erving
1961   *Encounters.* Indianapolis: Bobbs-Merrill.
1963   *Behavior in Public Places.* Glencoe, Ill.: Free Press of Glencoe.
1971   *Relations in Public.* New York: Harper-Colophon Books.
1974   *Frame Analysis.* New York: Harper-Colophon Books.
1979   Footing. *Semiotica,* 25:1–29.
1981   *Forms of Talk.* Philadelphia: University of Pennsylvania Press.

Goodwin, Charles
1981   *Conversational Organization: Interaction between Speakers and Hearers.* New York: Academic Press.

Gouldner, Alvin
1954   *Industrial Bureaucracy.* New York: Free Press.

Graham, Kenneth, and Leon Letwin
1969   Prosecutorial Discretion in the Initiation of Criminal Complaints. *Southern California Law Review,* 42:519–545.

Greenberg, David F.
1977   Socioeconomic Status and Criminal Sentences: Is There an Association? *American Sociological Review,* 42:174–176.

Grosman, Brian
1969   *The Prosecutor: An Inquiry into the Exercise of Discretion.* Toronto: University of Toronto Press.

Gulliver, P. H.
1979   *Disputes and Negotiations: A Cross Cultural Perspective.* New York: Academic Press.

Gumperz, John J. (ed.)
1972   Introduction. Pp. 1–25 in John J. Gumperz and Dell Hymes (ed.), *Directions in Sociolinguistics.* New York: Holt, Rinehart, and Winston.

Gurwitsch, A.
1964   *The Field of Consciousness.* Pittsburgh: Duquesne University Press.

Hagan, John
1974   Extra-Legal Attributes and Sentencing: An Assessment of a Sociological Viewpoint. *Law and Society Review,* 8:357–384.
1975a Parameters of Criminal Prosecution: An Application of Path Analysis to a Problem of Criminal Justice. *Journal of Criminal Law and Criminology,* 65:536–544.
1975b The Social and Legal Construction of Criminal Justice: A Study of the Pre-Sentence Process. *Social Problems,* 22:620–637.
1977   Criminal Justice in Rural and Urban Communities: A Study of the Bureaucratization of Justice. *Social Forces,* 55:597–612.

Hagan, John, John D. Hewitt, and Duane F. Alwin
1979   Ceremonial Justice: Crime and Punishment in a Loosely Coupled System. *Social Forces,* 58:506–527.

Hagan, John, Ilene H. Nagel (Bernstein), and Celesta Albonetti

1980 The Differential Sentencing of White-Collar Offenders in Ten Federal District Courts. *American Sociological Review, 45*:802–820.

Hall, Jerome
1960 *General Principles of Criminal Law.* Indianapolis: Bobbs-Merrill.

Haller, Mark H.
1979 Plea Bargaining: The Nineteenth Century Context. *Law and Society Review, 13*:273–279.

Handler, Joel F.
1967 *The Lawyer and His Community: The Practicing Bar in a Middle-Sized City.* Madison: University of Wisconsin Press.

Hanushek, Eric A., and John E. Jackson
1977 *Statistical Methods for Social Scientists.* New York: Academic Press.

Hasenfeld, Yeheskel
1972 People Processing Organizations: An Exchange Approach. *American Sociological Review, 37*:256–263.

Hazard, John N.
1962 Furniture Arrangement as a Symbol of Judicial Roles. *Et Cetera, 19*:181–188.

Heath, Anthony
1976 *Rational Choice and Social Exchange: A Critique of Exchange Theory.* New York: Cambridge University Press.

Heinz, Anne M., and Wayne A. Kerstetter
1979 Pretrial Settlement Conference: Evaluation of a Reform in Plea Bargaining. *Law and Society Review, 13*:349–366.

Hetzler, Antoinette N., and Charles H. Kanter
1974 Informality and the Court: A Study of the Behavior of Court Officials in the Processing of Defendants. Pp. 76–97 in Sawyer F. Sylvester, Jr. and Edward Sagarin (eds.), *Politics and Crime.* New York: Praeger.

Heumann, Milton
1978 *Plea Bargaining: The Experiences of Prosecutors, Judges, and Defense Lawyers.* Chicago: University of Chicago Press.

Hilbert, Richard A.
1981 Toward an Improved Understanding of 'Role'. *Theory and Society, 10*:207–226.

Hogarth, John
1971 *Sentencing as a Human Process.* Toronto: University of Toronto Press.

Homans, George C.
1958 Social Behavior as Exchange. *American Journal of Sociology, 63*:597–606.
1961 *Social Behavior: Its Elementary Forms.* New York: Harcourt, Brace, and World.

Hopkins, Andrew
1977 Is There a Class Bias in Criminal Sanctioning? *American Sociological Review, 42*:176–177.

Horwitz, Allen, and Michael Wasserman
1980 Formal Rationality, Substantive Justice, and Discrimination: A Study of a Juvenile Court. *Law and Human Behavior, 4*:103–115.

Hymes, Dell
    1974   *Foundations in Sociolinguistics.* Philadelphia: University of Pennsylvania
            Press.
Ikle, Fred C.
    1964   *How Nations Negotiate.* New York: Harper and Row.
Jefferson, Gail
    1978   Sequential Aspects of Storytelling in Conversation. Pp. 219–248 in Jim
            Schenkein (ed.), *Studies in the Organization of Conversational Interaction.*
            New York: Academic Press.
    1979   A Technique for Inviting Laughter and its Subsequent Accep-
            tance/Declination. Pp. 79–96 in George Psathas (ed.), *Everyday Language:
            Studies in Ethnomethodology.* New York: Irvington.
Jefferson, Gail, and Emanuel Schegloff
    n.d.   *Sketch: Some Orderly Aspects of Overlap in Natural Conversation.* Unpub-
            lished manuscript.
Jefferson, Gail, and Jim Schenkein
    1977   Some Sequential Negotiations in Conversation: Unexpanded and Ex-
            panded Versions of Projected Action Sequences. *Sociology,* 11:86–103.
Kalodner, Howard I.
    1956   Metropolitan Criminal Courts of First Instance. *Harvard Law Review,*
            70:320–349.
Kalven, Jr., Harry, and Hans Zeisel
    1966   *The American Jury.* Boston: Little, Brown and Co.
Kessler, Robert A.
    1962   The Psychological Effects of the Judical Robe. *American Imago,* 19:35–66.
Kleck, Gary
    1981   Racial Discrimination in Criminal Sentencing: A Critical Evaluation of
            the Evidence with Additional Evidence on the Death Penalty. *American
            Sociological Review,* 46:783–805.
Klein, John F.
    1976   *Let's Make a Deal.* Lexington, Mass.: Lexington Books.
Klonoski, James R., and Robert I. Mendelsohn (eds.)
    1970   *The Politics of Local Justice.* Boston: Little, Brown and Co.
Labov, William
    1972a   *Language in the Inner City.* Philadelphia: University of Pennsylvania
            Press.
    1972b   *Sociolinguistic Patterns.* Philadelphia: University of Pennsylvania Press.
Labov, William and David Fanshel
    1977   *Therapeutic Discourse.* New York: Academic Press.
La Free, Gary D.
    1981   Adversarial and Nonadversarial Justice: A Comparison of Guilty Pleas
            and Trials in the United States. Paper presented at the meeting of the
            American Society of Criminology, Washington, D.C.
Lagoy, Stephan P., Joseph J. Senna, and Larry J. Siegel
    1976   An Empirical Study on Information Usage for Prosecutorial Decision-
            making in Plea Negotiations. *American Criminal Law Review,* 13:435.

Lakoff, Robin
1975 *Language and Woman's Place.* New York: Harper and Row.
Langbein, John H.
1979 Understanding the Short History of Plea Bargaining. *Law and Society Review,* 13:261–272.
Levin, Martin
1972 Urban Politics and Judicial Behavior. *Journal of Legal Studies,* 1:193–225.
Lind, E. Allen, and William M. O'Barr
1979 The Social Significance of Speech in the Courtroom. Pp. 66–87 in Howard Giles and Robert St. Clair (eds.), *Language and Social Psychology.* Oxford: Basil Blackwell.
Lipsky, Michael
1980 *Street-Level Bureaucracy: Dilemmas of The Individual in Public Services.* New York: Russell Sage Foundation.
Littrell, W. Boyd
1979 *Bureaucratic Justice.* Beverly Hills: Sage.
Lizotte, Alan J.
1978 Extra-Legal Factors in Chicago's Criminal Courts: Testing the Conflict Model of Criminal Justice. *Social Problems,* 25:564–580.
Lofland, John
1971 *Analyzing Social Settings.* Belmont, Calif.: Wadsworth Publishing Co.
Loftus, Elizabeth, and John C. Palmer
1974 Reconstruction of Automobile Destruction: An Example of the Interaction Between Language and Memory. *Journal of Verbal Learning and Verbal Behavior,* 13:585–589.
Loftus, Elizabeth, and G. Zanni
1975 Eyewitness Testimony: The Influence of the Wording of a Question. *Bulletin of the Psychonomic Society,* 5:86–88.
Long, Lucinda
1974 Innovation in Urban Criminal Misdemeanor Courts. Pp. 173–206 in Herbert Jacob (ed.), *The Potential for Reform of Criminal Justice.* Beverly Hills: Sage.
Luckenbill, David F.
1979 Power: A Conceptual Framework. *Symbolic Interaction,* 2:97–114.
Lynch, Michael E.
1979 *Disclosure and Argument in Plea Bargaining Sessions, Part I: The Topicality of 'Plea Bargaining'.* Unpublished manuscript, Centre of Criminology, University of Toronto.
1982 Closure and Disclosure in Pre-Trial Argument. *Human Studies,* 5:285–318.
Lyons, John
1968 *Introduction to Theoretical Linguistics.* London: Cambridge University Press.
MacCaulay, Stewart
1963 Non-contractual Relations in Business: A Preliminary Study. *American Sociological Review,* 28:55–67.

Matheny, Albert R.
   1979   A Bibliography on Plea Bargaining. *Law and Society Review*, 13:661–687.
Mather, Lynn M.
   1974   Some Determinants of the Method of Case Disposition: Decision-Making by Public Defenders in Los Angeles. *Law and Society Review*, 8:187–217.
   1979   *Plea Bargaining or Trial? The Process of Criminal Case Disposition.* Lexington, Mass.: Lexington Books.
Matza, David
   1969   *Becoming Deviant.* Englewood Cliffs, N.J.: Prentice Hall.
Maynard, Douglas W.
   1979   *People Processing: Plea Bargaining in a Municipal Court.* Unpublished doctoral dissertation, Santa Barbara: University of California.
   1980   Placement of Topic Changes in Conversation. *Semiotica*, 30:263–290.
   1983   Language in the Court. *American Bar Foundation Research Journal*, 1983:211–222.
Maynard, Douglas W., and Thomas P. Wilson
   1980   On the Reification of Social Structure. Pp. 287–322 in Scott G. McNall and Gary N. Howe (eds.), *Current Perspectives in Social Theory: A Research Annual.* Greenwich, Conn.: JAI Press.
Maynard, Douglas W., and Don H. Zimmerman
   1983   *Ritual, Topical Talk, and the Social Organization of Relationships.* Revised version of a paper delivered at the annual meetings of the American Sociological Association, Boston, 1979.
McBarnet, Doreen J.
   1979   *Conviction: Law, the State, and the Construction of Justice.* London: MacMillan.
McDonald, William F.
   1979   From Plea Negotiation to Coercive Justice: Notes on the Respecification of a Concept. *Law and Society Review*, 13:385–392.
Mehan, Hugh
   1979   *Learning Lessons: Social Organization in the Classroom.* Cambridge: Harvard University Press.
Merton, Robert K.
   1968   Bureaucratic Structure and Personality. Pp. 249–260 in *Social Theory and Social Structure.* New York: Free Press.
Mileski, Maureen
   1971   Courtroom Encounters: An Observation Study of a Lower Criminal Court. *Law and Society Review*, 5:473–538.
Miller, Gerald R., and Judee K. Burgoon
   1982   Factors Affecting Assessments of Witness Credibility. Pp. 169–194 in Norbert L. Kerr and Robert M. Bray (eds.), *The Psychology of the Courtroom.* New York: Academic Press.
Miller, Herbert S., William F. McDonald, and James A. Cramer
   1978   *Plea Bargaining in the United States.* Washington, D.C.: National Institute of Law Enforcement and Criminal Justice.
Moerman, Michael
   1977   The Preference for Self-Correction in a Tai Conversational Corpus. *Language*, 53:872–883.

Mohr, Lawrence B.
  1976   Organizations, Decisions, and Courts. *Law and Society Review*, 10:621–642.
Moley, Raymond
  1929   *Politics and Criminal Prosecutions*. New York: Milton, Back and Co.
Morris, Norval
  1981   Punishment, Dessert, and Rehabilitation. Pp. 257–271 in Hyman Gross
         and Andrew von Hirsch (eds.), *Sentencing*. New York: Oxford Univer-
         sity Press.
Myers, Marsha A.
  1979   Offended Parties and Official Reactions: Victims and the Sentencing of
         Criminal Defendants. *Sociological Quarterly*, 20:529–540.
  1982   Common Law in Action: The Prosecution of Felonies and Misdemean-
         ors. *Sociological Inquiry*, 53:1–15.
Myers, Marsha A., and John Hagan
  1979   Private and Public Trouble: Prosecutors and the Allocation of Court
         Resources. *Social Problems*, 26:439–451.
Nagel, Stuart S.
  1962a Judicial Backgrounds and Criminal Cases. *Journal of Criminal Law and
         Criminology*, 54:33–39.
  1962b Testing Relations Between Judicial Characteristics and Judicial Deci-
         sion-making. *Western Political Science Quarterly*, 15:425–437.
Nardulli, Peter F.
  1978   *The Courtroom Elite: An Organizational Approach*. Cambridge: Ballinger.
Needleman, Carolyn
  1981   Discrepant Assumptions in Empirical Research: The Case of Juvenile
         Court Screening. *Social Problems*, 28:246–262.
Nettler, Gwynn
  1979   Criminal Justice. Pp. 27–52 in Alex Inkeles, James Coleman, and Ralph
         Turner (eds.), *Annual Review of Sociology*. Palo Alto, Calif.: Annual Reviews.
Neubauer, David W.
  1974   *Criminal Justice in Middle America*. Morristown, N.J.: General Learning
         Corporation.
Newman, Donald J.
  1966   *Conviction: The Determination of Guilt or Innocence Without Trial*. Boston:
         Little, Brown and Co.
Nimmer, Raymond T.
  1974   Judicial Reform: Informal Processes and Competing Effects. Pp. 207–34
         in Herbert Jacob (ed.), *The Potential for Reform of Criminal Justice*. Beverly
         Hills, Calif.: Sage.
O'Barr, William M.
  1982   *Linguistic Evidence: Language, Power, and Strategy in the Courtroom*. New
         York: Academic Press.
O'Barr, William M., and Bowman K. Atkins
  1978   When Silence is Golden—An Inquiry into the Nature and Meaning of
         Silence in an American Trial Courtroom. Durham, N.C.: Duke Uni-
         versity Law and Language Project (Research Report No. 18).

Perrow, Charles
   1979   *Complex Organizations: A Critical Essay,* 2nd ed. Glenview, Ill.: Scott,
          Foresman.
Peyrot, Mark
   1982   Caseload Management: Choosing Suitable Clients in a Community Health
          Clinic Agency. *Social Problems, 30*:157–167.
Phillips, Susan
   1982   *The Social Organization of Questions and Answers in Courtroom Discourse.*
          Paper presented at the annual meetings of the American Sociological
          Association, San Francisco.
Piliavin, Irving, and Scott Briar
   1964   Police Encounters with Juveniles. *American Journal of Sociology, 69*:206–214.
Pollner, Melvin
   1974   Mundane Reasoning. *Philosophy of the Social Sciences,* 4:35–54.
   1975   The Very Coinage of Your Brain: The Anatomy of Reality Disjunctures.
          Philosophy of the Social Sciences, 5:411–430.
   1979   Explicative Transactions: Making and Managing Meaning in Traffic Courts.
          Pp. 227–248 in George Psathas (ed.), *Everyday Language: Studies in Eth-
          nomethodology.* New York: Irvington.
Pomerantz, Anita
   1975   *Second Assessments: A Study of Some Features of Agreements/Disagreements.*
          Unpublished doctoral dissertation. Irvine: University of California.
   forth-
   coming Pursuing a Response. To appear in J. Maxwell Atkinson and John
          Heritage (eds.), *Structures of Social Action.* Cambridge: Cambridge Uni-
          versity Press.
President's Commission on Law Enforcement and Administration of Justice
   1967   *The Challenge of Crime in a Free Society.* Washington, D.C.: U. S. Gov-
          ernment Printing Office.
Pruitt, Dean G.
   1981   *Negotiation Behavior.* New York: Academic Press.
Reasons, Charles E.
   1977   On Methodology, Theory, and Ideology. *American Sociological Review,*
          42:177–180.
Riker, W.
   1962   *The Theory of Political Coalitions.* New Haven: Yale University Press.
Rosenthal, Douglas E.
   1974   *Lawyer and Client: Who's in Charge.* New York: Russell Sage.
Rosett, Arthur, and Donald R. Cressey
   1976   *Justice by Consent: Plea Bargains in the American Courthouse.* Philadelphia:
          J. B. Lippincott.
Ross, H. Lawrence
   1970   *Settled Out of Court: The Social Process of Insurance Claims Adjustment.*
          Chicago: Aldine.
Rossman, Henry H., William F. McDonald, and James A. Cramer
   1980   Some Patterns and Determinants of Plea Bargaining Decisions: A Sim-

ulation and Quasi-Experiment. Pp. 77–114 in William F. McDonald and James A. Cramer (eds.), *Plea Bargaining*. Lexington, Mass.: Lexington Books.

Roth, Julius

1962 Comments on 'Secret Observation.' *Social Problems*, 9:283–284.

1972 Some Contingencies of the Moral Evaluation and Control of Clientele: The Case of the Hospital Emergency Service. *American Journal of Sociology*, 77:839–856.

Rubin, Jeffrey Z., and Bert R. Brown

1975 *The Social Psychology of Bargaining and Negotiation*. New York: Academic Press.

Ryan, John P.

1981 Adjudication and Sentencing in a Misdemeanor Court: The Outcome is the Punishment. Pp. 93–136 in James J. Alfini (ed.), *Misdemeanor Courts: Policy Concerns and Research Perspectives*. Washington D.C.: National Institute of Justice.

Sacks, Harvey

1963 On Sociological Description. *Berkeley Journal of Sociology*, 8:1–16.

1967–

1972 Unpublished lecture notes. Irvine: University of California, Irvine.

1972a An Initial Investigation of the Usability of Conversational Data for Doing Sociology. Pp. 31–75 in David Sudnow (ed.), *Studies in Social Interaction*. Glencoe, Ill.: Free Press.

1972b Notes on Police Assessment of Moral Character. Pp. 280–293 in David Sudnow (ed.), *Studies in Social Interaction*. New York: Free Press.

1975 Everyone Has to Lie. Pp. 57–79 in Mary Sanches and Ben G. Blount (eds.), *Sociocultural Dimensions of Language Use*. New York: Academic Press.

1978 Some Technical Considerations of a Dirty Joke. Pp. 249–269 in Jim Schenkein (ed.), *Studies in the Organization of Conversational Interaction*. New York: Academic Press.

Sacks, Harvey, and Emanuel Schegloff

1979 Two Preferences in The Organization of Reference to Persons in Conversation and Their Interaction. Pp. 15–21 in George Psathas (ed.), *Everyday Language: Studies in Ethnomethodology*. New York: Irvington.

Sacks, Harvey, Emanuel Schegloff, and Gail Jefferson

1974 A Simplest Systematics for the Organization of Turn-taking for Conversation. *Language*, 4:696–735.

Sarat, Austin

1979 Doing the Dirty Business of Coping with Crime: The Contemporary 'Crisis' of American Criminal Courts. Pp. 59–79 in Peter F. Nardulli (ed.), *The Study of Criminal Courts: Political Perspectives*. Cambridge, Mass.: Ballinger.

Schegloff, Emanuel A.

1968 Sequencing in Conversational Openings. *American Anthropologist*, 70:1075–1095.

1972   Notes on a Conversational Practice: Formulating Place. Pp. 75–120 in
        David Sudnow (ed.), *Studies in Social Interaction*. Glencoe, Ill.: Free Press.
1980   Preliminaries to Preliminaries: 'Can I Ask You a Question?' *Sociological
        Inquiry*, 50:104–152.
Schegloff, Emanuel A., and Harvey Sacks
1974   Opening Up Closings. Pp. 233–264 in Roy Turner (ed.), *Ethnometho-
        dology*. London: Penguin.
Schegloff, Emanuel A., Gail Jefferson, and Harvey Sacks
1977   The Preference for Self-Correction in the Organization of Repair in
        Conversation. *Language*, 53:361–382.
Schelling, Thomas C.
1963   *The Strategy of Conflict*. Cambridge: Harvard University Press.
Schutz, Alfred
1973   *Collected Papers I: The Problem of Social Reality*. The Hague: Martinus
        Nijhoff.
Schwartz, Barry
1974   Waiting, Exchange and Power: The Distribution of Time in Social Sys-
        tems. *American Journal of Sociology*, 79:841–870.
Scott, Marvin B., and Stanford M. Lyman
1968   Accounts. *American Sociological Review*, 33:46–62.
Searle, John R.
1969   *Speech Acts: An Essay in the Philosophy of Language*. Cambridge: Cam-
        bridge University Press.
Sharrock, Wesley W., and Roy Turner
1980   Observation, Esoteric Knowledge, and Automobiles. *Human Studies*,
        3:19–31.
Sigler, Jay A.
1981   *Understanding Criminal Law*. Boston: Little Brown and Co.
Skolnick, Jerome
1966   *Justice Without Trial: Law Enforcement in Democratic Society*. New York:
        John Wiley.
1967   Social Control in the Adversary System. *Journal of Conflict Resolution*,
        11:51–70.
Smith, Alexander, and Abraham Blumberg
1967   The Problem of Objectivity. *Social Forces*, 46:96–105.
Smith, Dorothy
1974   The Social Construction of Documentary Reality. *Sociological Inquiry*,
        4:257–268.
Spradley, James P.
1980   *Participant Observation*. New York: Holt, Rinehart, and Winston.
Stanko, Elizabeth A.
1981   The Impact of Victim Assessment on Prosecutors' Screening Decisions:
        The Case of the New York County District Attorney's Office. *Law and
        Society Review*, 16:225–240.
Stevens, Carl M.
1963   *Strategy and Collective Bargaining Negotiation*. New York: McGraw-Hill.

Stinchcombe, Arthur L.
1963 Institutions of Privacy in the Determination of Police Administrative Practice. *American Journal of Sociology, 69*:150–160.

Strauss, Anselm
1978 *Negotiations: Varieties, Contexts, Processes, and Social Order.* San Francisco: Jossey Bass.

Sudnow, David
1965 Normal Crimes: Sociological Features of the Penal Code in a Public Defender's Office. *Social Problems, 12*:255–283.
1967 *Passing On: The Social Organization of Dying.* Englewood Cliffs, N.J.: Prentice Hall.

Swigert, Victoria L., and Ronald A. Farrell
1977 Normal Homicides and the Law. *American Sociological Review, 42*:16–32.

Terasaki, Alene
1976 *Pre-Announcement Sequences in Conversation.* Social Science Working Paper 99. Irvine: University of California.

Thomson, Randall J., and Mathew T. Zingraff
1981 Detecting Sentencing Disparity. *American Journal of Sociology, 86*:869–880.

Utz, Pamela
1978 *Settling the Facts.* Lexington, Mass.: Lexington Books.

Weber, Max
1946 Bureaucracy. Pp. 196–221 in Hans Gerth and C. Wright Mills (eds.), *From Max Weber: Essays in Sociology.* New York: Oxford University Press.

Werthman, Carl
1963 Delinquents in Schools: A Test for the Legitimacy of Authority. *Berkeley Journal of Sociology, 8*:39–60.

West, Candace
1979 Against our Will: Male Interruptions of Females in Cross-sex Conversations. *Annals of the New York Academy of Sciences, 327*:81–97.

West, Candace, and Don H. Zimmeraman
1983 Small Insults: A Study of Interruptions in Cross-sex Conversations Between Unacquainted Persons. Pp. 102–117 in Barrie Thorne, Cheris Kramarae, and Nancy Henley (eds.), *Language, Gender, and Society.* Rowley, Mass.: Newbury House.

Wieder, D. Lawrence
1974 *Language and Social Reality: The Case of Telling the Convict Code.* The Hague: Mouton.

Wilson, Thomas P.
1982 Qualitative 'Versus' Quantitative Methods in Social Research. Published in German as "Qualitative 'Oder' Quantitative Methoden in Der Sozialforschung." *Kölner Zeitschrift Für Soziologie und Sozial Psychologie, 34*:487–508.

Wilson, Thomas P., and Don H. Zimmerman
1980 Ethnomethodology, Sociology, and Theory. *Humboldt Journal of Social Relations, 7*:52–88.

Wittgenstein, Ludwig
   1958   *Philosophical Investigations.* New York: Harper and Row.
Zimmerman, Don H.
   1974   Fact as a Practical Accomplishment. Pp. 128–143 in Roy Turner (ed.),
          Ethnomethodology. England: Penguin.
   1978   Ethnomethodology. *The American Sociologist, 13:*6–15.
Zimmerman, Don H., and Melvin Pollner
   1970   The Everyday World as Phenomenon. Pp. 80–103 in Jack D. Douglas
          (ed.), *Understanding Everyday Life.* Chicago: Aldine.
Zimmerman, Don H., and Candace West
   1975   Sex Roles, Interruptions, and Silences in Conversation. Pp. 105–129 in
          Barrie Thorne and Nancy Henley (eds.), *Language and Sex: Difference and
          Dominance.* Rowley, Mass.: Newbury House.
Zimmerman, Don H., and D. Lawrence Wieder
   1977   You Can't Help But Get Stoned: Notes on The Social Organization of
          Marijuana Smoking. *Social Problems, 24:*198–207.

Author Index

251

Subject Index